INVENTING THE TRUTH: MEMORY AND ITS TRICKS

A GAY LIFE

LUCIEN L. AGOSTA, PH.D.

BookLocker
Trenton, Georgia

Published by BookLocker.com, Inc., Trenton, Georgia.

Printed on acid-free paper.

BookLocker.com, Inc.
2022

First Edition

Library of Congress Cataloguing in Publication Data
Agosta, Ph.D., Lucien L.
Inventing The Truth: Memory And Its Tricks by Lucien L. Agosta, Ph.D.
Library of Congress Control Number: 2022913590

FOR MY PARENTS

ANTHONY ALEXANDER AGOSTA
(1917-2011)

LOUISE ROSANNE LANDES
(1911-2000)

Tell all the truth but tell it slant.

--Emily Dickinson

Lies told for the sake of artistic effect ... can be, in a higher sense, the most beguiling forms of truth.

--Kurt Vonnegut

Narrative truth and personal myth are more telling than literal fidelity.

--Timothy Dow Adams, *Telling Lies in Modern American Autobiography*

What I do is take real plums and put them in an imaginary cake.

--Mary McCarthy

TABLE OF CONTENTS

Introduction..1

A Note To The Reader..9

Dress-Up Days...13

Diversity, Abundance, And The Conquering Of Time.....25

The Parents Of The Homosexual: A
    Coming-Out Story 39

Lust And Love 99

My Grandfathers...155

Thirteen Ways Of Looking At A Racist Past..................183

Darkness...211

An Articulate Courtship, An Eloquent Marriage............235

Conclusion: A Valediction Forbidding Mourning..........329

About The Author..335

INTRODUCTION

We can only understand life backwards, but we're forced to live it forwards.

--Kierkegaard

This is a book of memories. I cannot say that the memories summoned in this book are precise transcriptions of past events, a series of immersive re-experiences of bygone episodes in my gay life. Memory does not work like that. Memory is tricky. It wrests and twists, morphs and contorts one's past into shapes and designs bearing only a resemblance to the events memory tries to reconstitute from lost time. Memory reflects experiences of the past as if in a funhouse mirror, recollections recognizable as authentic though altered and transmuted. The "past," after all, is what we choose to remember, not what actually happened in any exact, immutable sense. A memory provides a strong gravitational core: Matter related, even matter extraneous to that memory can be drawn into its orbit, digested by it and germinated into extensions of it. But even such transmuted memories are true to the self they help to form.

For well over a century, neuroscientists have pursued memory's secrets, attempting to understand the complex workings of the extraordinary human capacity for remembering the past. They concur that memories are not preserved in a static state. Memories are never retrieved with perfect fidelity to the original events that prompt them. They do not emanate pellucid and unalloyed as diamonds dredged up from the coal-darkness of the mind's deep labyrinth. Memories are mutable and unstable. They are transformed each time they are summoned.

1

Retrieving a remembered event from its resonance in long-term memory initiates a system of reconsolidation, a process of aggregating to that memory present experience, linkages to similar memories, evolving attitudes toward and interpretations of what is remembered, maybe even details supplied by others who remember the event differently or more fully. This process of reconsolidation results in memory modification, a reshuffling of the narratives. We cannot retrieve a memory intact as from a storage cabinet. Our memories are not objective records of the past. We alter our memories each time we retrieve them. Thus, we do not remember an event; instead, we remember the last time we remembered an event. Memories are never infallible. There is an insufficiency in every effort at recollection.

Memory daubs like a Cubist: it slices events and reconfigures them, collages scenes from many odd angles all at once, shades in strange chromatics. It turns ventriloquist: it amplifies conversations and mouths novel dialogue, not bothering to disguise its moving lips. It snaps like a daft photographer, fiddling with exposures and overlaying images. It is an unreliable narrator.

Apparently memory works like this: Neurons, fired by sensory experiences and our reactions to them, encode memories in the cortex and hippocampus, regions of the brain activated during the process of remembering. Each time a memory is subsequently summoned from the complex web of memories amassed in these regions, that particular memory is re-encoded by a similar, but never identical, set of neurons. This re-encoding impacts how a memory is called up in the future: Aspects of the remembered event may be strengthened, weakened, altered, even substituted depending on which neurons are roused during the process of remembering.

In short, memories cannot be returned to in stable form as one can repeatedly revisit sculptures, forever frozen in marble. Memories are surprisingly malleable. Plato recognized this when he theorized in his dialog *Theaetetus* that human souls cohere around what amounts to an internal ingot of wax, the gift of Mnemosyne, goddess of memory. Our thoughts, perceptions, and experiences notch themselves in this wax, but whatever is imprinted there is susceptible to reconfiguring, remolding, even to melting away. Imprinting on wax is obviously less durable than carving in wood or etching in stone.

Though not employing Plato's adroit metaphor for memory, modern neuroscientists similarly explain these memory permutations and insufficiencies. No one, they argue, is capable of perfectly encoding in memory all aspects and details of an event or experience. Memory is selective. The missing information causes gaps in memories, lacunae, some possibly significant, others minor. The brain, a fussbudget busybody always pressing for greater order, coherence, and pattern, pushes in to fill these gaps and defaults. The brain fabricates details that coerce memories to make sense.

Neuroscientists refer to this effect as "confabulation," the human brain's insistence on providing greater coherence and a consistent pattern to a memory sequence. Confabulation is not lying: it does not involve a conscious intention to deceive the self or others. It is an unconscious process employed by the fastidious brain that requires memories to be lucid and rational, narratives complete, reasoned, and intelligible. In confabulation, the brain connects the dots, colors in blank spaces, and spans the gaps in memory.

Confabulation tends to increase with age. Memories grow dimmer, increasingly accumulative, arrayed in divergent interpretations, or tinted by evolving significances. I am keenly aware of this as I compose this book of remembrances in my 70s, as memory aids me in reading my life toward the end of it. In this book, I attempt to set down my memories before they evanesce in the solvent of Time. I recognize the vagaries and insufficiencies of memory, the inevitable effects of a brain busily confabulating. My memories recorded in these pages are thus necessarily both true and fictitious at the same time. Because absolute accuracy is alien to memory, the verifiable fictions that comprise this book are inventions of the truth, constructionist renditions of it. Both my confabulating brain and my conscious mind agree on their fabricated veracity. I can get no nearer to the truth of my experiences of the past than in these veracious contrivances.

I am not interested in facts as reflected in memory; I am interested in telling the truth. Granted, facts are important, particularly in the sciences, politics, and other areas of human endeavor where facts can be substantiated and result in serious consequences. But when laid out end to end in straight lines, the facts of one's personal life often lead nowhere. Personal significances float up from the facts that prompt them. One must always re-structure remembered events so as to locate the truth hidden within. Daily life is chaotic, far different from the orderly sequence one fabricates to understand it.

What is personally human can never be factual. As soon as the mind notices facts of a personal nature, these facts get screwed up. Motives and intentions and inferences warp facts. Events haze in interpretation, angle of vision, point of view, perspective, subjective filtering. They lie in a veiling mist of indeterminacy. What was said or done may not have been meant, may have been misconstrued. The witness who saw a shove and the witness who saw a playful nudge both report the truth.

These pages offer a mix of imagination and memory and fiction and narrative sequencing and myth-making. I have changed almost all names. I have at times invented settings to locate what I suppose happened. I have worded conversations to dramatize what I think was intended. I have occasionally created characters who elicit actions and reactions and motives that reveal who I imagine I was at the time. These pages are readings of moments interpreted in a language unavailable to me while those moments were occurring. I am telling the truth in the best way I know how to invent it. I swear this account is utterly reliable, though I had to make parts of it up for accuracy.

Recording one's memories is a challenge for another reason: Memories never present themselves according to a schematic chart. They arrive as annunciations, suddenly opened windows, unexpected apertures, epiphanies, slippages in sequential present time. To record them in any way that makes sense, memories must be coerced into a chronology, made to align according to a narrative time frame. This imposition of order upon memories results in a further fictionalizing. In writing this book, I brought memory and narrative order together. They loathed each other. "Chaotic fuck-up!" chronology muttered under its breath. Memory was equally uncivil: it hissed and hurled images without words. It glowered, flashing hues and shifting outlines just to be ornery. The pen struggles to record and structure memories, so jumbled and prolific are they. In recording memory, the conscious mind wrestles with the illogic of its interior world.

But in league, narrative chronology and I were fierce opponents. Together we managed to straitjacket memory into its necessary constraints. Memory conceded at last, but to the end it was a savage loser. The remembrances recorded in this book, then, offer narrative contrivances of my life's truths. I hope the book is readable and engaging. I would not want any reader to confront in these pages aboriginal memory scratching its nuts and snarling alone in a hoarder's house. I want to be kind to anyone who honors me by wandering into these pages and pauses to peruse them.

Granted, then: Memory is a shape-shifter, a fabulist rather than a historian, a storyteller instead of a tape recorder, a dauber and never a photographer—but memory is all any of us have to ground ourselves in our pasts. Memory, then, is my lifeline, securing me in the experiences that have formed me. As I have demonstrated, memory is a strange gift, unreliable, porous, susceptible to influence, revision, and interpretation, to being colored by shifting attitudes to what it summons. Nevertheless, in memory we locate ourselves. Our sense of integral personhood is established there and nowhere else. Memories exist to reinforce our life narratives, to provide us with a sense of identity and a place in the world's pattern.

Memory is also the abode of the beloved dead. Without our memories of them, the dead vanish. In not remembering the dead, we forsake them in their darkness. In these true fictions, I have attempted an animation of many of those whom I have loved and lost. I hope, to some degree, they live again in these pages. They were far too vital to fade into silence without leaving an echo.

The ancient Greeks revered Memory as personified in Mnemosyne, a Titan and mother of the nine Muses. The Greeks acknowledged Mnemosyne's continued power even after they had dethroned and dismissed her Titan siblings in favor of their newer gods. The Greeks praised their gods in a series of 87 Orphic Hymns, reserving the 77th one for Mnemosyne, whom they invoked in the following lines:

'Tis thine to waken from lethargic rest
All thoughts deposited within the breast;
And naught neglecting, vigorous to excite
The mental eye from dark oblivion's night.
Come, blessed power, thy mystic's memory wake
To holy rites, and Lethe's fetters break.
                    --translated by Thomas Taylor, 1792

The true inventions in this collection result from a summoning of my memories, rising like vapors from Mnemosyne's breeze-stirred pool and here encoded before they condense and sink forever in Lethe, the river of forgetfulness, its banks blanched white with crusted salt.

Mnemosyne, 1881 (or Lamp of Memory; also called La Ricordanza)   --Dante Gabriel Rossetti

A NOTE TO THE READER

This is my second published memoir (See *Losing Time: AIDS Lessons in Love and Loss*, 2019). We live in an age of self-disclosure: everything in everyone's life is now deemed worthy of documentation. Photographs of one's lunch, appetizing or not, regularly surface on Facebook; pictures of a daughter's third-grade finger-painted scrawls are posted on Instagram. Oprah Winfrey's program, which featured individual human dramas, was one of the most popular ever on television. "Reality TV" records the hyped-up interactions of "real housewives." Everyday people promote themselves as celebrities. Social media pervades our culture, for better or worse, introducing us to life narratives of sometimes noble, sympathetic human beings as well as to the malign stories spun out by lying self-promoters, wackos, narcissists, conspiracy theorists, and often witless purveyors of nefarious foreign propaganda.

In this atmosphere we are called to be perspicacious in our attention to the life stories everywhere thrust upon us. Nevertheless, this ubiquity of life narratives in our culture makes for a fascinating human terrain. It follows, then, that ours is a generation where memoir has begun to outpace fiction and other literary genres in demand and popularity. I hope readers of this memoir will find it engaging while it offers affirmation to its gay audience and an expansion of understanding and tolerance among any straight readers drawn to it. Those serve as the primary reasons for my having written it.

Born in 1948, I am now approaching my mid-70s. This gay memoir chronicles an extensive period of gay history, from almost universal homosexual condemnation before 1969's Stonewall Riots through the AIDS die-off (focused

9

on in my memoir, *Losing Time*) into the modified but shaky and precarious tolerance we gay people are currently experiencing in America. *Inventing the Truth* sets my personal experience within the historical context of my generation. I hope readers will find this memoir astute in its observations, adroit in its images and amassing of details, at times humorous in its depiction of gay life's incongruities, and well enough written to engage them throughout their perusal of it. Whether or not readers find in this memoir a satisfaction of all these descriptors, it remains nonetheless my story, told in the truest, most honest way I know how to invent it—and told without fear.

On another matter: I received occasional blowback about the explicit descriptions of gay sexual encounters in my recent book *Losing Time* (2019). The criticism was leveled by some of my straight readers whom I know to be sophisticated and urbane, neither prudish nor easily shocked. The sexual accounts in that first memoir as well as in this one are, I contend, no more erotic or explicit than similar accounts found in many straight texts and films. I can only conclude that these readers found the frank sexuality in my first book difficult because it outlined certain homosexual practices they certainly must have been aware of but had perhaps not confronted so candidly before.

In *Losing Time* I had attempted to construct a dialectic between lust and love. Apparently I presented the matter without adequate cuing or appropriate reader preparation. I had originally preceded *Losing Time* with a note to the reader similar to this one, but I omitted it at the urging of a consensus of my gay readers for whom the note seemed more defensive than explanatory. In *Inventing the Truth*, I do not intend this note to be apologetic for the book's occasional descriptions of gay sex. But I also intend to address this matter without flinching. That said, I might

Order of January 2, 2023

Qty.   Item

Inventing the Truth: Memory and Its Tricks - A Gay Life
Agosta PhD, Lucien L --- Paperback
B0BG6CRDM5
B0BG6CRDM5 9798885313025

Return or replace your item
Visit Amazon.com/returns

D/Gxcd92dJb/-1 of 1-//RBD5-MOR/second/0/0111-18:30/0111-16:59   SmartPac

A gift for you

Enclosed is your Zip Book. When finished, please return the item and note to the desk of any Sacramento Public Library. From Sacramento Public Library Zip Book

prepare a reader for the frank sexual discussions in Chapter 4: "Lust and Love." I would not want a reader skittish about gay sexual practices to wander away from the book's other chapters.

Throughout history, the straight world has molded gay discourse according to its strictures and has succeeded in forcing gay fluency into its own dialect, distorting our words and coercing our language and reining in our stories. In the face of this, gay men have had to prevaricate and edit and encode and drop hints and substitute pronouns and exercise restraint and sanction reticence and adopt duplicity. We have penned cautious and mendacious memoirs. We have projected inauthentic, self-edited, self-loathing personae. I can now write without needing the courage required of those before me who first worded gay silence. I cannot—I will not—ever speak in a borrowed voice again.

In *Inventing the Truth*, I do not suppress queer sexual languaging. In this chronicle, the fey heart words queer desire. I gift myself with the faggot-speak of a reclaimed tongue. Only 45 or so years ago, state sodomy laws in the U. S. criminalized gay sexual expression. Sexual acts acknowledged in these pages would be admissible as evidence against a gay man in a court penal trial or would have provided an excuse for confining him in a loony bin for his "psychosexual pathology." In a dozen or so countries in the world, such admissions would currently earn me the death penalty. Still. Being able here and now to write openly of gay sex—and of gay life in general—is celebratory and emancipating. This relatively recent freedom is ours for the first time in our long history. Even the Classical Greek pederasts and the uranians and inverts of early 20th-Century Paris and Berlin and New York had not this license for telling their sexual truths. I mean to take advantage of this liberating opportunity.

DRESS-UP DAYS

"You don't know me." I have just traipsed into Suzette's kitchen in one of my get-ups. I must be about five, maybe six years old. Suzette lives across the street and I like to play dress-up with her. I am wobbling along in my mother's cast-off high heels, an old graying black skirt cinched at my waist by large diaper pins with yellow plastic safety catches. I don't remember wearing a blouse, maybe just a t-shirt tarted up with tawdry necklaces and another diaper safety pin packed with religious medals. I have a champagne-colored window-sheer panel draped like a veil over my head and tossed de'gage' over one shoulder. I later got a long gypsy skirt with ribbons of shimmery rainbow colors all down it, after which I consigned the little black number to the bottom of my dress-up box. And I remember a fake leopard turban, too, though I don't remember ever wearing it. Suzette's father had asked who the new girl was when I had tottered into their kitchen. I knew enough not to reveal my identity to the questioner with the bright eye and the ironic smile.

I loved my get-ups and wore them often. Perhaps I am a master at repressing the unpleasant, but I remember only one time when I was taunted about my juvenile cross-dressing. What made this episode painful was that the jeering came from the girls I so loved to play with. There must have been four girls—Suzette, Nancy, Gloria, and my sister Mary—and then little ole anomalous me, all turned out in our finest. I think I was the smartest by far—the champagne sheer was magical. I felt like a fresh ingenue among time-worn matrons who took this dress-up business for granted.

We were sitting around a small chicken-wire cage in Suzette's side yard watching her black and white Muscovy duck with the red cancerous-looking wattles at the bridge of its black beak, the ugly grown-up version of the downy duckling, dyed pink, she had cuddled on receiving it the Easter before. I was poking a stick at the duck, trying to make it rise from its crouch and waddle over to the cement-lined puddle in the center of the cage. For some reason I wanted to see it in the mucky water. The duck was annoyed, dodging the stick and snapping at it with an outraged piping. When it refused to stand or move to the puddle, I began to jab it hard, and Suzette asked me to stop. When I continued, she started calling me a sissy and—where she got the word from I do not know—a "morphodike." This last word was news to me. The other girls immediately joined in: "Sissy! Sissy!" I remember being so outraged at this reminder of my slender attachment to their girl-community that I turned away from the duck, hoping the rejection would cease.

When it did not, I grew desperate. I tried to stand up—no easy matter in over-sized high heels that rocked and wobbled in the grass. At last I fumbled my skirt up and stepped out of the heels so I could rise. The name-calling was now a chant: "Sissy! Sissy!" I remember being furious, but even more hurt. I raised my skirt and bound it around my waist with one arm and with the other hand reached into the fly of my shorts and pulled out my penis. The chanting turned into shrieks and threats to tell. And then I started to whizz, flicking myself around and about to shower them. (I was too young then to understand the tyranny of phallic power I was exercising, but I clearly understood the problem-solvency of urine in this situation.) The resultant pandemonium startled the duck, which careened across its pen to the side farthest from us, adding its squawks to the girls' shrieks of terror and disgust. They all slid out of their

14

shoes and ran, skirts torrential. I picked up the stick, went to the other side of the pen, and gave that duck a vicious final jab under its wing. Then I did not know what to do, but I knew I was in for it.

That night, after supper, my eyes still bloodshot from crying during my whipping, I asked for the candy eye of a chocolate Easter rabbit my parents were dismembering for dessert. "An eye for the painter," my mother said sullenly, refusing to let go of the incident the day before when a neighbor lady phoned her to complain about my having daubed her clothesline pole with clots of bright blue paint I found in a small can in my father's garage. "No, an eye for the pissing demon of the duck pen," my father spat, his black Sicilian eyes ablaze.

I tried on a big, bright smile.

"Why is the simpleton grinning?" my father directed at my mother.

"Can't you see he's smiling to keep from crying?"

At that, I burst into tears and ran from the table. Later that evening, I emerged from my room to overhear snatches of conversation: "….the way he shrills and waves his hands about…." "He'll outgrow it." I crept back to my room, convulsed with shame.

My parents were clearly distressed about this dressing-up business and my early resistance to rigid gender conformity. It was one phase of my life they refused to document on camera, either still or moving. They also seemed averse to filming me playing with dolls, though the home movie camera caught me at it on several occasions. At the fourth birthday party for my younger sister, for example, she clapped her hands in anticipation as a large present was handed to her, but after she had unwrapped the present to reveal a dark-haired doll dressed up in pink gingham, the smile buckled into a deep frown abetted by a trembling lower lip. Suddenly, I lunge across the picture frame to snatch that doll away from her, startling everyone. The film stops abruptly at that point.

On another occasion, the movie frame catches my sister Mary and me fighting in the background over one of her Barbies, but the camera snaps to a stop after a brief glimpse of this. I have the doll by the legs, an advantage that I'm sure allowed me to win it away from her unless a parent intervened. I played dolls for a long time in my childhood, and I played house too, decorating the chicken-wire pen of our own Easter ducks after I traded them in for a cocker spaniel puppy when my father had had enough of stepping in duck splatter every time he went into the backyard.

My parents finally came to the conclusion that I was bending boy-gender expectations too far out of whack by the time I reached first grade. I came home one day from school in early September to find my dress-up box missing from under my bed. "Who stole my clothes!" I wailed. My parents were talking together in the kitchen. They glanced at each other quickly when I entered.

"We gave them to Pearlene, Lucien." Pearlene was our praline-colored maid who arrived each morning at 8:00 from the bus stop at the end of the street. We had no idea where she lived, though we knew her mother lived with her and that her husband was at Angola State Prison serving a life sentence for having fatally knifed a man at a bar one night while drinking and throwing craps. Pearlene was confident he would be paroled in a couple of years. After all, as she explained it, he had only knifed another colored man, not a White man, and the judge would let him out early.

"Pearlene already <u>has</u> nice clothes!" I shouted. In fact, Pearlene had some very stylish dresses: though she changed into crisp blue button-down work dresses when she arrived, I remember her coming to work occasionally in bright sundresses of a flowery print, tight in the bodice, flaring out full in the skirt below a thin belt. She wore these if she was going out after work and did not have time to go home to change. Hell, I wanted her clothes.

"Well, Pearlene is poor," my mother said. "We thought you should share with her." Actually, these people had just donated my dress-up box to the Purple Heart! Pearlene was in on the ruse because the next day she thanked me for the beautiful skirts which she was going to wear to church every Sunday.

"They're my clothes," I protested. "You give them right on back!" My mother reprimanded me for being ugly, and Pearlene cooed, "Oooh, now don't go be that mean way, sugar."

I could not stay mad at Pearlene for long. She brought me home the only comic book I ever owned, one she found on the bus one morning. My mother never bought comic books for us. She took us to the library every week or two instead. Pearlene's gift was a "Dr. Dread" comic book, depicting on its glossy cover a demented horror in a white lab coat midway down a stairway littered with skeletons and facing a rush of buff shirtless men, the man closest to the demonic doctor already skeletonizing at the point of injection with a huge hypodermic needle. This cover gave me screaming nightmares for a week at least, but I would not tell my parents where the terrors were coming from for fear they would confiscate this wondrous comic, the cover images of which were to provide me with some of my first masturbatory fantasies in the future, a fact best for me not to examine too closely.

Eventually I relented about my dress-up box, but I remember asking Pearlene's mother how Pearlene looked on Sunday mornings in the skirts I used to have. That was the only time I ever saw Pearlene's mother startle out of her stern mask to register anything even hinting at surprise.

I was fascinated by Pearlene's mother, who, we were told, was "from the Islands," wherever that was. She was short, not very old, her eyes and mouth three straight lines across an expressionless mask of a face. I was convinced that she, like the Sisters at school, had no hair: she wore a swath of brilliant fabric tied around her head, not like the bandanna of Aunt Jemima, but a headpiece of pure elegance. I never understood a lilting dialect word this woman ever uttered.

She was what my father called a "Hoodoo." The first thing she would do before entering our house was drop a small divot of blue powder on each of our steps and blow it away, her lips moving soundlessly. She would then proceed to the back steps and repeat the process. She preferred to sit in a metal lawn chair in a shady corner of the yard under a blooming white oleander if it was warm outside and stir the air with a heart-shaped palmetto fan. Pearlene would bring her things to drink, over which she waved her hands cautiously.

When she left with Pearlene around 3:00 PM, we raced to check the corners of each room where she would occasionally leave small coins scattered or coke-bottle caps filled with rum. We never saw her do this, though she must have had to go into the house to use the bathroom. When it was cold or rainy, she sat in the kitchen listening to the radio dramas always on while Pearlene and my mother worked about the house. Pearlene explained that these coins and liquor-filled bottle caps were offerings to the "loas" and to various spirits of the house, to appease them, to divert any mischief they might be conjuring up.

One day, Pearlene's mother presented my father with two small cans of paint, one a brilliant blue, the other ruby red, and instructed him to paint the window frames and door jambs with these powerful colors to ward off evil powers, spiteful loas, and wandering malign spirits. When my father declined, she advised him, second best, to spot a drop—a mere undetectable drop—of each color on the corners of the window sills to fend off the greatest malice, especially in a house so vulnerable to it, filled with five healthy, crowing babies and a pretty wife, enough to inspire envy in the groaning vacuity of the spirit world. My parents never followed this advice, a negligence I thought reckless.

Given my penchant for dressing-up, I had little regular interest in making-up, though I watched my mother when she sat on a cushioned low bench before the mirror of her vanity bureau and applied what she called her "allurements." I would stand right up next to her, the length of my body touching her arm.

"Wouldn't you rather go play?" my mother would ask.

"Git!" my father would say if he were in the room. I had designs on him too. I wanted to see him take off his pajamas and get dressed. I could not believe how big his penis looked when I was five years old.

If she were alone, my mother would sometimes guide me around to the left of her and sit me beside her at the bureau. "Now talk to me," she would say, "but don't fidget." I would chatter away, admiring my mother's dexterous moves among her puffs and potions. First she would rub some cream all over her face, then rub it all off again. Then came beige powder from a compact, patted on with a small frayed pad. Next came torture from a silver contraption with scissor finger-holes and rubber-lined jaws clamped onto her eyelids to curl the lashes. My mother's face would squinch up when this instrument was applied. "Don't move," she would breathe. Then came the drawing on of her lipstick, which my mother was never without and which she

19

refreshed often, unscrolling the pointed stick from its jet case. She wore only one color all her life, Revlon Super-Lustrous "Cherries in the Snow," a deep, muted red lightened with silver undertones. Usually she blotted it, leaving red kisses on a white tissue. Some days she would smudge a tiny bit of this lipstick on a fingertip and rub it into her cheeks a long time. "Good as a rest cure," she would say. This whole operation took maybe ten minutes, and when it was concluded, she looked the same to me, only better.

This litter on my mother's bureau looked benign, a little like my older brother's chemistry set. One Saturday morning, I sat at her bureau alone, commanding the array of bottles, potions, notions, and tubes. The blinds in my parents' bedroom had not yet been drawn; the beds were unmade. The smell of bacon and coffee and the canned laughter of a radio comedy came from the kitchen. I rubbed on the cream and rubbed it off, flicking the tissues stuck to my fingers until they let loose and floated to the floor. Then I applied the powder. Immediately I looked different, older somehow: my face was all one color and texture. The jagged pink scar on my forehead where I got stitches when I fell on the concrete steps was obliterated. Gone too was the white pucker scar above my upper lip, set there when the lid of the back hatch on the drugstore delivery motorcycle fell on me as I rummaged through the bin. The tight red stitches scar at the bridge of my nose had also disappeared, the one I got from following Pearlene too closely as she was swinging a bucket she had just emptied of its dirty mop water. My face now looked like a grown-up face—even, hard, settled—and it frightened me.

I uncapped the "Cherries in the Snow" and applied it to my lips, then immediately decided I had not colored within the lines. Red leaked below my lips; the sharp corners of my mouth were gone. My face had changed once again, this

20

time alarmingly: I looked all mouth, a great ragged wound. I scraped my upper teeth over my lower lip, backing them with a waxy sludge. I looked as if I had been gnawing raw liver. In a panic, I reached for gobs of tissue and started rubbing. The smear spread. It got up under my eyes. I sat still for a moment to do a little damage assessment. My image in the mirror swam in tears, but I fought them back, afraid to do any more rubbing.

And then I decided. I picked up the compact and powdered my face again. The red diminished in the dim light. With the lipstick, I painted semicircles under my eyes and two short diagonal stripes on each cheek. Then I ran a vertical line down my chin.

I went into breakfast. I thought if anyone noticed anything, I would say I was playing Indian, even though I had on my favorite cowboy shirt with the fake mother-of-pearl snap buttons and covered wagons rumbling all over it, raising little tan puffs of dust. My older brother Andy saw me first. He stared at me solemnly, then looked up at my father to learn how he should react.

"What the….!" whispered my father.

"Are you <u>bleeding</u>?" gasped my mother. She leapt up from the table, dropping the spoon she was zooming as an airplane to dump a cargo of Gerber plum-pap into the drooly mouth of my baby brother.

"Take them off! Take them off!" I bawled, shocked at the vehemence of their reaction to me.

"Them?"

"Cherries in the Snow."

"For goodness sake, Lucien. What possesses you?"

"A fiend," my father laughed, "like I've been telling you."

My mother ignored this and took me by the hand. My father sighed, folded the paper, and got up from the table:

"Here, let me take him." He march-stepped me into the bathroom, a firm hand on my shoulder. "Close your eyes and I'll make the cherries go away," he said. "But from now on, light on the lipstick, ok, cowboy?" He slathered camphor-tingly Noxema on my face to dissolve the "allurements" and my tears and any further desire to daub myself with make-up ever again.

Looking back at my early interest in dressing-up and at the loss I felt in being forced to donate my clothes to Pearlene, I am surprised that I never attempted to reassemble my dress-up box. Apparently this youthful foray into female drag was enough to satisfy me for the remainder of my days. Never again did dressing-up like a girl hold me in its swishy spell. When I look now at Helen Bedd, a 6'3" drag queen, her feet tortured into size 15 stiletto heels like one of Cinderella's stepsisters, her hair a vertiginous tease, her voice a disconcertingly deep baritone, her shaved cheeks shadowed blue-black beneath the pancake, I consider myself fortunate that I was a shimmering diva early on, that I knew the thrill and the despair of gender-fuck before descending into the everyday sunlight of the ordinary male with a penchant for khakis and button-down Oxford-cloth shirts for teaching—my "schoolmarm drag," as I called it. For parties and such, though, I do gay-up my wardrobe with flocked paisley shirts and designer jeans or leather trousers to remind me of the dress-up glory days I am relieved to have left buried deep in my past.

I do not know for certain what caused this early gender-nonconformity as manifested in my juvenile habit of cross-dressing and playing with dolls, though I suspect I engaged in these girlish pursuits because I did not want to play rough, competitive boy games and sports, preferring tamer, more creative play. I was never dissatisfied with or wanted other than the boy body I was born with, and I was exceedingly happy later on to possess a brisk post-pubescent penis. I never rebelled against the binary rules which assigned me to one definitive gender. I would have bristled had anyone dared use other than male pronouns in referring to me, nor did I ever desire to be considered anything other than a boy. It was just that women's clothes were more colorful and creative, more flowing and dramatic than the bland khaki shorts and t-shirt drab business I was given to run around in.

Would I have fared better in a family more accommodating to my early cross-dressing and interest in dolls? I doubt it. My family was tolerant of my temporary alternate gender expressions. Their concerns were voiced when they thought I would not hear them. They never ridiculed or belittled me over the issue.

From my perspective now, I am relieved that my parents were of a generation which had never heard of withholding a definite gender identity from a child until that child was old enough to choose one. It never dawned on my parents to create an atmosphere where I could free myself from "the restrictive prison of binary gender." I did not have "gender-creative" parents, and I am happy that they never questioned my cis-male identity, no matter to what degree I challenged it at times.

If I had manifested gender-dysphoria, been desperately unhappy, especially at puberty, with the male body and the gender identity assigned me at first glance in the delivery room, this would have been a different story. And I have never had any interest in experimenting with being "gender fluid." It just feels right to me to identify according to a fixed male gender—simpler somehow, though I am far from judging anyone whose gender identity is more complex or fluid than mine, no matter how I started out in life.

DIVERSITY, ABUNDANCE, AND THE CONQUERING OF TIME

I

I surfaced from the shielding of my childhood home in Baton Rouge to venture into two public spaces which were to fashion the person I was to become—the East Baton Rouge Parish Public Library on Laurel Street and Sacred Heart of Jesus Catholic Church on Main. In these two places I was to discover life's rich diversity, its plenitude and abundance. In addition, both places endowed me with a means of slipping out of diurnal time to realms where clocks and calendars relinquished their tyrannous sway.

I attended Sacred Heart Church and its affiliated parochial school my entire childhood. This church glowed in luminous frescoes lit incandescent by blue-tinted stained-glass windows inset with prisms which zithered sudden flashes of light throughout the church interior. Corinthian columns, balancing their golden acanthine capitals, marched down both sides of a wide nave and around the sanctuary to prop up a gilded dome dominated by a fierce Christus Pantokrator thrusting forth a book announcing "Rex Sum Ego," or "I Am King." The eyes of this stern Christ drilled congregants wherever they knelt in this large church. No milksop Jesus this—here was a grave cancellation of the blonde, white, effete Jesus so often presented to sentimental worshippers drawn to a divinity they could diminish and dominate.

Other fresco murals in this radiant church depicted Heaven as far from static, a realm charged with irrepressible exuberance and populated with celestial beings and Biblical personages potent with life: two strident warrior-seraphim

25

glowered out from the frieze of their stylized wings on pilasters siding the altar. Their hair white flame, their arms pulsed in a gesture both combative and reverential, they served as protective guardians around the altar's gilded tabernacle.

Biblical penitents occupied the lunettes above the confessionals. Shimmering in an aquamarine gown, the Magdalene cascades her golden tresses in sudden streams over the feet of a startled Jesus reclining at table in a maroon robe. The promiscuous Samaritan woman occupied the other lunette, flaunting her emerald brocade garment, a hand on one saucy hip and balancing a glowing alabaster water jar on a shoulder, standing insouciant before a Jesus perched on the rim of the well to hear her own up to having had five "husbands." The Gospels feature these women for their sexual transgressions, the implication being that women, like their wanton mother Eve, give rise to prurient temptation. Our celibate nun-teachers, those virginal superegos, seemed to imply that sexual waywardness was pretty much the only kind of sin worth revealing in the confessional anyway.

This richness of fresco imagery, of mantling stained-glass hues and dyes, of focused slashes of prism translucence suggested to me as a child the abundance of this world and the co-existence of a resplendent realm that spilled over into our sphere, stunning me with an awareness of the prodigal profusion that enclosed me at every turn.

Ritual, procession, liturgy, and chanting in this church furthered that heightened awareness, all suggesting that our human world resonated with an alternate divine world that would, with the eventual dissolution of diurnal time, succeed it.

At the rite of solemn Benediction, for example, the priest somehow appeared to float into the sanctuary despite

26

a ponderous cope, sumptuous with gems and embroidery. Billows of blue incense partially obscured him as he encased a white host in a crystalline occulus centering a golden monstrance which he lifted in blessing, rays darting from it in a gilded dazzle. Those so blessed received a foretaste of that Beatific Vision that we were told awaited us in Heaven, fulfilling all our longings and righting all our stumblings in an eternal perfected realm where bliss was the air we would breathe. This earthly world, we were everywhere reminded, was not the only realm we walked in.

After the priest vacated the sanctuary following Benediction, the lights in the church began to dim, the lemony scent of wood polish issued again from the pews, the sharp odor of Pine-Sol could again be detected from the terrazzo floors. Fumes diffused from expired incense and extinguished candles drew me back from the profusely abundant realm I had earlier glimpsed. Then the mundane world of home and school closed around me again—but haloed in a rich aura and echo that never quite faded.

II

The ritual splendor I participated in at Sacred Heart Church employed a rich accompanying language at once evocative, varied, and poetic. Prayer, psalm, litany, hymn, invocation, intercession, blessing—all were couched in a devotional discourse of sonorous beauty, suggesting an alternate divine realm where language took on a cadence and a tonality set apart from the domestic, academic, and practical commercial vocalizations one had recourse to in the human world.

The Mass of my childhood was still sung in Latin, a silvery tongue I thought echoed from God's realm, linguistically renewing our world of custom and habit. Even the prayers in English, especially the litanies, those poems of repetition with variation, employed powerful imagery. Litanies are prayers of call and response: the priest chants an invocation and the congregation answers with a supplication. There are litanies to the Blessed Virgin, to her spouse St. Joseph, to the Sacred Heart of Jesus, as well as to the Saints. The Litany of the Blessed Virgin implores her spiritual aid and protection under 53 appellations: Mirror of Justice, Seat of Wisdom, Cause of Our Joy, Mystical Rose, Tower of Ivory, House of Gold, Morning Star, Vessel of All Virtues, Star of the Sea, and Queen of Angels, to name a few.

The Litany of St. Joseph invokes the saint's benefaction under 31 titles, my favorite being "Terror of Demons," while another litany addresses the Sacred Heart as "The Burning Furnace of Charity" and "The Desire of the Everlasting Hills."

The abundance and diversity of the chanted appellations in these litanies grounded me in poetic images, infusing me with their power and imaginative resonance. I early grew to love the expressive imagery in church prayer so ardently that I would come in time to devote my professional life in the college classroom and in my writing to sharing with others the power and beauty of those images which underlie all poetry. Images, when bracing and original, startle us into an engagement with the richness of the world. They breathe freshness and animation into a world too soon rendered stale and habitual by our continued presence in it.

The abundance and diversity of the 10,000 saints recognized by the Church complemented the verbal richness of Catholic discourse. This thronged roster of saints offered a complete human inventory of genders, ages, occupations, nationalities, and experiences, a trove of narratives and life stories often admirable and inspiring—but just as often bizarre, even grotesque. The lives—and deaths—of these saintly martyrs, widows, philosophers, virgins, mystics, theologians, rulers, clergy, and simple, ordinary folk offer fascinating narratives which later would ignite in me a passion for fiction.

Each of these saints had a special Feast Day set aside in the year to venerate him or her, mobbing each of the 365 days of the calendar. On my birthday, July 10, for example, 72 saints are honored. My favorite is St. Amalberga. Though passionately wooed by Charlemagne, she sniffed at the dignity of becoming Queen of the Franks, opting instead for inviolable virginity and a black serge veil. When Charlemagne attempted to abduct this sturdy virgin during her evening prayers, she fastened onto the altar with such brawny determination that he was unable to budge her.

Most of the saints venerated on my birthday were martyrs, spanning the historical gamut from St. Alexander, beheaded during the reign of Antoninus Pius in 165 to Blessed Emmanuel Ruiz, a Spanish Franciscan martyred in 1860 along with eleven companions during a Druse uprising in Lebanon for refusing to accept Islam. Sts. Januarius and Maximus had the bad luck to be martyred along with 44 companions in Nicopolis, Armenia in 320, a full seven years after Constantine's decree of 313 proclaiming tolerance for Christianity throughout the Empire. News traveled slowly in the fourth century.

These martyrs met grisly ends, shivering me as a child with a thrilling if morbid turn as I imagined their tortures. My fifth-grade teacher, having assigned a paper on a saint honored on our birthdays, was alarmed by my particularly gruesome report on the martyrdom of St. Peter Tu, a Vietnamese Catholic who met his end in 1840 for his energetic evangelism among the Buddhists. In my grim report, I attempted to ratchet up interest by inventing macabre details—bamboo splinters pressed under his fingernails, tooth extractions with rusty pliers and without a numbing from novocaine, toes snapped into limp submission, climaxing with the saint's head hacked off with a dull hatchet to a torrent of blood ensanguining all standing within ten paces of the slaughter.

Proud of this virtuoso piece, I looked forward to high praise for it. Instead, my mother got a phone call from Sister Agatha who suggested she make an appointment for me with a child psychologist. Soon. My mother launched a defense of my bloodthirsty masterpiece, reasoning that its feverish details had their origins in my almost daily exposure to our church's niche statue of that arrow-pincushion, St. Sebastian; to the statue of St. Lucy proffering her eyeballs on a platter; to the Holy Infants run through with swords and hoisted up on lances wielded by Herod's henchmen pictured in the church prayer books in the pews. And, she added for good measure, the fourteen Stations of the Cross lining the walls of the church depicted, with satisfactory gore, the passion and death of Jesus Himself whose flesh and blood we feasted on every Sunday.

My mother consulted her buckram-bound *Lives of the Saints* to discover the identity of the canonized woman from whom Sister Agatha copped a name on professing her nun vows: "St. Agatha of Sicily" endured the interesting experience of being stretched on a rack during her martyrdom, torn with iron hooks, whipped, burned with torches, and—to finish the job—had her breasts pulled off with pincers.

The veneration of all these martyrs was designed to secure us in our faith were it ever challenged by secular or anti-Catholic forces—worldly, demonic, atheist, communist, especially the liturgical poverty of

Protestantism with its smarmy hymns, carnival-barker preachers, and alarming outbursts of gibberish. As these martyred saints testified: nothing, not even torture or death, was ever to cleave us from the fostering bosom of Mother Church, whose emblem is a pelican, wings fledged to protect her brood as she tears her own breast to nurture them.

III

The abundance and diversity of our natural world as it rests on the numinous divine world is insistently celebrated in the Catholic perspective. After twelve years of drilling, this perspective resonates in me to this day. So does Catholicism's mystical conception of time.

We Catholics were taught that time exists in two interrelated dimensions: profane or diurnal time and sacral time. Diurnal time passes in the ticking of clocks and in a calendar of time segments, numerically calibrated into days, weeks, months, and years, and, in larger measure, into the past, the instantaneous present, and the future. Diurnal time only seems to hold us bound in its thrall, however. In Catholic actuality, diurnal time drifts like a mirage or a rainbow oil slick on the eternal vastness of sacral time, a time subsuming time as we know it, our diurnal time being dissolved in the incomprehensible immensity of Eternity. We join the entire sweep of creation and history through our union with the Cosmic Christ who absorbs all of time. Thus God's sacral time is ever-present and continuous, without flow, passage, or succession. As the psalmist proclaims, "The heavens reach beyond earth and time; we swim in mercy as in an endless sea."

This understanding of time had important implications in Catholic ritual and liturgy. For example, in the Mass's Sanctus, that hymn of praise echoing continuously from His creatures to their Divine Originator, we join the angels of all ranks and all the denizens of Heaven as well as with human beings who have lived before us, all those now breathing, all those yet to come in a timeless laudation in the eternity of sacral time. In short, during the Sanctus, one stepped out of diurnal time into sacral time, just as one did at the Mass's Eucharistic sacrament. The bread and wine, believed by Catholics to be transubstantiated into the actual flesh and blood of the God-Man Jesus, transports the communicant's discrete body beyond time's diurnal illusion and unites it integrally with all those who have died, all those yet living, and all those to come in a single Body with Christ as its Head, a body that thrives eternally beyond the strictures of diurnal time.

Catholic theologians have historically seen diurnal time as essentially illusory, even as it claims our continuous attention during our earthly sojourns in it. But everywhere, Catholicism insists on the sublimation of diurnal time.

In the Catholic Mass, for instance, diurnal time dissolves into the sacral. Congregants present at the Mass's Consecration are subsumed into sacral time and are present at Golgotha, witnesses of the Crucifixion and standing before the Cross on that dark Friday, participants in the redemption of all humankind forever. Calvary is not re-enacted in the Mass. It does not re-occur in some symbolic masque. Calvary is forever and always occurring in God's sacral time. It is Christ's always-dying that forever refreshes all life, and the Mass grants us immediate access to it. Or so we were told.....

I was also told that at my birth, God gifted me with my very own guardian angel, a spirit from sacral time thrust into the diurnal to watch over me, my sacral double as it were, who went where I went, observed all I did, and supposedly kept me from harm. When I first got wind of this ghostly companion, I expressed strong reservations about having this officious spy always hanging around. "Don't think of your guardian spirit in that way!" my mother exclaimed. "Know instead that you walk this earth in the company of angels!"

The programmatic theme of Medieval and early Renaissance religious paintings rests on this Catholic temporal conception that God's sacral time pervades and grounds our profane time. Those old painted boards display a connecting spiral up from our linear human time into God's gilded and glowing ever-present. God's sacral time is coruscating simultaneity: all events occur at once, forever. Past, present, and future align as coterminous, their boundaries nullified.

Portraits of the donors who shelled out the money for these religious paintings occupy the lower margins. They kneel, stiff and diminished in profane time, hands folded, eyes raised in supplication to their intercessor saints, expansive in eternal time, one hand resting on a donor's shoulder, the other gesturing towards sacral time's depicted religious subject, a shy Madonna and her exuberant Child, for instance, shimmering in gold leaf and standing in imposing scale, as if they alone are real.

The Infant reaches out a pudgy hand from the enclosure of the Lady's arms to the solemn saints surrounding them, saints born long after the Infant's death in diurnal time but who here encompass Him in His sacral space. Fascinated, the Infant fingers a ruby-enameled crucifix, a refined emblem of his destiny pinned onto the surplice of some pious bishop, his miter backlit by a halo. An aged abbess-saint, dead long before this picture was painted, extends towards the Child an elegant ivory forefinger banded in the golden circlet with which she wed the Infant in a spiritual marriage centuries after His death.

All in this painting flourish in sacral time, the compressed loop of the continuous ever-now. Even the painting's kneeling donors seem granted a vision of the all-at-once. They and their saintly sponsors are rapt with the Infant and His Mother, circumventing diurnal time's constraints. Here, the infinite restructures the finite. All that ever was, forever is!

Though I would not, as I grew older in my time, sustain with any conviction this temporal Catholic vision, it nevertheless imbued me—then and now—with a sense that a richer, more abundant and diverse universe surrounds and sustains me than I am daily conscious of, that I am a creature immersed in mystery and wonder rather than one confined to a static, quotidian universe perceived only by my limited senses, a world of custom, habit, and stale, repetitious experience. My early Catholicism positions me as a creature who, in spite of the demands of diurnal time, walks in vast dimensions and who breathes the inscrutable. I confess a sad diminution of this confident bearing-up that I felt when I believed so firmly that my true home was in sacral time and that the profane time of my everyday waking life was but preamble, a stubborn and persistent illusion to be dispelled on that day when I would awaken at last in a luminous ever-now! Its hold on me diminished now or not, my early Catholic indoctrination imbued me with a sense of the profligate abundance of the world(s) I occupy.

IV

Bordering on the holy, the East Baton Rouge Parish Library also fostered in me an expanded awareness of the world's abundance and diversity and demonstrated for me that the boundaries of everyday diurnal time could be suspended, expanded, even circumvented.

Stately as a temple, stolid as are most government buildings erected in the 1930s, the East Baton Rouge Parish Library commanded a broad sweep of stairs. Stylized bronze garlands framed its large windows, its doors capped by a bronze filigree grille and flanked on each side by art-deco torches. Two terracotta inserts broke the building's blocky façade, one featuring an open book topped by a flaring Aladdin's lamp to represent the fire of knowledge kindled in the library's books. The second insert, framed by indented chevrons, proclaimed this substantial building a PVBLIC LIBRARY.

A cool reverential hush sobered a patron on entering. A large semi-circular desk, like an altar, anchored the library's first floor, from which radiated reading and reference rooms floored in cork tiles, their lofty ceilings supported by Ionic columns. Behind this desk rose tiers upon tiers of books repeated on an open mezzanine floor above, bordered by a bronze art-deco railing and tiled in opaque glass panels. Thousands of books lined these orderly shelves, secular counterparts to the 10,000 saints of my church whom I imagined as standing in similar rows around the throne of God.

These tiers of books promised an inexhaustible abundance, a profligacy of human lives lived or imagined, of experiences and experiments and histories and ideas all available to me, here preserved from the solvent vat of time and loss.

This library also offered me a way of transcending time! When drawn into a book, I could dislocate from diurnal time and pass into literary time, for want of a better term. I could experience a time expansion, indwelling in Medieval Dantean celestial realms, say, or in the realistic Dickensian gloom of 19th Century London, in the sprawling, feverish castle of Gormenghast, or in a dreamy red chamber in 18th Century China. Immersion in a book renders diurnal time irrelevant for a reader, absorbed in alien eras, cultures, lives, and lore. The world engendered in the book becomes for a time the reader's world.

In engaged reading, we plunge into other consciousnesses. Worlds other than our own become permeable. We empty ourselves out for a time, filling that inner void with lives and situations other than our own. In books, we can free ourselves from the confines of the historical and social structures that limit our lives.

My mother took full advantage of what this library had to offer. Every week or two, she bundled her five children into our two-toned aqua-and-white Ford sedan and drove us downtown to the library to select books she expected us to read, as many as eight each if we wanted. She would hand us over to the librarian in the basement's children's room with its pint-sized tables, squat chairs, and diminutive book shelves. After my mother selected her books from upstairs, she would return for us and hand out to each of us our own library card to check out our books, listing the titles on a pad as the librarian stamped the return dates on the inside flap of each book.

Once, when I was eight or nine, I crept out of the children's section and plodded up the stairs into the adult collection. I spied my mother in a stack on the mezzanine level. I climbed up to her, but rather than approach her, I began looking at the adult titles in a row one over from where she was browsing. Suddenly, a librarian, prickly in a tawny tweed suit, peered down at me over her cat's-eye glasses: "Little people do not belong up here. These books are not for you. Now you need to get on back down to the basement where the children's books are."

I could see my mother eying us through a gap in the books on a shelf in an adjacent row. Suddenly her face disappeared. She walked down the aisle where I was staring up at the frowning librarian.

"He can check out any book that interests him," she said, "anywhere in the whole library."

And there it was—my welcome into a limitless literary world in all its bountiful diversity. And I was thereby encouraged to conquer time through my reading, to free myself at will from a consciousness otherwise temporally and situationally bound.

I accepted my mother's invitation there and then, and in time I was hired as a page at that library, responsible for re-shelving returned books, my first job. My professional life would involve inviting students into this prolific literary world where they too could come to confirm the world's rich diversity, where they too could step out of time's constricting boundaries into abundance.

THE PARENTS OF THE
HOMOSEXUAL:
A COMING-OUT STORY

I

"You never wanted a woman to take you up to bed," my mother used to laugh, more prescient than she could then have known. "As an infant, you shrieked, balled up your fists, and squinched your eyes tight shut if one of your aunts tried to gather you up and place you in your crib. You always wanted a man to take you to bed, Daddy, an uncle, or one of Daddy's friends."

My mother told me I seemed so male-oriented as an infant that she and my father thought I would be a real "man's man," a "he-man," maybe also because I was a chubby baby, bald, a real bruiser, a "ruffian," as she described me in one of her letters. My parents rigged me out as a newborn in a Notre Dame football jersey in one photograph, in a little LSU sweater and beanie in another. Then they named me "Lucien"—an accident of birth: I was born the day before my grandmother Lucy's birthday.

"If a man were speaking in a room where you were drooling down my dress front," my mother used to recount, "you would turn immediately to his voice, as if you were powered by an automatic homing device. When women spoke to you, you started back, a frown dragging your brows almost down to your nose."

My mother relished telling these anecdotes to her friends and laughed at these memories of my infantile misogynist quirks and whims—until she learned I was gay. She had thought all this was cute at the time, but she seemed less certain of that after I came out.

II

I am puzzled by a photograph of me, aged 18 months, costumed for Mardi Gras 1950. I am standing next to my older brother, Andy, who is dressed like a matador. I am dressed like a little girl, staring bleakly out from a mask with distended, whorish red lips, an outsized bow tied around my head at a saucy angle. On the next day, Ash Wednesday, my mother described this costume in her letter to her sisters in Ohio: "Lucien made a very cute little girl in a pink dress and a pink hair bow which wouldn't stay on his infinitesimal hank of hair. I thought he made a very creditable girl until little Audrey from next door came and stood beside him and he greeted her in true Cagney style," meaning, I assume, that I pushed her down. My mother continued her description of this unlikely get-up: "He had a cute girl's mask and at first refused to keep it on, then when we went to his grandparents' house, he wanted it to stay on. Got real fond of it." There I am in this photograph, exactly as she described me, the pink smock draping halfway over the plastic pants covering a cloth diaper topping my stocky, dimpled legs.

I cannot figure out what this was all about. I wonder if, when my mother saw this photograph later, after I was older and treasured my dress-up box, or older still, when I finally came out to my parents, she felt this might have been a particularly ill-advised costume. Perhaps I announced a preference for this outfit as early as then? Impossible to believe, about as impossible to believe as that this unlikely costume resulted from some subconscious wish on my mother's part for a daughter. No, that could not be right. With each new pregnancy, including hers of 1950 which resulted in the birth of a daughter, my mother asked her sisters to pray "for a safe delivery of a normal and healthy baby <u>boy!</u>" So, did she intuit something about me that early that led her to costume me in this way? Beats me.

As things turned out, though, she was not far wrong in this intuition, if intuition it was. My gender-fuck days soon ensued, as I have recounted in my essay "Dress-Up Days" earlier in this book.

III

My new red nylon swimsuit shimmered like a fresh cherry, dewy and glistening, a tight little slip of a wedge to hide my four-year-old knurl of a pud. My father pulled my shorts and underpants off and told me to get into my swimsuit while he turned from me to don his own suit before the locker we shared at the city park pool. A man next to us held me transfixed: tall, blonde, a divot of light hair feathered between dark nipples, a penis as large as my father's—an astonishing size for a four-year-old to contemplate. Gaze I did, naked, rapt, holding tight to the slatted locker-room bench before me, my little sprout erect.

"Hey, little man," said the blonde, his large, smooth face approaching mine as he bent to slip on his own suit. "How's it hanging?"

"Put your suit on," my father demanded, turning me by the shoulder with one hand from the vision that held me spellbound. "Don't look around like that in here."

"He's only four years old," I overheard my mother say when we met up with her in the pool. "He's just curious. It's natural at that age."

So, I learned to guard my gaze very early on, to mind my glances, to keep them furtive and covert.

IV

I overheard my parents talking about me over coffee early one Saturday morning. They had not heard me enter the house from the backyard. I never let the screen door slam behind me like my brothers did.

"The way he waves his hands about," my father was exclaiming. "It's just not what boys do. Andy doesn't do that nor do the other boys in the neighborhood. And he fights with his sister over her Barbies. Shouldn't we do something about that?"

Home movies in which I appear prove all this hand-waving to be accurate. On one occasion I had been presented with my birthday cake, that year an angel food topped with miniature plastic cowboys galloping through patches of blood-red icing, just what I had ordered. I look to be about five, decked out in chaps, a holstered pistol, and a cowboy hat. My hands scallop in the air above this cake in emphatic arabesques, rococo convolutions, pirouettes, extravagant flutterings and stirring balletic swoopings. I look like a symphony conductor caught in a mad triple-time speeded-up musical tempo.

"As for the hand conniptions, he'll grow out of that," my mother said. "He's a smart, imaginative little boy who'll find his way."

"I just wish he'd imagine himself more a regular boy is all," my father sighed.

"We don't want to do anything to dampen his imagination and discourage his intelligence. As for the Barbies, let's give him more assertive toys for Christmas this year. This is all a phase he'll leave behind soon."

My mother got up from the table to pour herself more coffee.

"Maybe," my father said, "but we've tried that before. Remember how he reacted to the red dump truck we gave him for his last birthday? 'But what do I do with this?' he'd asked, close to tears. Andy immediately took it over, straddled it, and pushed himself along on it with his feet. Lucien just put that truck in his bedroom, stuck some Barbies in it, ran over that boy doll with zip between his legs, and left him beneath the wheels."

"Unfortunate, that gift,'" my mother laughed. "The boy doll is named 'Ken.' Lucien used to dress him up in Barbie's clothes. Do you think Lucien's too young to learn chess? Maybe he'd like a set this Christmas? He likes art. Maybe we can get him a paint set?"

"Not exactly what I had in mind," my father sighed. "Maybe a tennis racket?"

"Or a croquet set to get him out of the house and in the yard more?"

I burst into the room. "I don't want any of those," I shouted. "I want paper dolls!"

"Stop spying on us!" my father thundered.

V

Because I was adept at making friends, my parents felt no need to worry about my social skills or my integration into the neighborhood or school child-culture. I was never a lonely child, was never really bullied. The Catholic grammar school I went to was attended by children from close-knit parish families. I always had a best friend, always was welcome in neighborhood games, parties, and outings. I was a Cub Scout, turned out perfectly in my uniform: I loved the merit-badge sash, the neck kerchief, and those pins over the blue flap shirt pockets.

I did venture out a bit to make a friend or two beyond the immediate neighborhood. I remember going over after school to the house of a boy I met on the public park playground near our house. When his mother saw my khaki parochial-school uniform, she asked me if I knew why the nuns and priests at my church wore those long black dresses.

"I don't know," I replied, taken aback by the sneering vehemence in her voice.

"To hide their cloven hooves and forked tails, that's why," she spat. "And those priests are all queers."

"I don't want you ever to go over to that house," my mother replied when I told her of this. "And don't be friends with that boy anymore."

After I told this rejected friend I did not want to play with him again, he and his brothers used to wait for us to be let off the school bus near their house.

"Fish lickers!" they would call after my siblings and friends, clad alike in our school uniforms. "Mackerel snappers!"

"They call you that because we eat fish on Fridays," my mother explained. "Ignore them."

"You can hit them back if they ever hit you," my father added. "But don't start anything."

VI

I did see in these priest cassocks a way to dress up and at the same time win not just acceptance but downright approval. I frothed with anticipation, twitching my forked tail and clattering my cloven hooves at the prospect of becoming an altar boy in fourth grade, even though it meant having to serve at the 5:00 A.M. "Fisherman's Mass" on occasion and having to look at dead people in carnation-scented mortuaries when called upon to serve at funerals. But those cassocks were magical dress-ups!

The sacristy at Sacred Heart Church was outfitted with rows of wooden lockers for altar boys to hang up their cassocks and surplices between services. I disdained the cassock and surplus supplied me: new boys got old cassocks missing some of their buttons on fabric worn to a grayish smudge, smelly, tattered old things tossed onto locker hooks by boys who could not appreciate what a cassock could do for one! My cassock had to be a deep ebony and long enough to cover the backs of my scuffed brown school shoes. The surplice had to be dazzlingly white and fall in crisp pleats well below my waist.

In order to attain this liturgical splendor, I had to steal. In church. I rifled through the sacristy's unlocked lockers until I eyed the perfect combination of cassock and surplice—rightful owners of these be damned. Once attained, these wondrous garments went home with me after I used them on the altar. Not for these perfections the rank and rumpling lockers! Once I grew out of these consummate cassock/surplice iterations, I had to return to scrounging through the lockers again until I found their desired replacements. No one ever caught me at these illicit trade-offs, nor was I ever particularly bothered by the dismay of another altar boy on his discovery that I had replaced his cassock with a changeling that cramped his shoulders and rose way above his shins.

If I had had my way, I would have worn that cassock at home every day all day, but my mother made sure that was not to be. "This is not something to sashay around the house in," she would scold. "These are church things, to be used in church."

On the sly, I tried to persuade my Aunt Jo who liked to sew that I needed darts at the flanks of my cassock to accommodate extra fabric for that full effect I envied in the cassocks of real priests.

"You are not a priest, that cassock is not yours, and," my aunt would emphasize on denying my request, "I do not intend to set about damaging church property at this time in my life."

I could not make her understand that since I was going to be a priest in the future, now was the time for me to start practicing with the amplified, perfected cassock she could make for me.

VII

I was devious: there were approved ways for me to satisfy my yen for dressing up without wearing the female clothing I was no longer interested in. The cassock dodge was but one of them.

That year in fourth grade, I somehow persuaded my parents to make for me an angel costume for Halloween. I had had it with being a hobo or a cowboy or a pirate, was done with the burnt-cork-smeared beards and ripped clothes, the chaps and vest and cowboy hat that I already wore on regular play days, the bandanna, eye patch, sash, and such. After my parents concurred that angels were in fact male, there ensued a network of cooperation to bring this costume into being. My sewing aunt designed for me a long white gown banded at the hemline in two gold lame' stripes to match those around the wide sleeves. My mother bought me a short wig of preternaturally yellow acrylic that looked like Barbie's wiry hair and, in the sunlight, like spun glass. My father abetted all this by fabricating a pair of large wings cut from cardboard, tight-sheathed in layers of gold foil and attached by cords hidden under the sleeves. These wings were awesome. Once hitched into them, I felt ready to levitate and soar beyond this earth,

There is a home movie of me in this get-up. My older brother Andy, dressed as a fireman, stands stolid and resolute to my left. On the other side of me is my sister Mary dressed as a gypsy girl. Heavily made up, she looks as if she is being offered up as a virgin prostitute child, a pedophilic delight. My sister Felice stands scowling beside her, dressed as an Indian princess in a short white-satin shift dotted all over with sequins arranged in Indian patterns, the relic of a school pageant she had been in the year before. Finally, my little brother Damian is decked out in a cowboy outfit, radiantly smiling as he takes pistol potshots at everyone. I keep turning around for the camera to capture a full view of my dazzling golden wings.

I wore this angel business to school for the Halloween party that year. Sister Grace stopped me in the hallway: "Are you a boy or a girl?" Indignant, I held up my gown to reveal the scuffed brown boy shoes my parents made me wear with the costume.

"Well, I'll be!" the nun laughed. "It's you, is it? I only wish you were an angel in my classroom." She was the teacher who always gave me a C- in conduct on my report card and checked off two notations: "Wastes Time" and "Annoys Others." I spent most of my recesses punished, standing in a corner of the playground with my arms folded. I just could not sit still for very long in a classroom but had to be up and visiting....

That same year, I was in a school pageant. The boys and girls in fourth grade had to wear cowboy regalia for some song cycle to be performed for those parents dedicated enough to endure such spectacles. The nun conducting the singing cocked her ear down to me while I was yodeling away during rehearsals and whispered that I was just to move my lips during the songs. "Don't really sing," she whispered conspiratorially. "Just look like you are...."

My sewing aunt made my cowboy shirt out of azure satin and tarted it up with ruby rhinestone rosettes on the collar tips and on the shirt back. I loved that shirt, but the makeup we had to wear under the bright stage lights—lipstick and rouge—was addictive. My mother's cosmetics got an occasional workout on the sly. I knew by then how to remove makeup with Noxema.

Home movies show me wearing this shirt and my first pair of blue jeans, stiff as fiberboard. I am jutting my hip out and up and down, arm akimbo, like I thought real cowboys did at the saloons while throwing back their whiskeys, one boot hooked on the bar rail, but instead I look more like some cross-dressed western floozie impatient for a drunken cowboy to scoop up his winnings at the poker table and join her for a romp in a room upstairs.

I saw immediately on the first showing of this home-movie reel that these hip moves were just not right, more images to add to those cinematic embarrassments I had to endure whenever we had home movie nights.

"Gah," my brother would say when I appeared on the screen, "What's going on with the hips?"

VIII

When I was eleven, my sewing aunt was stricken with ovarian cancer that had metastasized to her liver, causing her almost constant nausea. She was never without a basin, ironically liver-shaped. I used to visit her daily that summer: she lived with my other maiden aunt across the street from us.

I thought I was doing my aunt a kindness in these visits, relieving her of her loneliness, but in retrospect, I am not so sure. She apparently had not been able to tell me that she would have preferred to ride out the nausea waves alone, waiting for her sister to comfort her after work.

I must have caught her on a particularly hard day. "What's wrong with you?" she raised her voice. "Why don't you act like a regular boy?"

I stared at her, stunned.

"I'm tired," she sighed. "Why don't you go out and play now. Play with the <u>boys</u>, not the girls," she stressed.

When she died in the fall, I served as an altar boy at her funeral. I held the crucifix at the head of her open coffin at the funeral home before she was taken to church for her Requiem Mass. I was distressed to see a smudge of bruise-purple on her chin where the embalming fluid had apparently begun to fail. At church, I headed the procession down the aisle to the altar bearing the crucifix. I was crying.

The acolyte to my left taunted me: "You cry like a girl. Only sissies cry," he whispered, but loud enough that my parents might possibly have heard, following close behind the coffin. A few days after this, I edged this boy's book bag with my foot into a deep mud puddle on the playground after he had laid it down before running off to play tag. No one saw me do it. I relished his dismay on fishing out his dripping bag and then trying to explain to our teacher why his homework was sopping wet. Thus I learned to even out affronts on the sly with anyone who slighted me. In time, however, I would come to realize that these "slights" against me were prompted by heterosexist feelings of privilege, especially among white males and already incipient in their young sons. I would develop more effective strategies for countering them, like gaining an education that centered me in a career that granted me compensatory privileges I might not have attained in other fields, a career wherein I could help to empower others, including, especially, others like me. I came in time to have no more need for petty retributions, however satisfying they were at the times I resorted to them.

IX

One day on the playground of the Bernard Terrace public school at the end of our street, I stumbled on a root-raised crack in the sidewalk and toppled a kid's brand new red Schwinn bicycle, denting the back fender and knocking off the round red reflector, faceted like a fly's eye. He had just gotten the bike for his birthday and had been showing it off. He was furious with me, rubbing his short sandy hair into an angry bristle. He ran at me and grabbed me by the neck of my t-shirt, his eyes orange with rage.

"I didn't mean to!" I shouted. "I tripped."

When he pulled back his balled fist, I twisted free and high-tailed it out of the playground and down my street. My father was out front washing our 1953 black DeSoto when he saw me running as fast as I could make sinews, bones, and muscles mesh. He did not see the boy chasing me, who, on spying my father, turned away.

"You're fast as a devil on the scent of a sinner!" my father laughed. "You tear around like you've got salt on your tail. You'd be a good runner at track."

Wishing to maintain my father's rare approval of anything I ever did that smacked of the athletic, I decided at the age of ten to try out for the track team at my grammar school a week later.

"Good for you!" my father applauded.

"You want to do <u>what</u>?" Sister Grace chuckled when I told her I could not stay after school to clap her erasers clean of chalk dust the day of tryouts. "You have to be joking! Who put you up to this?"

"My father tells me I run fast!" I told her and gave her the fish-eye when she shrugged and turned away.

The grass in the field behind the church had just been mown, pungent with the green scent of cut grass and wild onion. Two shaky white chalk-lines had been laid out by hand some distance apart, and the usual school jocks were standing around engaged in a bantering I did not know how to assume, athlete culture being as alien to me as the Buddhist traditions of Tibet.

"What are you doing here?" asked Brett, wiry as a rat terrier, his hair sheared short all around except for an upright fringe above his forehead. His mouth sneered open, teeth gapped like a falling-down fence.

"Why do you think I'm here? I'm trying out for the track team," I said, immediately drowned out by snickers and guffaws.

"He can try out if he wants," said our math teacher, dragooned to be the track coach, who had come up unnoticed. "Anyone can. But where are your Keds?" he asked me. "You can't run in your brown school shoes."

"Oh," I said, to renewed jeers.

"Try running barefoot then," the coach suggested.

The next thing I knew, I was lined up with four boys prepared to run from one line to the one farther off. The other boys all touched right fingers to the grass, stretched right legs out behind them, left arms balanced on flexed left knees. I just stood there, this stance being completely foreign to me. When a whistle sounded, I took off running.

"I'm doing great!" I thought. I was way out in front of the other boys who all lagged behind. I pounded away, all systems go. "I'm winning!" I panted. "Who's laughing now?"

My breath began to sound in my ears like an old vacuum cleaner with a busted gasket. Then, out of the corner of my left eye, I saw Brett closing in on me. Another boy appeared at the corner of my right eye. As they passed me, seemingly effortlessly, each gave me a light tap on the back of the head. Then the other two runners hurtled past, the last of them clapping me on the back as he passed, sending me pitching forward. I came in dead last, after the four other boys had passed the line and bent over to catch their breaths. I could not talk, I was breathing so hard.

"Okay, the next five of you step up to the line," the coach bawled. Then, turning to me: "Ready to go again?" he laughed.

"How did tryouts go?" my father asked after supper that night. "We'll buy you some Keds if you make the team."

"I didn't try out," I said. "The trophies they give out are plastic."

This incident illustrates how my childhood was often sited along seismic lines: the desire to be the boy my parents would have been comfortable with versus the stronger personal desire to be what my natural inclinations prompted me towards. I had parents who, fortunately, let me follow my own instincts for the most part, however troubling some of those instincts may have been for them.

X

"I love Superman. He's better than cowboys."

I am eleven years old. I am spending the weekend out in the country at the home of the grandparents of my best friend Kurt. Kurt has a thin face, a slim, taut body, and hair slicked straight up in front. He hates sports too. We are sitting up in a high double bed together reading his comic books, a ceiling fan whirring overhead and strobing the light socketed above the rotating fan blades.

"Superman's okay, but Roy Rogers has Trigger, and I like horses. Besides, Roy Rogers is real and Superman's made up," Kurt counters.

Lightning bugs glimmer and locusts chirr outside our open window on the second floor of the big white clapboard farmhouse with dark green shutters and a wide porch floored in glossy gray cypress boards. We have just had our baths after a day of swimming in the coppery-green water of a pond on the property. Underwater, sunlight glinted on sand suspended like flecks of mica in jasper. Water gliders floated above, each leg a black etching dimpling the water. Little fish nibbled at the incipient hair on our legs.

"Roy Rogers is made up too. He doesn't really ride the range all day wearing that white hat and those starched shirts and looking for bad guys. He probably lives on a city street in a brick house and has a stable boy look after Trigger somewhere out in the country."

"He's not a comic-book man, though. He can't fly. He doesn't have x-ray vision. He's just a real man," says Kurt.

"Yeah, but I like Superman's cape and his outfit. And his face is so clean and sharp."

"In the comics, yes, but the TV Superman is old and fat," Kurt observes. I had to admit that the TV Superman did look like a 50s television dad, minus the gray flannel suit and the advice he would be dispensing to a TV son given to minor infractions against expected suburban behaviors. I did not like the TV Superman much either.

"Well, Roy Rogers is old too and has a little pinched-up face like a possum."

I hear grown-ups talking above the clink of dishes and flatware being laid in the kitchen below where fish are frying. Someone calls a cat in. A screen door slams.

"At least Roy Rogers has a normal life. He's got a wife and he's got friends like that fat man who talks funny and drives around in a beat-up old World War II jeep."

Someone is cooing to the cat in baby talk. A car drives up, wheels crunching on the oyster-shell driveway.

"Superman only has Lois Lane who is dumb as a crowbar because she can't even tell that Clark Kent is really Superman. And Superman has no friends, and everyone laughs at Clark Kent because he's clumsy and clueless," Kurt continues.

"But Clark Kent is not who Superman really is. Superman fools everyone all the time. He hides his true identity."

Kurt's grandfather appears in the doorway, unknotting his tie and telling us to get ready for supper.

"But Superman's not <u>normal</u>! He's this weirdo with freaky clothes who's always hiding. He locks himself in that frozen green ice palace all alone. Clark Kent can't make any real friends or get married either because he's nothing more than a disguise. Both of them are lonely. Roy Rogers has a house, some horses, and a wife. I want to be like him when I grow up. Who'd really want to be like Superman?"

Kurt throws his legs off the side of the bed and slides down until he is standing, shuffling his feet about trying to slip on his flip-flops.

Kurt's grandparents, his mother, and his two sisters sit at the table. Kurt takes his place with a sense of belonging. I sit, kindly invited, but aware of being an outsider, a consciousness that would remain with me far into the future until I would finally summon the courage to throw off my disguises and sexual subterfuges, to fuse my hidden and my public selves in order to live a unified life in plain view at last.

XI

My parents were happy when I told them I wanted to be a priest. Catholic families usually consider it an honor to have produced a priest, none more so than my parents who had been praying for a priestly vocation in their family even before I was born.

They encouraged me to follow what, prompted by the nuns at school, I called my "vocation," my "calling from God." So, after graduating from the eighth grade at the age of 13, I packed up my clothes and my parents drove me some 70 miles away from home to a Benedictine Abbey-sponsored seminary for the training of prospective diocesan priests.

I sometimes wonder at my parents' willingness to allow me to leave home so young. Was it more than their strong desire to see one of their sons ordained? I doubt they ever said or even consciously thought as much, even to themselves, but could it have been a relief for them to see me as a priest because the vow of chastity I would take at ordination would place me outside of traditional male gender roles, the priesthood being a respected enclave where one was not expected to be a man in traditional capacities— husband, father, fully vested member of the patriarchy. Perhaps at some subconscious level, they comforted themselves that a boy like me who did not conform to the usual societal expectations of my gender would find a fitting sinecure in the celibate priesthood.

I was away from home for a month before my parents were allowed to visit me. On that Sunday, I emerged from the abbey church after Mass. Parents had gathered at the church doors to meet their sons. My father, bobbing this way and that, scanned the boys as they filed out. On seeing me, he made a dash for me, picked me up in a brutal hug, pressed his lips to mine, and burst into tears. My mother, more restrained, hugged me to her for several moments, held me away from her, her eyes darting over me, then pressed me to her again.

On these monthly visits, families brought hampers of food for picnics. I was required to write a letter to my family every Saturday afternoon, letters filled with an adolescent's account of his limited doings and ending with scrupulous adjurations for all to remain in a "state of grace" so we could be together for eternity in a heaven I could not envision but believed passionately in.

I did not at this time understand the implications or characteristics of homosexuality. Where and how would I have learned such things? I did not even have the term down yet for what I would eventually come to accept about myself. I did know that I was attracted to boys in a kind of generalized, nebulous way, but I was so removed from the idea of sexuality as it pertained to me that I was unable even to name that attraction.

XII

My understanding of homosexuality and my eventual acceptance that I was a homosexual had a protracted dawning, its delay abetted by the several priests who served as my spiritual directors at the seminary, part mentors, part confessors. I afforded them clear opportunities to help me into an understanding of my gayness, but they remained as obtuse as I in the face of manifest evidence.

"I think I like boys, Father. I'm dreaming about them." I am 14 years old and seated across from Father George, a Benedictine monk of then indeterminate age, though now, from my adult perspective, I suspect he was in his mid-fifties. Even now I see the coarse weave of his scapular folded neatly over his knees. His black serge habit has a man-smell: pipe tobacco, shaving lotion, laundry soap, the mustiness of the cloister.

"Do you touch yourself when you think about boys?" I am in my first year at the seminary preparing for the vocation I had been envisioning for myself throughout childhood. About the third month of my stay in seminary, however, it began to occur to me, with a devastating gradualness, that this priestly closing down of the world was precisely the opposite of what I really wanted in life. Being a priest involved more than flowing cassocks, jeweled copes, and brocaded chasubles.

This realization initiated a heavy time for me: I dreaded revealing to my parents my increasing doubts, now petrifying into certainty, that the religious life was not for me. I knew how disappointed they would be. I stopped eating. I stopped studying. I stopped sleeping. I mooned about in a solitary dismay in the pine forests surrounding the abbey. I even prayed not to live through the night. This was not histrionics: I butt up against this juvenile despair even now with that flattened sense experienced when one crashes headlong into a boulder one did not see when starting out on a clear path.

One evening after supper, I sat watching the gray evening sifting in over the abbey's lake, smutting the bronze burn in the west. The lake slow-hemorrhaged light. Red leaves dripped late autumn's blood and ticked on the dry grass. The sky deepened a dark auburn, a distant cautery. I made my way into the abbey church and was discovered sobbing on my knees in a darkened chapel by three awed boys who had stolen in to try the door to the belfry where they planned to sneak some cigarettes. I remember their shocked faces in the red flicker of the sanctuary lamp. They reported me at once to the first monk they met—Father

George, a shockingly loud priest of large gestures, hearty laugh, little nonsense, his mouth perpetually screwed around a black cauldron of a pipe blasting cinders and belching clouds of gray smoke that smelled to me like burning rope.

After that tearful night, Father George became my spiritual director. Suspecting simple homesickness, he recommended that I complete two years at seminary before making a final decision about leaving, thus delaying revealing my change of heart to those who, at least in my imagination, lived solely for the day I would celebrate my first Mass at ordination.

Father George asks again if I touch myself. He seems in no way alarmed by my confession, his hazy blue eyes slowly scanning my face, my clenched hands. In spite of his calm, I cannot suppress a painful thudding of my heart. Nearly apoplectic, I had thought to alarm and repulse him with my revelations.

I was a preternaturally dense student of sexuality. I seemed to have little normal curiosity, little facility for processing information concerning the region south of the waist. Innocence vied with stupidity: I was trophy for both. I had been informed about the "facts of life" when I was nine years old after coming home to relay a preposterous version of the sex act I had gathered, gaping with consternation, from boys in the neighborhood.

My father, incredulous at the ineptitude of my understanding of sex, corralled me and my older brother in his upstairs office where he further confounded me with some black-and-white line drawings depicting the penis in cross-section, showing the spermal pathway through the testes and their mystifying duct work, through the urethra, and finally out in a blinding white pleasure gush.

I gazed with utter stupefaction at the diagram of the vagina and uterus from a 1930s nursing manual: I still remember this drawing with its lines connecting words to areas anatomically meaningless to me. I have a mental image of myself standing agog and dumbfounded by my father's desk, shorter than my brother and considerably more confused. I remember that my father asked me if some night or other while showering I might have accidently rubbed my penis until it released a white fluid. I had no earthly idea what he was talking about, but as a result of that evening's revelations, I concluded that a man had sex with a woman when he inserted his penis into her anus, a notion which Father George scornfully dismissed.

"Well, do you get aroused when you are undressing with the other boys for bed or in the showers?" I studied the wiry gray hair erupting from the priest's nose and ears. He asked the question casually, thumbing an age-spot on the back of a hand with a nicotine-yellow forefinger.

My mind ranged over the bodies of the naked boys I was accustomed to seeing daily in the dorms. I was so shy about undressing in public that neither my mind nor my eye was licensed to linger over the bodies I was dreaming about: over Jeff who was muscular and precociously hairy, whose prognathous jaw and close-cropped black hair lying like a bristly pelt on his foreshortened skull made him resemble an ape; over Carl whose pearl-white skin seemed to glow and whose gleaming copper curls made him resemble the painted angels swirling around and around the abbey church's cupola; over Ben, so compactly hewn, muscle system gliding effortlessly into muscle system, whose ease and self-assurance were to provide my model for the desirous, who became the prototype for the golden boys I would search for much of my life. Images of male pulchritude glimpsed in the gray-tiled showers flooded through my mind, but I had no memory of arousal.

"No, Father."

"Do you get erect at the swimming pool or afterwards in the locker rooms?"

"No, Father."

I was so self-conscious about the freckles and marks that spotted my pasty skin in that rally of slim, bronzed ephebes that I usually ran from the dressing rooms with a towel draped over my shoulders, flung it hurriedly onto a chain link fence, and cannon-balled into the pool, to emerge only when I saw a dwindling of the lines retreating into the dressing rooms after swimming period had concluded.

I was perpetually guarding my gaze, monitoring my actions, impulses, even my thoughts and desires, though in sleep my surveillance surrendered to that impish panderer, the Id, as it swept aside the gray silks of nighttime reserve and ushered me into saturnalian dreams of boys, my naked classmates aureate in a lubricious light.

"Are there times when you find yourself aroused other than in your dreams?"

"Yes, Father. Sometimes I get hard in class, even sometimes in church, sometimes at dinner or in study hall."

"Okay, that's because you're 14. Do you consciously attempt to excite yourself by looking at pictures or fantasizing in your mind?"

"No, Father. It just comes and I have to put my hands into my front pockets to hide it."

"You're not a homosexual. Your body is just hormone-bedeviled. You're in an all-male environment, so some of that hormone interference is directed at your classmates, which makes you confuse attraction for mere admiration for some of them. Try to avoid the occasions of sin, dismiss impure thoughts when they arise, and think of Our Blessed Mother when you are tempted to touch yourself. For the rest, you can't control what your body must do, nor are you responsible for your dreams, wet or dry. Don't worry anymore about any of this. Try sleeping on your back or side, not on your stomach anymore. This will help to keep the nighttime arousals down. You're perfectly normal."

I think I emitted a little shrill shriek of relief.

XIII

The year following, I am 15 and sitting before Father Maxim, my new spiritual director.

"I think I like boys, Father. I am thinking about them all the time."

Father Maxim, elderly by anyone's reckoning, is sitting across from me, his lined face a study in stern concentration. His hair, pitched up into a corona of fantastic wisps, is hay-dry, the texture of someone's hair just before it falls out after a dose or two of chemotherapy. His black eyes are hawk-like, hooded under dense eyebrows brushed up into spikes like the astonished eyebrows painted on a 19th-Century porcelain doll's face. But in spite of this sharpness of aspect, an ineffectual play hovers about the corners of his mouth, about his receding chin.

"And how do you come to be thinking about them all the time? What are you thinking about them?"

I am not sure how to answer this question because my concentration on my classmates was not then recognizably sexual: There was little consciously erotic about my obsession with the boys I was cloistered with in such close quarters day and night. I would, for example, obsess about Ben's forearms, about how his watch cinctured his wrist securely when my own watch slipped up and down on me like a bangle bracelet, at the musculature that brocaded his forearms, at the light hair sprinkled down his legs, glinting a gold that somehow made my throat constrict. I would obsess at the perfection of Rich's nose, at the deep furrow above his upper lip, the shaved skin there hard and polished as if molded of warm marble. I would obsess about Rob's thick brown hair, sun-bleached at the borders; at Scott's long torso, telescoping down from square shoulders to a narrow column of a waist, at his nipples, pinched into tight brown puckers.

In contrast, my own nose jutted a monumental hooked beak from a long, thin face saddled by a pair of heavy black-plastic eyeglass frames that highlighted the thickness of my lenses. Thinking back on all this, I simply could not have been as ugly as I then judged myself to be. To make matters worse, I had sporadic acne, never seriously invasive but bad enough to cause occasional severe consternation as some hideous rose-fester would bloom over night on chin or nose.

"So that's it." Father Maxim blew air out of his nose in a billow of exhaled relief after I had enumerated all the perfections I envied in my classmates. "All you have to do is give time a chance to work on you. You're not finished yet. Look here: if you want Ben's forearms or Scott's chest, go to the gym. Go every day. There are weights and older boys to show you how to use them. If you like Rob's hair, grow yours longer, and maybe you might want to choose a lighter frame for your glasses so people can see your eyes. As for Rich's nose, well, give your face a chance to catch up with your nose. Three years from now, all this anguish will be over. A lot of young people like you think you're ugly. All this is perfectly normal."

I resolved to go to the gym every day and grew to admire the bodies of the boys who worked out so assiduously there. I resolved to ask my parents for new glasses. I resolved to let my hair grow out. It would, of course, have been more helpful to me then and in the future if my spiritual directors had been able to affirm that I was a homosexual, if they had tried to help me understand my condition and prepare me for a life of acknowledging and affirming it. But that was not to be. They were simply unequal to the task.

XIV

Two school acquaintances in my second-year class, more mature and self-assured than I, had progressed into a fuller understanding and acceptance of their homosexuality by that time, outpacing me by leagues. They were always together, though I doubt they had yet crossed over into full sexual participation, perhaps even yet a naïve judgment on my part. They took great pleasure in posing as sexual sophisticates. They singled me out as a person of interest.

These boys were both from New Orleans. They were bored in the seminary: neither could believe that their plans to jettison their dim-witted families and dull neighborhoods had gone so far awry. They indicated that they had landed on a planet swarming with yokels and hayseeds so corny and provincial as to be beneath contempt. They scorned the seminary hootenanny sing-alongs, the organized sports competitions like horse-shoe throwing, the Saturday night movies like *The Robe* or *Spartacus* (which they grumbled even their torpid families had viewed ten years earlier), the dumb skits mounted by the upper classmen. They were dark, sneering presences in the background of each such event.

One day when I was alone in the open showers, one of these boys wandered in and stood gazing at me as I was lathering up. I thought he wanted to borrow some soap or shampoo. Finally he said, "You're coming along nicely!" He continued to stare at me, eyes roving up and down my adolescent body with its fine brush of pubic hair just beginning to migrate toward my abdomen. I grew shy and turned my back to him, whereupon he thwacked my soapy butt with a rolled-up towel.

Several days later, this boy and his taller companion invited me to go for a walk with them along the river and down the trails into the bordering pine woods. I had walked with them before as well as with many other boys in my class. I liked these two: they were humorous, ironic, and irreverent, given to gossip about our classmates but especially about our teachers.

Well into the woods, we sat companionably on a fallen log, slender shafts of sunlight slicing the air around us. The wind through the pines soughed with the sound of ocean waves. The boy who had encountered me in the showers then announced that I had joined them on the first of what they hoped would be many congenial "gutter walks."

"Gutter walks?" I asked.

"Well, we go on these walks to talk about what boys we find sexy and what we would like to do with them. Some of the priests too!" said the taller of the two boys.

The boy who had eyed me in the showers then told me he found me sexy. He wondered what I thought about him. I told him, truthfully, that I had never given him much thought at all.

He immediately put his hand on the bulge at my crotch and began to unzip my pants. "What do you think of me now?" he asked.

I stood up and dashed his hand away, suddenly afraid to be alone in the woods with them. Seeing how startled I was, they set out to calm me.

"Just wanted to see how you might react," said the boy from the showers. "If you're not interested, it's all right."

What they could not know was that for the first time in my life I felt a throb of sexual desire for another human being in the flesh instead of one dimly outlined in the safe space of my imagination. That I could feel this stirring of desire for this boy puzzled me: I heard this boy's smarmy nasal voice with annoyance and viewed his cheap appearance and limp, colorless hair with repugnance. He looked oily, white and fleshy as a garden grub. And yet I <u>did</u> want him to unzip my pants, curious about what he wanted to do with what he found there.

But this was all way too fast, too far advanced. My innocence then was spectacular, my tastes unfocused, my sexual impulses comatose. I did not know what to say, standing there poised for flight.

Arriving at this dead end, they changed tactics. "Don't go," coaxed the taller boy. "He didn't mean to upset you. Sit back down and let's talk."

I found him even less attractive than his friend. He was doughy and disheveled, his shirt always resisting confinement, his belt slung low where he wore his pants down below his hips. At least one long shoelace always slapped against the sidewalk as he lifted one clumsy foot after the other just high enough to propel himself forward. He always looked as if he were rolling rather than walking.

Though wary, I sat again. They told me their sexual fantasies, tentatively at first, but when they saw I was receptive, gradually advancing more graphic, including particulars that made me blush with a fascination I could not help but reveal. This emboldened them: they ventured on descriptions of boys they had catalogued in the showers and what they wanted to do with them. On hearing their conversation, which I was unprepared to join, I began for the first time to imagine a sexuality that until then had remained inchoate. Desire stirred in me, now with a clearer focus.

These moments in that still, sun-sliced forest intrigued and repulsed me. This "gutter walk" served as my initiation into a sexual imagination. I was fifteen. I was devoutly religious. I had never even masturbated. Though I was having wet dreams, these clotted outlets visited me when I was unconscious, rapt in sleep.

Though captivated by these boys' fantasies, I soon judged them to be sinful. They goaded each other into more and more salacious elaborations, describing sexual acts I had never imagined, enjoying the shift of my facial expressions, the reddening and blushing that came and went. This "gutter walk" was my homosexual initiation, my awakening from childhood's erotic slumber. I gained what my limited resources could not yet supply me—what was sexually possible between men. Oral sex? Anal sex? News to me.

On that long-ago afternoon, wind sighing through the bending pines, the river nearby breathing a scent of water, I underwent my baptism into sexual desire. For the first time, clearly and without doubt, with full intellectual and emotional force, I recognized that I was attracted to my own sex. My eyes were now opened, my thoughts engaged, my imagination aroused. Here was Adam's Edenic fall into a full sexual awareness played out again in my own psyche. I had, at last, bitten into the apple.

This plunge into sexual awareness did not sit easily with me. Within a week, disturbed by an ingrained guilt produced by a too-scrupulous conscience and with the mortal sin I felt these boys had burdened me with, I sought an appointment with Father Maxim and, in confession, provided him with an account of these newly codified desires and an acknowledgement of how they arose—place, time, cause, instigators.

Several mornings later, both of my companions on this "gutter walk" were absent from class. They had decided, we were told, that they wanted to leave the seminary and return to their families. The one who had peered at me in the showers left me a note: "Lucien—You were a grade A friend. Whenever I was in the dumps, I could turn to you." Clearly, these two boys had not figured out the role I suspect I played in their expulsion.

I knew why they were gone. No one else in the class did. It was not unusual for boys to leave suddenly, no reason given. Once they had decided they did not wish to become priests, their families came for them, often over a weekend, occasionally overnight. It was clear to me that these boys were asked to leave—and I was behind it.

Corroded with guilt over this, I went immediately to Father Maxim. He assured me that I had simply precipitated the inevitable, that on questioning them, these boys confessed that they had no intentions of ever becoming priests and were simply waiting for the earliest opportunity to leave. I provided the catalyst which brought on the conclusion they had wished for. I was in no way to feel guilty about any of this. I was, this priest persuaded me, not really a homosexual, only susceptible to suggestion and liable to the usual adolescent confusion.

So ended this incident, but like a stone dropped into a lake, this "gutter walk" would ripple far out into the coming years when, belatedly, I would embrace at last my sexual maturity. This "gutter walk," so troubling to me then, would prove fortunate in the future, though it occasioned much confusion and consternation in the short run.

XV

I never doubted for a moment that my parents loved me, though during the 1950s and 60s it did not seem the fashion to express that love directly in words. I never feared that my parents would ever stop loving me, even after it had become clear to me that I did not want to be a priest after all. On

Mother's Day of my second and last year in seminary, I broke this news to my visiting parents.

"You're sure?" my father inquired. "This is not just a case of homesickness?"

While I was making these halting disclosures, a group of men rushed down to the banks of the Bogue Falaya, the shallow, sandy river that bordered the seminary grounds. Soon they found the missing four-year-old, his drowned body wedged under a submerged log.

The day after my parents returned home from this visit, my father penned a letter to me:

> Well I guess yesterday was one of those days that we have to meet with once in a while. I was very much disturbed when I found out the youngster had died, and then when I found out about your decision, I couldn't talk or think. Most every father and mother look forward to having a member of their family have a religious vocation. We both did in your case. I told Mother last night when we got home that I guess the Lord didn't see fit to let us have a vocation at this time.
>
> Your change in plans will cause no change in your and my relationship. I will stand up for you in your decisions and know you will come through in whatever vocation you choose. I will hold nothing against you because of this change. I find it so hard to realize you have made the change. I am willing to accept it and will soon make the adjustment. We all love

you very much and look forward to your
return home.

Even at 15, I recognized the disappointment which
prompted my father's letter. It hurt me that he and my
mother seemed to feel that they were unworthy of having a
son called to the priesthood. But emanating through every
line of that letter was the love beneath their letdown that
guided my father in composing it.

I only fully realized the extent of my parents'
disappointment in my turning away from a vocation they so
ardently wished for me, when, shortly after my 72nd
birthday, I began to read my mother's preserved letters to
her sisters in Ohio, penned during my birth year. On March
18, 1948, she noted that the Church in Louisiana "needed
priests desperately," and concluded that she hoped she and
my father "will be able to produce at least one." On July 6,
a scant four days before my birth, my mother concluded her
letter by asserting that she hoped this child about to be
delivered would be "a little boy as we were definitely
praying for a vocation to the priesthood" for either me or my
older brother. In her letter of July 12, announcing my birth
on the 10th, she notes that my father "savored the following
words on his tongue: 'Father Lucien.'"

With the exception of my father's letter to me after I
told them of my decision to leave the seminary and abandon
the priesthood as a vocation, my parents never indicated to
me how disappointed they were that I had dashed their
deepest hopes for me.

XVI

During my last months at the seminary, I was assigned
a new spiritual director tasked with helping me transition to

the secular world. This monk was homely: a hooked nose supported black-framed glasses with lenses of such an astonishing thickness that his crossed eyes seemed to have retreated into crystalline caves. A pouty little mouth bottomed a pock-marked face, the remnant of what must have been an acne-agonized youth, assuaged, no doubt, by his early enclosure in the abbey cloister. He was slight in stature and, I suspect, gay. He had a tell-tale queer tone of voice accompanied by a readiness to laugh in a high register in order to diffuse the distaste he suspected he inspired, a crisp self-possession to counter the fragmentation many gay men experience who cannot evade the sense of disconnection from the straight world. He had a way of walking and positioning his body, a clipped near-prance, a tight precision unlike the easy lope of many heterosexual men. He had a penchant for full canonical vesture, the hood of his white alb crisply aligned above the scarlet or emerald or pearl of his brocaded chasubles.

Like therapy, effective spiritual direction depends on a degree of mutual affinity. This monk apparently disliked me as much as I him. I suspect he and I each saw echoed in the other some personal traits that we both despised in ourselves at that time. During our sessions, I held back information on the recently awakened sexual interests I had decided to be ashamed of and to deny for the rest of my life.

(I am chagrined to admit that even as late as June 1971, while in graduate school, I was writing to my parents, in a letter they preserved, about "Orlando, the queer who lives below me, who just <u>adores</u> my new shirt, tra-la, tra-la." Such is the durability of denial and self-loathing....)

I had determined to eradicate the desires and fantasies awakened in me on my recent "gutter walk." I figured there was no need to confess what I would struggle against for the remainder of my life and never give in to. This decision may have preserved me from an intensification of guilt and shame at this priest's hands, or it may have been a missed opportunity if, in the unlikely chance, this priest had advised me humanely that mine was not a sinful choice, that I was gay by divine design, "fearfully and wondrously made" (Psalm 139) in the divine image like all human beings, and that I now had the responsibility, without any help from Mother Church, to develop strategies for living a full, rewarding, honorable life as a homosexual man.

During one of our sessions, he offered me advice both unsolicited and deeply wounding. Suddenly he was full into a denunciation of what he termed my "effeminate behaviors." "You will spare yourself much misery in the future if you could act in a more manly way," I recall him saying. "Speak in a deeper voice if you can. And when you talk, do not gape your eyes so wide. Keep your hands by your sides rather than waving them about. Never squeal or gush or simper. Certainly never giggle. Try to find at least one sport you won't embarrass yourself playing—tennis or volleyball or something. Choose smart friends but don't parade your braininess. You don't always have to blurt out answers in class like you do. Above all, try to fit in. This will preserve you from much ridicule and rejection if you can pull it off. Imitate Paul Geddings for a good role model. Notice how calm and even his temperament is, how slowly he speaks in a deep and modulated voice. The other boys respect him; his teachers like him; he will make a good and wise priest if he stays in seminary. It's a good idea to have someone to imitate. I suggest Paul for you."

Two thoughts surfaced immediately: first, this priest was in love with Paul Geddings. Second, I knew I would never approximate the handsome, athletic Paul Geddings who rarely spoke because he had so little to say, whose deep voice was slow and deliberate because his mind was

71

tentative and sluggish. But I did have to agree that Paul was a desirable and enviable young man, widely admired, generous and kind and open, displaying an effortless masculinity that this priest encouraged me to imitate. Paul Geddings, by the way, ended up in the Louisiana Legislature, representing a group of rural parishes outside of New Orleans. His political career was brought to an end by an ugly divorce and two DUI infractions in a single year.

Inevitably, this priest's advice stimulated in me a dark period of damaging self-judgments of my nature, mannerisms, interests, and physical characteristics as unappealing. My resulting self-consciousness led to a negative self-image that would take me years to replace. Here is a passage from my diary, dated Thursday, August 20, 1964, several months after this priest had at me: "My self-consciousness is giving way to more manly sentiments. I want to be very masculine now and I am very attracted to girls." This pathetic scribbling of a 15-year-old was prompted by a priest who was neither a psychologist nor a realist, merely a dabbler in the lives of those vulnerable to him. Simply telling someone to change ingrained habits and behaviors does not provide one with the means to accomplish the desired transformation. The natural result of such advice is self-loathing. Some never escape that onus. Others, like me, escape it, but with a struggle sometimes lasting years.

From the sessions with this priest I derived one clear advantage, though I did not recognize it as beneficial at the time: This priest recognized that I was as gay as he himself probably was and treated me as such, though he intimated that I should do all in my power to suppress my gayness. But here at last was clear confirmation of what had been up to that time only a strong suspicion. Now I knew that I was a homosexual. No more evading that. No more denying it. No more trying to pray it away. But no practical acceptance of my gayness either and all it meant for me and the life I had to construct with that confirmation. I could then, and did, decide never to act on my gayness, never to live as a gay man in spite of my acknowledging that condition in myself.

Everyone is on a learning curve into understanding and accepting the self. But gay men often undergo a more difficult process, more disturbing, flushed with doubt, even fear, before coming into full self-understanding, eventual acceptance, and the strength to live fully as the man one irrevocably is. I could wish that my process of coming out had been made easier, more supportive, but such was not the case. I hope it is different now for young gay men trying to come out, though I suspect it is as difficult for many now as it was for me so long ago.

So, this was the condition I was in on leaving the seminary and being sent by my parents to an all-boys Catholic high school with its emphasis on the sciences, mathematics, and athletics, disciplines for which I had little interest or talent. I had decided that I would not be the boy I had learned I was at the seminary. I would not be a queer, especially because that sobriquet was passed around so liberally, attaching to any boy who wavered even slightly from expected norms of male behavior, a machismo intensified in this all male world by no ameliorating feminine influence in the faculty or among my fellow students. Instead, I elected to become invisible, easy enough to do in a school where masculine jockeying for top ranking prevailed.

Many signals flashed for me at this school, semaphores warning me that suspect behaviors, even fantasies or silent desires, were to be suppressed. Constant vigilance was required. These warning vibrations came principally from other boys, but teachers and coaches contributed their shares.

One particular instance of this came in a health class, taught by a coach whose duties on the athletic fields did not completely justify his meager salary and who thus had to be given academic classes to flounder in to create the illusion that he was carrying a full faculty load. This coach concluded a class on nutrition one afternoon by warning us not to loiter after school and never to accept a ride from anyone we did not know. "There are men who drive around the streets surrounding this school looking for young men to get into their cars with them," he said, brows furrowed. "They have dark desires and are willing to pay boys to satisfy them. They are mostly harmless queers who just want to pay you to let them suck you off, but some of these queers can be dangerous."

I remember wondering if this was how I would end up, lonely and desperate, driving around a school in a futile search to pick up boys to pay them to revile and despise me. And I was well aware of what some of my classmates alleged, almost certainly fictitiously—that they spent Saturday nights downtown "rolling queers," meaning, I assumed, that they bashed them and then took their wallets.

In my desire to disguise any wayward tendencies that might reveal themselves, I submitted in my junior year to the tedious expectation that I should be dating girls. My older brother Andy was a senior the year I entered this school as a junior. He had a serious girlfriend whose parents would only allow her to go out with him on double dates, so Andy persuaded me to ask a girl on a date so we four could go out together when others of his friends were not available to double date with him.

I wish I had had the strength of mind or character at that time to forego this expected dating ritual. It would have

74

saved me from so many wasted evenings, including the worst experience of my unsatisfactory high-school dating career, which happened the first year I was back from the seminary. I asked a girl I knew from the neighborhood to go out with me and my brother and his girlfriend. She told me that she had to help her mother with something that night. I was so naive that I did not recognize this dodge for what it was—an indication of a complete lack of interest in me. When next I asked her out, she countered with yet another flimsy rejection. The third time I asked her out, she told me that she was having a little Christmas get-together at her married sister's house on that Saturday night. Then, apparently realizing that she should not have mentioned the party, she allowed a long pause to intervene before asking if I might be interested in attending.

When my mother dropped me off, I found that there were only eight kids there, none of whom I knew except for this girl. They were all paired up, my presumptive date clearly involved with a boy from a public high school. There was a Santa Claus toy there that, when wound up, climbed a little ladder on the side of a miniature house and surrendered a gumdrop down a chimney. I was ignored by the party guests: they did not even bother to respond to any of the conversational overtures I attempted. I repaired to this girl's sister and her husband in the dining room, exclaiming over and over how cute the Santa was and putting it through its trick repeatedly. After about 30 minutes of this humiliation, I called my mother and asked her to come for me, leaving by the backdoor to wait in the street, making some lame excuse for leaving before dinner. It is terrible to be an object of pity by adults who see what is happening but can do nothing to help a young person save face.

When this girl turned up pregnant later that year and had to leave school, I experienced so vivid a retributive satisfaction that I felt the term "Schadenfreude" I learned in literature class had been coined specifically to describe this petty salve to a wound that I am, almost 60 years later, yet able to scratch open again. Such moments of acute embarrassment and unease—no matter how trivial and inconsequential they now seem when looked back on from so far in the future—remain in the mind and notch the soul, ironically eclipsing other exhilarating moments of real triumph and accomplishment in memory's repository.

XVII

What did my parents know about homosexuality? What did any parents of the 1950s, 60s, even 70s know about it except how pathetic and pathological queers were, how sick and perverted, perhaps even how twisted and vicious they could be. Other than that, I do not think my parents knew much about it, though they could not help but scent a few whiffs emitted from poufters around them.

My father, for example, attended LSU in the late 1930s, living in a shared stadium dorm room on campus. Every weekend he would hitch a ride from the university to downtown Baton Rouge to catch a ferry over the Mississippi River where he would pick up another ride to take him to his small hometown of White Castle some 30 or so miles downriver. On several occasions during his four years at university, he reported being propositioned by a few of the men who had offered him rides. Apparently the offers were subtle and off-hand but unmistakable, and when he quietly declined, these men did not persist.

Once when my family was riding downtown in our 1950s beige and finned Ford Farirlane 500, my father indicated to my mother in a low voice that he had heard that the Mirror Room on 3rd Street was a bar where men went to meet other men. I overheard him, bolted up, knelt on the back seat, and faced the rear for a better view.

"Sit back down!" my father demanded.

When I did sit down and faced forward again, I caught my father's frowning eye regarding me in the rear-view mirror.

My father was one of the first men I knew who was into physical fitness. He took up jogging in the mid-60s when I was a teenager and contemptuous of such doings. He jumped rope like a boxer, criss-crossing his rope in front of him. He lifted weights in the garage. One summer afternoon while he was jumping rope on our back patio with only his jogging shorts on, a group of young men hanging out on a balcony of an apartment in a building overlooking our backyard called out to him, martini glasses raised high and glinting in the sun: "Ooh, Daddy, bring some of that up here!" and "Hey, Handsome, how'd you like to party with us?" My father simply laughed it off and went in the house. I stayed on the patio watching the men on the balcony, envying the good time they were having.

"If we can't have the rooster," one of the men snickered, "maybe we can get the chicken up here," pointing at me. I was probably all of fifteen.

"Always were a chicken hawk, right, Conrad? He's got to be too young even for you," laughed one of his companions. At this sudden burst of laughter, my father called me inside.

"A sad thing," my father said to my mother one evening when he walked into the house after work. "The police arrested Abe Kellogg's son in the men's room at Rosenfield's Department Store yesterday. Apparently he propositioned an undercover police officer at a urinal. It was in the paper this morning. Abe is going around telling everyone that his son's a 'goddamned queer.'"

"Now what kind of father would turn on his own son like that?" my mother sighed.

"A deeply humiliated one," my father said. "I'm glad none of my children have shamed me like that." Then he turned to look directly at me and added, "yet."

Abe Kellogg's son was later killed in a crash in his Volkswagen Beetle returning on a late foggy Saturday night from a gay bar in New Orleans. According to a companion in the car who survived the accident, he was drunk, must have been sleepy, met an inconveniently placed culvert, had disregarded his seat belt, and was thrown through the windshield. Later that same year, my father returned home one evening from work and burst into sobs while telling my mother that Abe Kellogg had gone behind the Mississippi River levee and blown the top of his head away, mouth to shotgun barrel.

My mother, even after all this, seemed clueless about homosexuality; either that, or she simply refused to give it any room in her imagination or in her world. Perhaps she thought it was so aberrant, so rare that it had nothing whatsoever to do with her or anyone connected to her.

Neither of my mother's older two sisters ever married. One of them, my Aunt Helen, was born in 1901, the year Queen Victoria died. Before I really knew her, when she was living in Ohio before she and her sister, my Aunt Jo, moved down to Louisiana to be closer to us, Aunt Helen was inseparable for many years with a man who served as my godfather shortly before dying in a car accident in Ohio. He was lovingly remembered by my mother and her sisters. From all I heard about him, I could only speculate that he might possibly have been gay, though my mother scolded me roundly when, in an unguarded moment, I mentioned this suspicion to her.

It was, however, no long stretch to think so about him. He was a church organist and master of revels at every party, organizing riotous skits and practical jokes, precise in his ideas of stagecraft, costuming, and accents, a master at riposte, banter, and gossip, though never mean or vicious. He was a jovial life-of-the-party kind of guy, a good dancer, an excellent singer. And he accompanied my aunt everywhere for years, maintaining a rigorously virginal distance from anything even suggesting the erotic. After he died relatively young in that car crash, he left my aunt a diamond ring that had belonged to his mother and a sizeable portion of his estate.

After their move from Ohio to Louisiana, my aunts, who did not cook for themselves, joined a "supper club" at a downtown cafeteria attended nightly by a few married couples and by a coterie of unattached women, some of whom I would later recognize as almost certainly lesbians, though my aunts were clearly not of the Sapphic persuasion, being, as far as I could tell, completely and utterly asexual. One of these women I suspected of being a lesbian shared her name with the first name of the invert author of *The Well of Loneliness*. I suspected she had assumed the name "Radclyffe" in homage to the earlier lesbian whose work she must have admired.

I think that because I was so completely devoid of any macho flavor, my Aunt Helen favored me, inviting me often to accompany her and some of her lady friends on their drives to New Orleans for symphony, opera, and summer pops. Their pimpled squire, I enacted courtly rituals with these ladies as I was trained by my aunt to do—opened doors, walked on the outside curb of the street, carried parcels, rose from table when they left to powder their noses, levitated again when they returned in order to attend to their chairs, helped them on and off with their coats (lift the coat collar high when the first arm slides into its sleeve; the other arm will find its way effortlessly and the coat will fall onto the neck and back in its natural position). I was the perfect courtier, a cavalier retainer who sat still, did not fidget or interrupt, was solicitous, discrete, had perfect table manners, never chafed at my collar or sport coat, guarded my tongue against ever uttering anything inappropriate, looked to the ceiling when my aunt settled our bill, a little asexual Prufrock gigolo, happy to be so and grateful to my aunt to this day for introducing me to social skills I exercise and entertainments I enjoy even now.

My aunt believed a gentleman ought to have a cocktail before dinner, so she allowed me to order a small gin martini. In those days, legal drinking age in Louisiana was 18, give or take three or four years. She always made a dinner reservation at Antoine's in the French Quarter where we ate at her usual table in a back room reserved in advance and attended by Sylveste, a black creole waiter in a tuxedo, who called her "Madame" and me "M'sieur," even before my voice began to crack.

My mother seemed so breathtakingly clueless about homosexuality that even when it confronted her directly and, to anyone else, unmistakably, she seemed unable to recognize or credit it.

"Who?" my mother asked over the phone. "Who is this calling, please?"

"Francis, an old friend of Pat's, the organist who was your sister Helen's friend. I knew you also when you worked at Springfield General as the medical records librarian there. Francis: I was a nurse there before the war."

"Francis! It's been such a long time!"

He and "his companion, Albert" were making a cross-country journey from San Francisco to Florida to visit

Albert's sister and were passing through Baton Rouge. They suggested a visit.

"Would you like to stay with us?" my mother felt compelled to ask.

"For a day or two, if we wouldn't be too much trouble."

My mother gave them the room I shared with my two brothers, and she made us sleep on floor-pallets in the living room, one of the reasons I did not like these two guys from the start. Our room had a double bed for my older brother and twin beds for me and my younger brother.

In the arrogance of my youth, Francis struck me as unforgivably old and doddery. Albert was a tad younger but had a hitch in his step from having suffered a stroke several years before. He was bald as a pecan and reeked of cigars. Though he was the one who hobbled, he was excessively attentive to Francis, steering him down the hall and up stairs with a hand ever at Francis's elbow.

Francis carried a shoulder bag, a "man-purse," the first man I ever knew to do so, and he wore what looked to me like rouge and something dark at his eyebrows. He sported a diamond ring on his pinkie and a silver bracelet on one wrist. His white hair was fluffed up around his ears to a roll over his forehead. He crossed his legs at the ankles and folded his hands in his lap when he composed himself at a side angle on the seat of a chair.

The morning after their arrival, I realized I had forgotten my toothbrush in the boys' bathroom and had to enter our bedroom to retrieve it.

"Come in," I heard when I knocked on the door. On entering, I discovered they were together in the double bed instead of the twin beds my mother had made up for them. Albert was in a white undershirt, which we used to call a "wife beater." He had a tattoo on his upper arm, which must have been an anchor or a heart at one time but which had

81

now dribbled into a gray puddle. Francis had on scarlet silk pajamas buttoned all the way up to his chin.

That day my parents drove them for a tour of some of the antebellum plantation mansions along the Mississippi River, a usual pastime we offered out-of-state visitors. While crossing the Mississippi River Bridge in Baton Rouge, Francis peered out of the car window and asked if the river below was the Gulf Coast.

"Gah," I exclaimed. My mother frowned at me when I snickered contemptuously.

The next morning, still resentful at having to sleep on the floor, I walked into the kitchen while my mother was frying bacon.

"These guys are queer," I said, "and they're stupid on top of it!"

"Well, yes," my mother admitted, "they <u>are</u> odd, but you seem to have forgotten that you are not allowed to call adults stupid."

"<u>No</u>!" I shouted, "They're <u>queers</u>! <u>Fruits</u>! Francis wears make-up!"

My father lowered the sports page. "Keep it down," he whispered.

My mother turned to me, blinked a few times: "How would you know about that? Where did you hear that word? Don't you remember they are still in this house?"

Homosexuality played the most minimal part in my parents' lives—until it played a large part indeed….

XVIII

My coming out to my parents was not voluntary. I was over 40, and as far as my clueless family was concerned, still in the closet. I had early decided I did not need to come out to my parents. I was then living in Sacramento and came home to Louisiana for only a week or so at Christmas and again for a short visit in the summer. With this infrequency of contact, I had decided that there was no need to divulge anything about a life they so rarely shared, especially if divulging my homosexuality would trouble them. Besides, I was single and sluttish with no intention of ever having a serious boyfriend I would feel compelled to introduce them to. So, they were the last in the world to know that I was gay.

I was wrong about these decisions. Once I was forced out, we had to re-shape a relationship that had been constructed on false premises in that they did not know or accept me for who I really was. There was pain for them on learning that I was gay, but we resolved that over time and grew to love each other for the people we really were—me a gay man, they parents whose unfailing love for me rested on a more honest, more secure basis.

So this is how my closet door was forced open from the outside:

My parents owned a beach house on Dauphin Island, Alabama, a long barrier island stretching across the mouth of Mobile Bay, essentially defining the bay as distinct from the bronze-tinted waters of the Gulf of Mexico. My siblings and I could reserve the beach house for as much as a week or two at a time.

At home for ten days one summer, I chose to spend a weekend at the beach house with three gay friends of mine from New Orleans. We would sun, swim, go crabbing, eat seafood, gossip, quaff copious cocktails. One of the three, my oldest friend Roger, had introduced me to the other two, both librarians with him at Tulane. The one I knew least well, Gus, was taciturn and grumpy in a droll way, complaining about everyone and everything with a dry raillery. His sharp repartee and bitchy observations often cracked me up. He was fat and homely but with a tongue that could etch aluminum.

"I'm consenting to participate in this little debauch at the beach only because I have never had a tan in my life, and I figure it's high time," he said on my inviting him. "I've heard everything those other two tarts have to say who are accompanying us, so I'm proposing to invite a new trick I picked up a month or so ago at the Club Baths. He's young and cute and occasionally campy, a counterpoise to the four old hags we've become. What do you say?"

"Just assure me he's housebroken," I said. "Will he steal the silverware—or know how to use it?"

"Oh, he's presentable, and we can at least bear to look at him. He'll liven things up."

I had misgivings.

"Bring him along," I decided, "but you'll have to drive over separately in your own car to dispose of the corpse if he displeases."

Gus and Ferdy arrived impossibly late on that Friday evening and demanded dinner, though we had eaten and washed up three hours earlier.

"Kitchen's closed," I said. "You'll have to drink dinner. Why didn't you eat on the way over?"

"Of course we ate on the way over. I just wanted to see if I could nettle you up into a fluster."

Ferdy: Many gay men would probably find him cute, but in a cheap way, a blurred cute. And young too, embarrassingly so, apparently over 18, but not by much. Smart? Let's just say he was headed toward flunking out of cosmetology school before he could even supply himself with curlers. Witty? I have laughed harder at crows picking over a dead armadillo by the side of the highway.

Ferdy had short-cropped white-blonde hair, longer in front, which he gelled up into a kind of tsunami cresting over a narrow forehead. His features were regular but had that undefined outline characteristic of those who have not lived long enough for either life or intelligence to etch themselves on them. His lips were full and red as if he had been sucking a cherry popsicle, but they seemed smudged, without clear borders. The real problem for me with the "cute" descriptor was Ferdy's skin tone, the color and too creamy texture of suet. He was small and compact, an ideal size for a bottom, but I suspect that he ventured into sex without much enthusiasm, lying there passively, eyes shut, perhaps murmuring vacantly to himself.

Shirtless at the beach, his small nipples were pink, tightly pinched rosebuds. His Speedo was a slip of an envelope that barely registered his genitals. He was plush as a toadstool and equally hairless. I was both attracted and repelled by him: attracted to his youth; repelled by his insistent physicality unrelieved by personality or intelligence.

When we arrived at the beach the next day, I noted offhandedly that the tide was out, whereupon Ferdy assured me that we could buy more in time to do the laundry before we left.

"Har, Har!" Gus exploded. "Brilliant!"

Though he merits just a brief dismissal, I write of Ferdy so fully because he was to play the pivotal role in the drama of my parents forcing me out of a closet I was, in the long run, happy they helped me escape.

Here's how that happened:

My younger brother was to take the beach house at 3:00 on the Sunday afternoon we were to vacate it. We were changing linens, doing laundry, and sweeping up the sand from the tile floors when my brother unexpectedly walked into the house at 1:00, his wife and children waiting in the car.

"I just wanted to see if you might have left early," he explained. "No hurry. We're off to have some lunch."

"I'd like to have you for lunch," Ferdy piped up, edging closer to him. "You look delicious."

My brother looked at Ferdy as if he were a tick, then glanced at me. As my brother was heading for the door, Ferdy made to follow him. I yanked Ferdy by the upper arm so hard that his head bobbled. "Cut it out," I hissed.

That was in the summer. Though I was not there to hear it, I suspect that my brother reported this encounter with Ferdy to my parents after returning from the beach house. Though I cannot be sure this ever happened at all, I can almost hear him saying something like this: "He was there with a bunch of fags, every single one of them a queer from New Orleans. How do I know? One little fruit followed me around like a puppy wanting to be petted. Lucien stopped that, but I could tell he was embarrassed. I couldn't wait to get out of there."

"So, do you think Lucien's gay too?" my father probably asked.

"Well, what do you think?" my brother would have replied.

"He's just got a gay friend or two is all," my mother would have interjected. "He told us his old friend Roger from seminary was going to be there. Roger's not gay. Besides, Lucien dates women," my mother would have concluded. "I think you should stop suggesting that he's gay."

On my Christmas visit following all this, my mother was out grocery shopping and I was sitting with my father over coffee the morning after I had arrived home.

"Well," my father began, creasing a section of the paper down and facing me, "tell me one thing. Are you attracted to women at all?"

"Do you mean sexually?" I asked. "If you do mean that, then the answer would be no."

He looked at me for awhile, then lowered his eyes and raised his coffee cup for a sip. "Then you're gay?"

"Why do you need to know that?" I asked, hedging.

"Because you're my son?"

"Then yes, I am gay," I said.

"Well, tell your mother. We've been speculating about it for months now."

Almost immediately following this disclosure, I heard the car door slam outside and my mother walked in with a full grocery bag in her arms.

"Mom," I said, before she got very far into the house, "I'm gay."

Her face fell. She looked around for a place to set down her groceries. Then she opened her arms and folded me in them. "You can't help it," she sighed. "I know you did not choose this."

"I hope," I whispered to her in this embrace, "in time to bring you to a happier place about it than this. You make it sound as if being gay is a disease or a birth defect."

She just hugged me tighter.

My father said, "Let us tell your brother and sisters, not you."

"Why?" I asked.

"We just think it will be better if we tell them," my mother said. I think they feared that my siblings might say something sharp or wounding on first hearing this news. My parents would provide a buffer.

So, I was out of the closet then, irretrievably so. Each time one comes out as gay, it is a gain. Ironically, I always felt coming out to be a loss as well. Before I came out to anyone, I harbored a secret self all my own that I chose not to reveal. There was a certain solipsistic power in that private knowledge. I know that others must have surmised that I was gay, but it was in my purview to keep from them a certain knowledge of my true self, my private, inviolable identity. This secret fashioned for me a life set apart, divergent, one true to me alone and outside the common run of men.

While I held this secret, I was all-in-all to myself—apart, other, whole within my own regard. This perceived distinction, while lonely, conferred a power, a pride and strength that dissipated as soon as I shared my gay secret, hung it out like a banner in the bleaching light of day. But with that disclosure came also relief that I was now woven into the whole-cloth of a richer human pattern, that I had assumed my rightful place in a world capacious enough for me to breathe more fully in. A gay identity, after all, is not meant to be hoarded or hidden. Such hiding eventually portends damage to one's self and to others.

I figured that since my parents had outed me, I had been given permission to share with them my gay life—whom I was dating, the bars and parties I went to, issues of gay politics. I was wrong about that. They seemed not to want me to share any of this with them. On our weekly phone calls, as soon as I opened up about my gay life in Sacramento, the line seemed to go dead and a hollow silence ensued. I nevertheless persisted in attempting to share the life they had come to recognize that I was living. I thought it important for straight people like them who are attempting to come to terms with a gay person they love to meet other gay people so that they can see the common humanity we all share, regardless of our sexual orientations. And it was important to me that my parents were assured that I was living largely and richly. Were I reticent with them, they would have concluded that my life was sad, narrow, and circumscribed, and that would not have made them happy for me.

I regret now not being more sensitive towards my parents at this juncture. What I should have realized was that they were at some level still burdened with the attitudes towards homosexuality prevalent during the 1940s and 50s: for my father, the Army's rigorous anti-homosexual stance; for both my parents the prevalent attitude back then that homosexuality was a psychosexual pathology and that homosexuals were dangerous sexual perverts, so mentally ill and/or susceptible to blackmail that they had to be prevented from working in any capacity for the government or in any job that brought them into contact with children. In addition, homosexuals were, by their sinful sexual perversions, criminals who could be locked up for their felonious sexual behaviors. They had lived much of their lives during the "lavender scare" that pervaded every aspect of American society during the 50s, 60s, and 70s. In short, my parents had been indoctrinated by their culture early on to see homosexuality through the lenses of sin, crime, and sickness. I regret now not being more solicitous in helping them to work through these dark residues and to show them more patiently that these outmoded ways of considering homosexuals did not apply to me, the gay son they continued to love but grieved to learn was other than the son they thought me to be.

My parents' refusal to engage with the gay issue went on for months, but on one particular phone call, I was buoyantly telling them about someone I had just started dating who happened to be in his twenties, then a full seventeen years younger than me. I would soon tire of the stupid financial straits this guy got into trying to maintain an old beat-up Saab which balked at running for more than three consecutive days, his constant job hunting, his speeding tickets on good days with his bad car. I hated that he always dialed my radio into heavy-metal head-banger stations. After the usual silence with which they greeted my dating news, my mother said, in a dry tone: "Just assure us that you won't have to pay for his college tuition."

As was usual for them when they faced anything troubling—my brother's divorce, my sister's conversion to a fundamentalist, born-again Christian religion—they consulted a priest about me, their gay son. They always had the good sense to select a smart priest, usually a Jesuit.

"Is your son a good person?" the priest asked them. "Does he have a good job? Friends? Is he happy and engaged with life? Well-adjusted?"

On hearing affirmative answers to all his questions, he told them: "It doesn't sound as if your son has any issues to be concerned about here. He can't live the life you would apparently prefer him to live—and that's not his problem. That's your problem. You can solve it by loving and blessing him in the good life he's living. Consider yourselves fortunate that he's happy and thriving."

Several months later on a visit to me in California, my mother and I were sitting together at a picnic table in Yosemite. I had invited a boyfriend along, though he had gone with my father and sister on a hike. I had stayed behind to keep my mother company.

"Do you like Doug?" I asked her.

"He's nice," she said. "He smiles a lot."

"I'm not sure we'll go very far together in life, but he's fun to be with for the present," I said.

"Is he aware of this? Does he expect more from you?" she asked.

"I suspect he's on the same page as I am," I said. "I just don't think either of us is in it for the long haul."

"The Catholic Church acknowledges that being gay is not a sinful choice," she said. "I know now that you are born that way, but the Church still condemns gay sexuality. You do know that you are called to the single life since you can't marry and did not receive a vocation to be a priest."

My whole body pivoted toward her on the picnic table bench: "Mother, is it really your wish for me that I live alone, that I never love anyone or let anyone love me, and that I deny myself all sexual satisfaction for the rest of my life? Is that really what you think will make me fulfilled and happy?"

She was silent for several moments, looking away from me and out over El Capitan. Then she turned to me, her eyes like my own—a hazel whirl of green, gold, soft brown. "No," she whispered, "I do not wish that for you."

Years later, after she had died, I was helping my father sort through my mother's clothes. In the top drawer of her dresser I found a book, apparently given her by the Jesuit she had consulted years earlier, published by the Catholic Press: *The Parents of the Homosexual*. Its opening sentence went something like this: "No matter what you think or did, no matter what you fear, no matter what you may try to blame yourself for, you did nothing at all in any way to determine that your son or daughter would live a homosexual life. That was beyond your control or your ability to cause or prevent."

My mother had underlined this passage five times. I hope it relieved her of the guilt she was so prone to, the responsibility she might have thought she bore for my gay life and how it turned out. My mother was wrong in thinking that she was responsible for and could determine the direction her children's lives would take, that she was solely accountable for the adults her children would become. I am grateful for the fostering and teaching and guidance she so lovingly provided me during my childhood, but she could not control the choices and the direction my life would eventually follow. I hope she did come eventually to have the easier time my father seemed to have with my being gay. I hope she saw that my being gay in no way deprived me of the enjoyment and satisfaction I have taken in my life, that my being gay—open and out about it—only increased my happiness. I could not have lived any other life with the engagement and fulfillment my parents would have wished for me.

XIX

I have every reason to believe that my parents were too intelligent, too informed to accept the old canard that a gay man could trace his "pathology" to an "overbearing, over-protective, domineering mother" in league with a "passive, abusive, or absent father." My parents could never be tagged with either of these descriptors. Though they would have consciously rejected this wounding misinformation from psychologists of a bygone era, harmful to parents and their gay sons alike, I do wonder if the poisonous resonances of this malign explanation of the origins of gay sexual orientation resounded at some level for them, being adults when this dominant theory held sway in psychological handbooks that also described homosexuality as a pathology, a form of mental illness.

My mother had a tendency to take on a misplaced responsibility for any variation in her children from her strongly held socio-religious convictions—like homosexuality in my case, or divorce, or apostasy from her deep Catholicism. She seemed to accept, on an intellectual level, that she had done nothing to cause me to be gay, though I suspect there echoed in her a nagging sense that she must have contributed to it in some way.

This most earnest of women once told me that she never really felt forgiven for whatever sins she conjured up for a priest in the confessional, even after receiving absolution. Certainly my mother, who bore four heterosexual children in addition to one gay one, could never be described as a domineering or over-bearing mother. A co-equal partner in her marriage to my father, she was ever buoyant, cooperative, and gently encouraging with all in her family.

I remember her as nurturing, inviting me during my second-grade year to read to her as she fried veal cutlets in the sundown shadows of her kitchen with its green wallpaper of looping ivy tendrils. I was proud of being able at that age to read from the Grimm fairytales she had read to me years earlier.

"Sound it out," she would suggest when I would get stuck on a word.

"O-gah-ree," I had said on one occasion.

"Well," she laughed, "sounding out doesn't always help. It's pronounced 'o-ger.'"

My father on several occasions referred to me as my mother's favorite. My siblings concurred. If this were so, I was unaware of it. That I loved to read, made high marks in school, was imaginatively mischievous, and was articulate beyond my years may have induced her to see mirrored in me her own gifts, and thus she may have felt a corresponding affinity with me. Or, as it now occurs to me, if indeed she evinced towards me a greater attention, she may have done so because she perceived at some subconscious level that my path in life might be harder because I did not register gender characteristics and avocations expected of typical boys and that my reception in the larger world would be cooler than if

I had tailored my actions and interests to a boy-culture applauded by society.

My father was in no way absent or weak, though, son of parents whose own stringent parenting could have been moderated by greater leniency, he was occasionally verbally harsh, venting his impatience or frustration with one or the other of us by calling us "good-for-nothing" or "useless." But he was most often playful and indulgent, encouraging us in our interests, engaging with us in our pleasures, rewarding and praising us in our accomplishments.

I never doubted that my father loved me and was proud of me, though over the years I have pondered the cooler relationship I had with him as a child, as an adult, than my brothers had. I did not share with him the easy familiarity, the free banter, the companionability he displayed with my younger heterosexual brother. Understandable, perhaps. Men of my father's generation were socialized to meet with distaste any display of atypical gender behavior in boys or men. Though he never belittled me or made any negative comments directly to me about some of the challenges I made to expected boy behavior when I was a child, I know he was uneasy with them. I must on some level have been aware of his tacit discomfort ever vying with his love for me, and that made it more difficult for me to identify completely with my father. I suspect most heterosexual fathers recognize that something is different about their gay sons and do not know how to relate to those differences, meeting them, certainly in my father's case, with a brew of love, reserve, perhaps anxiety and discomfort, a melding of these reactions that I intuited in him and that colored our relationship.

My father did not, for example, understand my choice of majors at the university. "What can you do with an

English major?" he would ask. "What are your plans after you graduate?

"I'm not sure," I would reply. "Maybe teach? Maybe go to graduate school?"

"But why?" he would frown. "And how exactly does teaching students about poetry help them earn a living?"

My father was the son of Sicilian immigrants who fled the hopeless poverty of the scant, rocky soil on the outskirts of arid Palermo. In America, they had sought practical vocations that gave them the assets they needed to thrive in their new country. They had little time for literature or art. Poetry? What use was it? My immigrant Sicilian grandfather was a cobbler who made his living re-soling for 50 cents a pair the heavy, muddy boots of men who labored in area sugar cane fields. My father became an accountant as did his brother, and their unmarried sister worked in payroll at a chemical plant. They had little time for careers without clear trajectories and a demonstrable monetary benefit. My matter-of-fact grandmother, on encountering me reading a book when I was a child, would ask me why I did not have anything to do. And when I received my Ph.D. in English, she is reputed to have asked what kind of doctor I was and was disappointed to learn that I could not operate on people.

So my choice of a career was yet another perplexity for my father. To give him credit, he never said anything to discourage me in my pursuits even if he could not fully understand what value could be derived from them. He was proud, however, of my Ph.D. and of having a university professor for a son. He always addressed letters to me with "Dr." before my name.

This nexus of emotions I felt for my father—and he for me—led me to become an over-achiever in order to win his approval in ways other than manifesting traditional boy behaviors, the usual routes to father-son bonding. I made outstanding grades and never needed his help with my homework as my siblings occasionally did, something he often congratulated me on.

Interestingly, when my parents learned I was gay, it was my father who had the easier time accepting it, differing from the more usual pattern where a mother accepts her son's homosexuality more readily than his father, who is often the last to be told, if he ever is. Perhaps this resulted from questions my father may have harbored all along about my sexuality while my mother was in denial.

I suspect that my parents, even after they recognized that my homosexuality erected no barriers to my living fully and richly, were never wholly comfortable with my homosexuality. Though they welcomed my partners, I think they continued to struggle with my openness about my orientation and the manifestation of it in my selection of friends. When, for example, I married my husband in 2008, long after my whole family knew I was gay, I received wedding acknowledgements only from my sisters. My mother was dead by then. My father and brother ignored my marriage, responding to news of it with absolute silence. My brother is to this day uncomfortable with me as a gay man. At one point, my father asked one of my sisters if she thought I was the wife in my marriage, demonstrating a continued anxiety about my masculinity as well as considerable ignorance of how gay men in a marriage usually relate to each other. Perhaps at some level, he doubted his success at having formed and fostered my manhood.

This knot of father-son love provides me with scope for further pondering. As I see it now, fathers of gay sons often manifest their love differently than they do to their straight sons, not knowing exactly how to relate to them. But love is love, no matter the challenges it rises above or the nuances that circumstances force it to take on.

Many gay men navigate these difficult waters in parsing their relationships with their parents. Of one central point I am certain: my parents loved me and strove to help me make the most of my life. I reciprocated that love, and I add to it my gratitude.

XX

When lonely, when sad, when lush with gin, when goals are not met and love occasionally seems to falter, when I am feeling those downcast emotions my parents would not wish for me to feel, I remember them with a poignant acuteness and wish I were with them again, having known them in ways I can never know another person, loving them in ways I could not realize fully when they were still with me. I am fortunate to have people in my life who love me and promote my happiness, but none of these do so as completely and unconditionally as my parents once did.

Every morning when I peer into my mirror, I see my father's face, long and narrow, his prominent nose a demarcation between my two cheeks, sunken now that I have aged. I regard myself through eyes the same hazel twinkling of green, gold, and soft, pale brown as my mother's eyes. As I gaze at this record of the both of them remembered in me, I seem to hear the two of them say again what they had told me on many occasions: "You are our son. We love you, as we always have. And we are proud of you." Their words of acceptance are words I still need to remind myself of every day.

LUST AND LOVE

I

I did not believe in romantic love until it ambushed me as I was nearing 50. I did believe in lust. My body acquainted me with lust at puberty. I was diffident with lust at first, timorous and chary as a trout circling a clumsily tied lure. Fool that I was, I listened to priests and nuns and teachers who would have me deny lust and the flesh as sinful, a vice to be purged. Their urgings echoing in me, I diverted all full physical expressions of lust for a while, became a puling peeping Tom, holing up in bookstore sections I was ashamed to be seen in and scanning the pages of gay magazines I was too fearful to present at the cash register.

But I was lucky: lust battered its way through my restraint at last. When it did, I gave myself up to it so thoroughly that I coined a new identity for myself: Promiscuous Hedonist. I set out to earn that epithet. I pinned that badge on proudly, but only after trying on false identities until finally I slapped some sense into myself and came into my own after my college years had ended.

My repudiation of romantic love was to be expected. As a queer boy, youth, then man, I could never figure out where I fit into this omnipresent component of the culture that formed me. Where would I have learned that romantic love had anything whatsoever to do with gay me? I had no gay handbook or manual for love, no precepts that did not appear to me as anything other than coercions. The only option for romantic heterosexual love open to me necessitated the sublimation of every desire my body urged me to. Growing

99

up queer in the 50s, 60s, and 70s, I recognized all models for love as denials and negations of my body's urges.

I attempted that sublimation, those negations—for far too many years of feigning and posturing. At last, belatedly, I threw all that heterosexist romantic crap aside. I concluded that queers fucked. That was it. Only then did I self-actualize. At that point I earned a self.

II

As I have indicated, the fire of this new freedom took a long time to kindle. For a dutiful, timid Catholic boy from a family with high moral and academic expectations of me, the desire to conform to heterosexual presumptions overrode my queer carnal desire, for a time at least.

As expected of me, I endured clumsy dates in high school with girls whose ratted Aqua-Netted hairdos, inept makeup, cheap, cloying colognes, Sears Roebuck pastel sweater-skirt twin sets, and vacuous conversations repelled me. I just could not get interested in dating, no matter how hard I tried.

The rituals of dating during my time in high school struck me then—and even more so now—as preposterous: one had to call a girl at least a week in advance to set up the date; meet the parents for an inspection and a detailed account of the evening's plan; promise to return the girl by a certain curfew; jog around a car to open the door for a healthy girl perfectly capable of lifting a car-door lever; pay for everything; insure a date's enjoyable time; feign attention to inane chatter sprinkled with words like "cute," "adorable," and "precious"; attend to the chair for one's date, some of whom could likely pin me down in a wrestling match; hold a coat open for a girl to shrug into; and end the pedestrian evening fumbling for an expected kiss—either tolerated or disdained—on a doorstep glaring with hostile porch lights. As I surmised from what I so often heard in the boys' locker room at school, the apparent goal of all these dating rituals was for a guy to somehow persuade a girl to engage in a necking session or to let him thrust his grabby hands down her panties, the very last thing I ever wanted to do.

My high-school dating was unenthusiastic and cursory at best. After all, only teens who cannot envision a future for themselves beyond high school ever get involved in serious love affairs while trudging through the arid high-school desert stretching endlessly between adolescence and young adulthood. Dating in college, however, took on a more resolute tone because college dating often leads to future couplings. Since I attended a local university and still lived in my parents' house during my undergraduate years, my college dating continued pretty much as it had during high school, though much of the earlier outlandish formality was eased. By college, however, this dating business had for me grown stale, no longer enlivened by the novelty that had given it some tepid earlier interest in high school.

The nadir of my lackluster college dating experience came one freezing Saturday night during my junior year. I had asked a girl from my biology class to go with me to an LSU-Ole Miss football game at Tiger Stadium, tickets to home games being included in our tuition. After the game, we were to thaw out over drinks at a campus dive. I had shared my class notes with this girl and had tutored her over coffee at the Student Union into a C- on her biology midterm. Her invincible inability to distinguish between mitosis and meiosis had so frustrated me that I had nearly slammed her textbook to the floor and stormed off.

The post-game dive was packed. We met up with several of her friends out with guys I knew from high school, including my friend David, renowned among his dates for his migratory hands. After a half hour or so, my date and her cackle of friends rose together from the table to repair to the toilet. It never failed: when one had to go, they all had to, as if they shared a bladder.

Soon after they left, those of us remaining at the table heard, even above the loud buzz of the crowded bar, those girls intoning, over and over: "Lukie's a mouse; Davie's a rat." They must have been joined by other girls in the bathroom because their chanting sounded clearly over the bar's chatter and blaring Rolling Stones racket. I looked over at David. He was pointing from himself to me, eyebrows raised.

I stood up when the girls returned to the table. My date thought I was offering to attend to her chair. Instead, I wadded up her coat and thrust it out at her.

"Are we going somewhere else?" she asked.

"Back to the dorm for you," I said. "I'm dropping you off."

"But it's early," she whined. "I haven't finished my rum and coke."

"Chug it," I said. "I've got to scurry on home now."

She scanned my face, then looked down. "That's alright," she mumbled. "I'll have someone drop me off later."

"How about you ask 'Davie'?"

Difficult to believe, but even this experience did not put an end to my college dating endurance. I manned my way through this heterosexual requirement for the remainder of my undergraduate years, largely because I would have had difficulty explaining to my parents and friends why I was going it alone every weekend night. I would have much preferred hanging out with guys—sexy, ripe, roguish beings! Male bodies were so keen, so tightly structured! Female bodies struck me as loose and pliant. Pendulous....

III

Everywhere I turned, my culture placed before me its panoply of heterosexually insistent signals: Dance lessons. Sock hops. Proms. Cotillions and debutante balls. <u>Romeo and Juliet</u> as required reading in junior-year English class. Straight couples holding hands and kissing in public wherever I looked. Hetero porn, soft and hard-core. Rom-coms. Flirting. Valentines. Sex-ed, strictly hetero-version. Going steady. Hollywood sex goddesses. Miss America. Strip joints and bawdy houses on Bourbon Street with their drugged, purple-bruised pole dancers and pathetic men leering up at them, barkers at the street doors yelling "Girls, Girls, Girls." Promise rings. Engagement rings. Wedding rings. Bridal showers. Stag parties. Rehearsal dinners. Weddings. Receptions. Wedding cakes, their top tiers miniature stages for tiny brides and grooms. Anniversaries, each year tied to a special gift. Harlequin Romances. Starry-eyed couples in magazine ads for Caribbean cruises under swaying palm trees. Society's whole moon-spoon-June confluence everywhere I looked....

Now where was there a place for little ole gay me in all of this?

All of these cultural traces, rituals, and heterosexual customs and expectations bristle with homosexual exclusions. Add to these cultural eliminations the heterosexist verbal bombs lobbed at gay people. Gay slurs are more linguistically developed, abundant, and diverse than those affronts hurled at any other stigmatized group, whether racial, social, religious, or ethnic. Every gay man has been taunted, perhaps even threatened, by the following terms, which either target directly or poison the air that gay men breathe. I do not even attempt to list those smears lobbed at lesbians, bisexuals, and transgendered folk, though some of the following aspersions serve for the entire LGBTQ community: Faggot! Fay! Fruit! Fairy! Pansy! Pederast! Pervert! Ass-fucker! Dick-licker! Cocksucker! Queer! Queen! Homo! Nancy boy! Mary! Maricon! Mariposa! Poof! Poufter! Ponce! Invert! Uranian! Deviant! Girlie Man! Sissy! Sodomite! Sword-swallower! Bugger! Fudge Packer! Nelly! Flamer! Flit! Swish! Twink! Limp-wrist! Light-in-the-loafers! Pillow-biter!

Did I miss any? Oh yeah, Pecker-pocket!

Even more effective at excluding gay men from love than these affronts are the violence-inciting gay condemnations pronounced by the world's popes, prophets, priests, prelates, preachers, rabbis, televangelists, ayatollahs, mullahs, muftis, and imams close-leagued with conservative, right-wing moron politicians and, not so long ago, with psychiatrists, psychologists, social workers, and therapists of all descriptions who placed us among the mentally ill as sexual psychopaths and plagued us with electro-shock, pre-frontal lobotomies, and various other suicide-inducing conversion therapeutic tortures that never even had a chance of working. And certain parents, teachers, school policy makers, and far too many fascist Republican politicians are still after us—even now! "Don't Say Gay!" as they say in Florida....

I suppose I strike one as angry? That's not even the half of it.....

Excluded from heterosexual romance as the only love allowable, proscribed by smears spread liberally and with impunity, denounced by the guardians of a narrowly available God and a stringently defined normality, is it any wonder that I—and so many gay men of my generation—

would find in lust a sure value, anchored in the certain urges and demands of the body as our one unwavering and reliable guide?

Love? Not for us…. And who needed it, anyway?

IV

In spite of all this, I remained craven enough, lacked inner strength and self-respect enough to try to force myself into the heterosexual world that had rejected and condemned me. I attempted to shrivel myself into that alien mold against the certain sexual promptings that sought to rule me, against, in short, my very nature. Excluded, marginalized, yet pathetically desperate to belong in the only world I then perceived as open to me, I forced myself to plod the hetero-normative path straight-paved by my culture. No one benefited from that forcing—not me, certainly not the women I wove into the tangled subterfuges I felt I had to weave.

This dating pretense extended beyond my undergraduate years, even after I knew what would sexually satisfy me as made obvious in my well-thumbed pages of <u>Playgirl</u> magazine. With those glossy male bodies I could throw off the masquerade and become myself. The idea of dating a man was beyond any behavioral model I could then conjure up, even in imagination. No possibility of love for another man—lust was my portion. And lust my body was eager to espouse.

I remained a virgin throughout college. Once, in my senior year, a co-ed let me slip my hands under her blouse. She undid her bra and I played with her breasts; these pillowy mounds of dough I was kneading did nothing for me. We were parked in the driveway of her house. This all came to an abrupt halt when I noticed the lifting of a blind slat on a front window. On another occasion, I French-kissed a girl while parked with her at the levee before returning her to her dormitory at LSU by curfew. On my drive home, I stopped at each traffic light and opened the car door to spit. I still feel a robust resentment over the whole dating business I forced myself to endure, with its utter waste of time and resources.

I had finally started to masturbate in college—a late spouter. I made imagined love to every pictured bare-chested man in the underwear pages of the Sears Roebuck catalog who appealed to me. I took mental snapshots on the sports fields at LSU of shirtless young men for later use. These compliant fantasy men occupied niches in my imagination for no other purpose than to service me. I did not have to open their car doors, buy their dinners, drape their sweaters over their shoulders when we were ready to depart a place. I simply dismissed them from further thought once I had had my way with them.

Thus, to all appearances, I was squiring girls; inside, I was romping with boys. A sad loneliness registers yet with me at this strange gulf between reality and fantasy, between perceived expectations and insistent desires, between the actual and the achingly unrealized at this time. I could not then have evaded this waste of psychic, emotional, and sexual energy. I could not at that time have poulticed what I then referred to as my "wound." I did not have the models, the counselors, the courage, or even the conception of how to make desire and its fulfillment conform. I congratulate myself that I came through all this integrated and happy at last. But the process was slow and tenuous and caused pain to myself and, I fear, to others.

V

Following my undergraduate years and opposing what I knew and felt, I thought to engage a woman for companionship and for the passport she could afford me in the straight world, the only sphere for me that I could then imagine existing in. With a woman by my side, I could forge an acceptable life, could screw myself into my culture's expectations for me. A woman I had known since grade school indicated an interest in me. That was always how my connections with women began: I never took the initiative.

This woman and I made each other laugh. She disregarded the wacky dating rituals most women expected. She was up for anything, including sex, which she was curious about. With her I shared my first sexual experience. Did I enjoy it? Of course. In our early 20s, we had sex often after that first fumbling, quickly climaxing opening. I came close, during our years of dating, to asking her to marry me. She indicated an interest in it; her family encouraged it; my family expected it. Fortunately for us both, I could not bring myself to propose. Still friends with her, though separated by distance and by our disparate lives, I am confident that both of us are grateful now that we did not approach the altar together, no matter how high my regard and affection for her was then and still is now.

Too many gay men of my and earlier generations conformed to hetero-normative pressures to marry women, never having been offered more suitable options. After years in these stifling marriages, after children, after sneaking around on the down-low, brokering clandestine hook-ups with men on the side, they at last dragged their middle-aged wives into divorce courts. These gay men, having ditched their spouses, often then went on to meet the men they were supposed to be with all along, having deprived their cast-off wives of relationships that would have been fulfilling for them. Because society's coercions are so forceful, these gay men, in fairness, bear only partial responsibility for having caused these marital misfortunes. Social ordinances are difficult to withstand. I can testify to that.

VI

Early in my Ph.D. program at the University of Texas, I shared graduate classes with a woman I will call Frankie. She came from a stringent religious background, the inflexible Texas brand of Southern Baptists. She hit Austin determined to shuck off the austere strictures promulgated by the evangelical church she claimed had brainwashed her. She could not wait to dispense with the pinched canons that had long chafed and cramped her at the small southern Oklahoma Christian college she had detested. No dancing. No beer, wine, or liquor. No cards. No cigs. No movies. For God's sake, no sex. Not even dating was allowed. Frankie was determined to engage, immediately and fervently, in all of these transgressions. She was hell-bent on aborting her barren religion and leaving the flat land of Oklahoma behind without so much as a glance over her then still modestly clad shoulder.

Frankie first arrived in graduate school wearing the armor of the Bible-belt: home-sewn buttoned-up, waist-cinched dresses hemmed low enough by her mother to hide her knees; lace-up oxfords; woolly eyebrows; helmet-bouffant hair with a perfect pre-tied bow color-matched to her dresses and bobby-pinned in her hair exactly above the middle of her forehead; vinegary East Texas twang.

For the first several weeks, Frankie took her bearings. Her classmates and I were startled one morning when she strode into class. The Little-House-on-the-Prairie dresses and the boxy shoes that came with her from the sticks had been stuffed into a Salvation Army give-away box in a Walmart parking lot, replaced with designer jeans, breast-perky Liz Claiborne tops, and Nike sneakers I could not have afforded. She got herself a smoldering Veronica Lake peek-a-boo hairdo, one kiss-my-ass dark tress seductive over her right eye; brows plucked and arched like Cupid's bow; intrepid make-up: lips an incendiary red, eyes smudged wide into lilac-shadowed pools.

Then Frankie was ready for sex. She selected me for the deflowering. After the initial smart occasioned by that breach, she grew keen. Hers was a fierce sexual upheaval after all the years of airless Christian continence. We met often that first year: after classes several nights a week, every night on weekends. Frankie would leave her study carrel in the library to clank up the outside metal staircase at the back of my apartment building and, regardless of the time, lean out from the top landing to strum her varnished fingernails over my bedroom screen, zithering a pre-coital psalm.

Occasionally I had to feign not being home, burdened with homework or simply exhausted by the sexual expenditures. On encountering Frankie in the department halls after these little sexual evasions, I had to conjure up the most plausible pretexts I could for my not being available the evening before when she needed me. Suspicious as well as insecure, she never credited any of these excuses that had so taxed my ingenuity.

Years of sexual renunciation whirled Frankie into a dynamo in bed. One Sunday afternoon, she and I joined friends over cheap pitchers of beer, more froth than brew, at an outdoor German biergarten. On returning to the table from the toilet, I overheard Frankie crowing about the number of times she had goaded me into arousal the night before. I sidled into my chair, managing the shadow of an embarrassed smile under the sidelong glances of our sardonic friends.

Later that evening, I implored Frankie to be more circumspect. She chided me: Being secretive is miserly, she claimed. One need never be reticent about one's carnal episodes, particularly when one is in one's 20s. As we conversed, we were rounding the perimeter walk at Barton Springs Park, frequented by families. As the sun set, we wandered off into a grassy soccer field away from the trees so as to gain a view of the western sky streaked with plumes a tatty drag-queen gaudy. As the light leached somber, Frankie initiated sex in the grass, distant mothers giving hell to balky children loath to leave the seesaws. Slamming car doors and engine ignitions sounded across the damp grass. Frankie frequently preferred alfresco diversions to the tame sinecure of the bedroom.

After well over a year of this, graduate school intensified for me. I was teaching two sections of freshman composition, reading for oral examinations, and researching possible Ph.D. dissertation topics in addition to taking grad classes to fulfill degree requirements. Trysts with Frankie had to be confined to weekends—with occasional week night lapses.

One night Frankie clanked up the metal stairs, her footsteps trailed by a lighter tread. When I lifted the sash to her strumming on my screen, I saw that she had brought in tow a younger woman with suspect hygiene. A gamin. A street waif. Her hair, dull oily in the street light, was chopped off shorter on one side of her head, longer on the other, imparting an unsettling lop-sided look to her face. Sometime in the recent past, she had apparently tried to persuade those she encountered that she was a blonde.

"How old are you?" I asked her.

"Old enough for anything you can do with me," she smirked, teeth nicotine-tan, a puckered scar over her upper lip, turning her sneer ominous.

"Grading papers," I begged off. "Can't tonight."

They clattered back down the metal stairs. I returned to my novel. I heard a motorcycle cough into life on the street below.

Frankie began to diversify her sexual partners in earnest, sometimes sex with me, but increasingly with a selection of women she shrank from introducing to her graduate-school friends. She acquired a motorcycle, which I chained up for her to a post under the metal stairs on the rare occasions when her florid father and acquiescent mother visited her. During these brief interruptions, I was pressed into service as the boyfriend, Frankie herself stowing the Veronica Lake hair-droop securely behind an ear and pawing through the back of her closet to drag out the remnants of what she called her "Jesus clothes."

VII

Like Frankie's "Jesus clothes," I myself was stuffed way deep in my closet, pushed back even further by my experience with a neighbor who lived in the apartment below mine in the shabby old house shared by six other tenants. Orlando was a gay Black Hispanic man given to drag, though he was far too homely to be successful at it. He contented himself with painting his long fingernails white and his lips pearl. There was little he could do about the deep acne scars, clogged with bronze face powder, which his adolescence had bequeathed him. His hair, marcelled into oiled waves, had ebbed far back from his massive forehead. He billowed about in a blousy crimson silk kimono figured in gold Japanese fans.

On my first meeting Orlando, he asked me if I liked men. My denial prevented his asking any further direct questions about the possibility of my being gay, but he nevertheless behaved to me from then on as if I had answered his initial question in the affirmative.

Many men frequented Orlando's apartment: I could hear them hooting and carrying on at all hours. Up through the old building's floor cracks wafted the reek of incense and marijuana and the gaudy blaring of Hispanic yi-yi-yi music accompanied by the rhythmic pounding of the foot of an old sprung Murphy bed against the uneven floor below. Whenever Orlando heard me trudging up the wooden stairs to my apartment at the top of the house, he would swoop out onto the landing and insist that I come in to meet his friends. The men there sized me up knowingly. The sneers that curled the corners of their mouths told me of their disdain for my gay denials.

These men were never attractive to me: I assume Orlando picked them up on the streets or in gay bars I never frequented. Invariably they were young, not overly attentive to personal grooming, sometimes sinister and dangerous looking. I was as fascinated as I was repelled by them, following them in imagination into torrid bedrooms rank with rumpled sheets, black-velvet paintings of bullfighters on the walls. I pictured them sitting around all day, shirtless and shiftless, waiting to take advantage of the people, events, and situations floating down to them on the haphazard stream of their lives.

Aimlessness was distasteful to me, too threatening to the orderly life I had contrived, ruled by strict time schedules, high purpose, carefully delineated plans, and the impulse always to play it safe. Seeing these young men, I tried to envision myself throwing over all convention and goals to live a feckless and compulsive sexual life.

Attraction, like an annoying itch, vied with revulsion at this life I saw lived before me. Like a voyeur, I kept accepting Orlando's invitations even after his friends tired of my upright presence among them, my sobriety of intention and persistence of denial of the gayness they accurately intuited in me and tried their hardest to break through to. I apparently liked the proximity of the gay life I knew I was called to lead but could not yet embrace. Knowing them was a vicarious gay exercise for me.

During the spring of my last year in Austin, I returned home one afternoon to my neighbors gathered in tight little knots on the sidewalk outside the building, convulsed with gossip: Orlando had been discovered tied naked to his iron Murphy-bed frame, his hands and feet swollen and blue-black from his struggles against his tight bindings. A bandana had been stuffed into his mouth clamped shut by several over-lapping strips of duct tape. He had been beaten, then bound from early the night before until nearly 3:00 the following afternoon when our snooping landlady, sure he was away from home, had stolen into his apartment as was her wont in the absence of her tenants. She had called the police, who unbound Orlando on their arrival and called for an ambulance.

Orlando was in the hospital. He had had to be tranquilized. I told the police truthfully that I had heard nothing in the night, no arguing, no loud noises. Orlando knew the man only as C.J. who had bound him, raped and brutalized him with a wooden dowel rod, and stolen his wallet and his car. The police found the hulk of his car smashed up and minus its motor and tires three days later.

Orlando returned to the apartment after his release from the hospital, his wrists bandaged, one eye swollen shut. He did not want to talk about what had happened to him. I came home from school the afternoon that he moved out to find gay porn magazines stacked in a box he had left by my front door, a note appended: "I know you will find these of interest."

From Orlando's experience, I concluded that I would never be happy in such an unrelentingly bleak gay life. Here before me was a vivid cautionary tale. Accordingly, I made an appointment at the university counseling center for the psychological help I could engage as a student. I suspect that the therapist, Pam, was a lesbian, large and fleshy, her disconcertingly narrow shoulders melting down to an enormous splurge of hips and butt. Her mannerisms were large, her voice loud: she paused after each utterance to study my responses.

I confessed my strong sexual attraction to men but my disgust and fear of gay life. I sought help from her about ways I might suppress my homosexual urges, which I always referred to as "my wound," a code I used in my journals. I assured her that I did not want to be gay and that I found gay men abhorrent and repulsive in their mannerisms and tones of voice. As I made these avowals, Pam stared at me intently with a look similar to those I registered on the faces of Orlando's friends on meeting me.

For Pam—and she was right—I was a pathetic personification of self-loathing, holding myself at arm's length and describing myself with revulsion, rejecting and reviling my very person. After this outpouring, Pam said nothing for an uncomfortable several moments. Then she indicated that I might want to avoid being trapped by stereotypical renditions of gay life, that certainly not all gay men were as I had described them, that even those who did manifest some of the traits I found so objectionable were harming no one and had every right to be themselves with dignity in a world capacious enough to foster us all.

Then she asked me a question that propelled me right out of further therapy: "What exactly do you want to accomplish with me? If you want to stop being sexually attracted to men, that will not happen in these sessions. Therapy will never help you to achieve that impossible goal. If you would like to explore ways you might live a full life as a homosexual man, perhaps we can work together, though our preliminary task will be helping you to divest yourself of the prejudices about gay men you are coming to me with. Neither of us will find those prejudices and stereotypes productive. I think you had better figure out what you want to accomplish before we continue with our sessions."

I did not make any further appointments with Pam. The fear and disgust instilled in me by Orlando's life and the violence done him confirmed my decision to avoid living openly as a gay man or giving into my homosexual desires. Pam's assurances that she could not support that decision or help me live it were conclusive. The closet remained at that time more comfortable for me than even a tentative entry into the realities of the only life I had been given to live.

VIII

Frankie and I both earned our Ph.D.s in 1977. My family hosted a reception for the graduate-school friends I was sorry to part with, many of us having secured academic teaching positions throughout the Midwest. By the time I received my Ph.D., my first girlfriend and I had both come to the realization that a marriage would have been for us a misadventure. That decision confirmed that heterosexual love-and-marriage was a dodge that would never work for me and should never again be tried. In spite of this conclusion, I was not even yet ready to embrace my true nature.

I went to an assistant professorship at Kansas State University in the small Flint Hills town of Manhattan. Frankie secured a more prestigious appointment at the flagship university of a neighboring state. She deserved it: she was among the brightest of the newly minted Ph.D.s Texas awarded that year, adroit at disentangling the turgid French literary theory then in vogue. My attempts at deciphering Derrida and Barthes and Cixous and their tribe sedated me into a miasmal brain fog within a matter of minutes. Frankie stunned me one evening, post-coital, by announcing a predilection for abstract literary theory and little tolerance for fiction or poetry.

Every other week or so that first year of our exile from our beloved Austin, I would hop a Greyhound out to Frankie's university city on Friday afternoons to keep Frankie company in a city she found unfriendly and for me to escape the great silence of Kansas. Soon, sex between us ended. She had taken up with Misty, a feral minx with a tic under her left eye which made the small mole there twitch like a midge on a hot plate. On one of my visits, Misty blurted out that she was afraid Frankie would leave her for me.

"Like that would ever happen!" Frankie hooted. "I keep telling you he's queer, even if he hasn't sucked dick yet."

One evening, Frankie and the minx persuaded me to join them at a lesbian club. I sat at the bar grimacing at each sip of a martini so ghastly that I could not fathom how it had been concocted. Suddenly something thwacked me solidly on the back. I turned around to behold a brawl around the pool table, a tangle of substantial lesbians pummeling each other with fists, pool cues splintering across heads and raised arms. The clash proceeded in a tense silence except for the thuds of landed blows. A shattered cue point had flown across the bar to hit me between the shoulder blades, leaving

116

an angry bruise for weeks. I slid off my bar stool and cowered on the floor beneath the bar overhang. Frankie grabbed me by the upper arm and hoisted me to my feet, Misty shoving me harder than necessary toward the door.

I began to feel more and more unwelcome at Frankie's apartment. Misty had grown increasingly hostile, glowering at me when I tried to speak with her. She was angling to move in with Frankie, unaware that this would hasten Frankie's intolerance of her illiteracy and low habits.

Years later, I learned that after having been consistently denied tenure at several major universities, Frankie had invested in a lesbian bar which limped along for several years before folding. Frankie had witnessed too many lesbians with blue-collar jobs and consequent low wages cadging ice at the bar to refresh drinks they poured for themselves and for their friends from flasks stowed in their bags while cruising the bar for tricks and enjoying the swirling colored lights pulsing to the music of the bar's DJ-directed dance floor.

I liked Frankie. Affection certainly played a part in our attachment, though lust cemented our bond, a comfortable connection for us both. But lust's bonds, soon strained, lack staying power. Lust always grows indiscriminant, seeks a more diverse trade. I would come belatedly to learn that only the love I was then denying had any chance of fixing me in a coupling. That love did not factor for Frankie and me. She had the same wrapper over her emotions as I had. It repelled love. I thought then that love had nothing to do with the sighs accompanying the carnal urges and thrusts we shared. We both got what we wanted from our intercourse.

IX

During my first several years at Kansas State, I tried to play it straight, not knowing how I would fare as a gay man trying to earn tenure in this Midwestern English department. Those first years were a stark, lonely time, grading endless papers in a cold, cramped basement apartment, walking downtown alone so many Saturday evenings to eat braised heart with sage dressing at the Horseshoe Grill, sliding through blue snow to attend early morning Mass each Sunday at Seven Dolors Church, praying in penitence at having been born a fearful fag. My heart cringes between hunched shoulders at these memories.

My final attempt at a heterosexual connection was with a colleague at Kansas State who arrived in the department several years into my lonely time there. She was then married to a gay man who held a position at another university, though that marriage had already foundered. She figured out I was gay before I was open about it.

Undeterred by this and sharing a mutual isolation in our small college town, she proposed that we explore together the surrounding hamlets and the subtle beauty of the Kansas countryside, savoring the bounty of rich farm stands, the austere offerings of Mennonite thrift stores, and the homely fare cooked up in country diners. Always gastronomically intrepid, I sampled "rocky mountain oysters" at one of these rural diners—bull testicles sliced thin and fried up in a light batter.

Our comradeship soon led to a sexual connection, a deep mutual affection, and, eventually, several years of cohabitation. She surmised that our relationship would not be permanent: "You strike me as someone who keeps a pair of running shoes by the front door, laced up and headed out," she said to me once. "I expect you'll put them on one day and not look back." That did happen. No matter how deep the regard is for another, one cannot settle when one's body is restless for other satisfactions.

No matter how much I valued this relationship, it inevitably shifted ground one summer when I secured an NEH Fellowship in Boston and met Owen there, a man with whom I had my first gay sexual relationship. I was then closing in on 34; he, 32. I invited him out to dinner one evening in Cambridge and then enticed him to watch the sunset with me on the bank of the River Charles. I attacked him on that embankment with a forceful kiss, apparently not unexpected because he returned that kiss as avidly as I had initiated it. I put my hands under his shirt, but when my other hand strayed below his belt, he grew uneasy, pointing out that we were in plain sight of the strollers on the pathway by the river. We went back to his Cambridge apartment, and I tasted sex with a man for the first—but far from the last—time.

I found it impossible to have enough sex with Owen. I was sharing a Beacon Hill townhouse near the corner of Beacon and Charles with another NEH Fellow, an older man, embittered by life for some reason. He took to imitating me with an exaggerated gay sneer, having wised up to my happiness at this promiscuous coupling with Owen that I made no attempt to disguise.

Though Owen was smart, assertive, and seemingly self-assured, traits I was still nurturing in myself, it was sex that secured me in this connection. Owen and I drove together throughout New England in his wheezy Volkswagen Beetle: I watched the highway race beneath us through a hole rusted out of the car's floorboards as we sped to the North Shore communities of Salem and Marblehead; to Provincetown and up and down the Cape; to Bar Harbor, Maine; to Newport, Rhode Island for a tour of the Breakers and other cottages; and to the Berkshires and to Tanglewood where Owen treated me to a Lena Horne concert on the night of my birthday, a red moon then in full eclipse.

Every night at about 10:00, after I had completed the day's research and writing, I listened eagerly for Owen's car horn in the street below, two rapid beeps, a mating call. I would fly down the stairs to join him for dancing and drinking until last call at Buddies, our favorite gay bar. I remember that enchanted summer with a fierce wonder and a joy rarely matched since. How very happy I was!

I had experienced deep sexual pleasure with the three significant women in my life, but sex with Owen was revelatory. It was as if a new sun had soared erotic from behind a bar of clouds, its beams irradiating every nerve-ending, every ganglion, atom, tendon, and strand of my being. My body stirred to life, galvanized and pulsing.

I thrilled at touching a male body in three dimensions, at such exquisite variance from the imaginary fleshing out of the flat images in gay porn magazines. Every feature of Owen's body fascinated me—his rough cheeks, the divot in his chin, his chest dusted with light hair, his bronze nipples, ribs, the sinewy saddle join at his belly and thighs, the elegant sculpture of his back, his tensed buttocks, the rigid musculature of his downed legs—and his penis with its marvelous permutations and effusions, so like my own in its workings that I intuited every pleasure I was affording him.

Sex with Owen was stern, never malleable or supple: every angle, plane, and surface of his body was obdurate, dense, arousing in me an intrinsic quickening so distinct from the pleasure I had earlier derived from the smooth, ductile bodies of women.

I was saddened by the certainty that my connection with my colleague in Kansas would now have to change, that, as she had predicted, I would lace up my running shoes.

Fortunately, our relationship continued as a friendship I value to this day. At first I tried to pass myself off as bisexual from fear that I would lose my way in a gay world, allegiance to which I then felt would target me for strictures from every source—familial, societal, legal, religious, and professional. This bisexual dodge did not last long. I met a few gay men in Manhattan, grew ashamed before them of the bisexual fiction, and finally came out completely. I was a homosexual. No more evasions, no more hedging. And no more fear.

It took me that long to determine that I no longer wanted to be a man ever at odds with himself, a man who loitered alone in his shower imagining that he was joined there by one of the smooth young swimmers ogled on a recent broadcast of an Olympic event or by the stolid construction worker spied on through the slats of an office mini-blind toweling sweat from his bronzed biceps after a stint on the jackhammer. I did not want to end up like the pomaded, ingratiating weatherman on my local television channel nabbed by a plainclothes policeman in the local park and fired from the nightly news after the report of his arrest made the papers. I did not want to be the respected businessman with a family busted in the men's room at Macy's bobbing up and down in a stall like a jack-in-the-box every time the men's room door opened, or the subsequently de-frocked priest discovered by an altar-guild lady sucking the cock of the church organist in the sacristy. I would not be the married school principal who committed suicide after being discovered by the night janitor being fucked across his desk by a feral young man picked up in a dark alley outside a downtown gay bar. I would no longer be the man whose inner desires conflicted with his outer life. That way destruction awaited, unhappiness and shame.

X

This final owning of my true nature brought with it an invigoration, a striding into my own life at last. I felt mended, renewed, as if I had molted a crabbed carapace that had cramped me. An unexpected exhilaration animated this new life: I was now a sexual outlaw, beyond and outside the inhibiting strictures I had always tried so fearfully to adhere to. As a sexual deviant, I would possibly be reviled, certainly disapproved of, possibly pitied, but I was also free, careless of the revulsion or the disapproval, my own person in a world now open to me in ways I had never expected. It is a revolutionary release to adopt one's self in that self's wholeness, consequences be damned.

Did I love Owen, who propelled me into this richer hedonistic life that all-too-brief summer? Could his spell over me have ripened in time had our circumstances been luckier? Was his allure a magic already seeded by a growing awareness that I would soon come to accept myself for who I was? My focus that summer, other than on my research, was having sex with Owen. I suspected even in its freshness that this intense passion would in time flare out. I did not even consider that this besottment could be a prelude to love. Deep affection, even need? Certainly. But all I could count on at that time was my lust. It was enough.

At the end of that summer, Owen bade me a tearful, lingering farewell before he left for his university, I for mine. On Labor Day, I answered a phone call from him. He was out of breath, jogging, as he explained, car horns blatting in the background, a bus grumbling by.

"I just wanted to call to tell you that I love you," he panted.

"Where are you?" I asked.

"I'm on my honeymoon."

"You're <u>what</u>?"

"I got married yesterday to a woman I have known since graduate school. We've actually been living together for years. I knew you'd hear about it sooner or later; I wanted you to hear it from me. I will never forget that astonishing summer we just spent together in Boston."

Several years after this, I returned to Boston on a yearlong sabbatical to write my first book. I rented an apartment with a fourth-floor bay window overlooking Commonwealth Avenue at Berkeley in the heart of Back Bay. I could look up from my writing desk to glimpse the swan boats in the Public Gardens, a long block down. From this aerie, I winged my way into a blithe gay life, a soaring I had never known before. I was not looking for love. I did not give it a thought. I was seeking sex. Then 36, I had lost time to make up, a lust-carnival to wander through over a year's lubricious reprieve from the gay desiccation of Kansas.

After that concupiscent gay year of sparkling sexual license, I, now an anointed Promiscuous Hedonist, returned to Kansas to an upstairs apartment in an old house, my bed tucked into a gable reflecting the green of the bird-filled tree branches that brushed my windows.

Sexual options for me in Manhattan, Kansas, were meager, a near-starvation regimen after Boston's sexual splurge banquet. I was driven to sipping tepid sex every Tuesday evening with a lab researcher in the chemistry department, grazing him with raw rug burns on his back while fucking him roughly, as he demanded, on my living-room carpet. His wife, who saw our assignations as necessary to maintain her marriage, actually scribbled me a note thanking me for satisfying her husband enough to keep him away from the bush boys lurking in the dark city park, as if I were some little sexual attendant dishing out manageable portions of dick to someone on a diet. So, I became a sordid matrimonial convenience. That I could countenance this humiliation defined my depletion. Love here? Get real.

One morning after I had seen him and his wife the evening before at a ballet performance by a touring troupe on a weeknight stop-over from more lucrative gigs in Kansas City or Denver, Professor Fuck-Buddy dropped by my office where I was enjoying coffee with two of my straight colleagues during a break between classes.

"My wife and I saw you at the ballet, Lu," he began. "Did you ever see so many dainty mincers as the flit-fruits on that stage last night? I saw a number of flamers in the audience as well."

"Both of us were there too," I frowned.

Such self-loathing steeled my resolve to get the hell out of Manhattan, Kansas, and far away from the kind of gay man I had been fucking on Tuesday nights.

XI

In 1987, I secured a near-perfect position at California State University, Sacramento. Just after leaving Kansas behind for good, I took a call from Owen, my usher into the satisfactions of gay sex. He invited me to visit him in Baltimore while his professor wife was out of the country on a research project. I declined, absorbed as I was in the effervescent gay life then opening for me. I was swimming in a louche new sexual sea in Sacramento. Sequestered in Kansas, I had missed the high flourishing of gay sexual awakening, that crimson budding of sex and exuberance and identity and pride in ourselves at last, that lovely foliation of the 70s and early 80s. Sacramento still echoed with that energy, though considerably tempered by AIDS then grimly stalking through the gay community there.

By the time of my move to Sacramento, I had become a committed love-atheist: love, I avowed, was a heterosexual construct that had nothing whatsoever to do with gay men. Love for me was a fever dream, a delirium, a delusion, a hoax, a con, a fraud, a sentimental mirage blown up by breeders to constrain them together long enough to put their kids through college. As a gay man I felt myself everywhere excluded from love and all its trappings—its signs, slogans, songs, symbols, and rituals—that clogged the culture. Fine with me. Lust was enough.

Besides, sex for me had never had anything much to do with love. Sexual panting and thrusting concerned the body, never rippled the deep lake where love reputedly welled. The lust-waves that flushed me out to sea, helpless and blind--what did they have to do with love? Coitus is clench-faced king of astonished moments. His chaotic anarchy is brief. Love is supposedly lord of length, of duration, of diurnal succession. I knew nothing much about that, nor did I much care to know.

My new life in Sacramento involved tenure-attention to teaching and scholarship, with near equal emphasis on disco, drink, and dick. I was new-cru vintage in town, fresh Eucharistic flesh—an object of at least temporary notice in the cruise bars where I trawled on weekends for tricks and one-night-stands. I spanned numerous courtships-honeymoons-divorces of two hours duration on first arriving in California. I relished tricks I termed "catch-and-release" encounters. I soon gained a succession of fuck-buddies, men whom I allowed to return, without attachment, for more dalliances following the fleeting one-night tumblings in tempestuous beds.

One particular fuck-buddy was running the lust gamut as I was. Having been married for 31 years to a woman, having fathered three children all now safely tucked away into independent adulthood, and having been on the down-low with innumerable men during his long marriage, Miles had belatedly thrown over his heterosexual camouflage in his divorce and embraced his perversions at last. He thought to establish with me a simulacrum of his marriage with all its seeming stability and permanence, maybe even, in his eyes, a type of respectability. On understanding that I, then much younger than he and not long out of my own gay constraints, was having none of what he had to offer, Miles turned wayward indeed.

Miles purchased an old pontoon pleasure boat from a dead queen's estate on Lake Tahoe and docked it in a berth on the American River from which he skippered out every Sunday afternoon, me in tow as first mate. We would load it up with nine or ten cases of cheap beer and a dozen bags of chips and anchor it upriver in a willow-screened cove. Miles welcomed aboard whoever approached.

Miles christened the vessel "The Love Boat," or, when its cranky engines gave trouble, "The Rust Bucket." I dubbed it "The Lust Bucket" or "The Tramp Steamer." Sometimes, when notified by someone or other of an infestation, "The Crab Pot." I was squeamish about the riff-raff clientele, often down-and-out street people, who mobbed the boat each week for the free beer and the prodigal sex. After a citation for public nudity from a police patrol boat cruising the river, Miles ordered all overt sex acts consummated below deck on the grimy galley sofas with their stained butterscotch-plaid upholstery, its piping frayed into clotted fringe. That usually left the upper deck empty. There I would sit in the willow shade, smoking, drinking beer, chatting with others resting from their carnal exertions, drowsing to the chuckling of the river against the bow while the sex carnival cavorted in the cabin below me.

Oh, the sideshow sexual acts I witnessed! My fastidious, squeamish refusal to engage in acts of lust too squalid even for me earned me the sneering sobriquet— Princess Prude. Prudy-tight, for short.

I soon abandoned these Sunday sodomite river bacchanals after Miles, way too drunk to be sailing, passed out at the helm one dark night and piled The Love Boat into a pier. I drove his car home for him while he spent a DUI night in the pokey, and on picking him up the next morning, I bowed out of his life, jumped ship in order to continue my lust spree with more attractive, younger, certainly cleaner tricks in less seedy surroundings.

I was then traveling around the country to academic conferences where I frequently delivered research papers. What sexual jamborees these meetings often turned into. I remember one wild night at a Hilton in Parsippany, New Jersey, where I was delivering a paper on diverse spirituality in young adult literature at a meeting of the American Academy of Religion. The computer geek running the A/V equipment at the conference levered me up in his bulging arms in my hotel room, my elbows bracing me back against a mirror. I pulled three used condoms, coiled up like garden slugs, off the floor in the morning. The evening after delivering a paper at a conference in San Diego, I met in the Caliph Bar a winsome young sales rep who schlepped upholstery swatches all over southern California. I remember his elegant body offered to me in a red plush chair back in my hotel room, his haunches bucketed up to me, my nipples grazing his crinkled auburn hair.

Certainly not all of these sexual encounters proved satisfactory: physical and/or personality miscalculations made in dark bars near closing time after a boozy night were amended in less bibulous states and in more salubrious light, warily edged away from or rapidly aborted in time, or, at the least, never repeated. But these misadventures were rare. I knew what I wanted, and I quickly intuited who could reliably supply it.

Carnal, sensual nights: ribbed condoms, scented lube, tit-clamps, cock rings, blow jobs, threesomes, Greek sex, French sex (of course), group sex, hand jobs in back alleys, sex parties, orgies, the Steamworks Baths in Berkeley, the Water Garden in San Jose, tricks, porn, poppers, peep shows, nudist gatherings, fuck ads in the gay rags, encounters in porn shops, massages with Kama Sutra oil and happy endings, nude Halloween parties (I went to one strapped only in bee wings and toting a toy machine gun— a killer bee): all the lusty offerings enriching the lewd paradise I then luxuriated in. Fifty shades of gay, so to speak. Hollow? Empty? Meaningless?

Exhilarating.

And love? Please. I neither credited it nor needed it. After several years of screaming and carrying on in the bars, after bedding whomever wherever, I determined to sober up a bit, to generalize love, transform it philanthropic, add a tasty sauce of agape as relish to my hot eros. I would transmute the love I was excluded from into compassionate humanitarian action by volunteering at the Sacramento AIDS Foundation to assist those whose earlier sexual behaviors, which mine mirrored, were pursued while unaware of the life-preserving information I had earlier garnered during my safe sexual sinecure in Kansas, information which allowed me to evade the HIV virus then clear-cutting the gay men of my community. (See my memoir *Losing Time: AIDS Lessons in Love and Loss*, 2019, for an account of life in Sacramento during the plague years.)

XII

One cannot escape one's past. Indeed, the past never really stays past. It has a way of treading on one's heels, dogging one's footsteps. During those early, lusty Sacramento years, two figures materialized from time's tenebrous shadows.

First, Frankie. One early spring morning, long before dawn had daubed the eastern horizon, I was startled awake by a telephone jangling in my dark bedroom. I reached over the fuck-buddy asleep next to me and fumbled for the phone on the bedside table. Though we had not spoken in years, I recognized a voice that shook me immediately to attention from my dream fog. Frankie was coming to San Francisco. She wanted me to join her there for the weekend.

"What are you doing these days?" I asked, having heard about her job-jumping and tenure disappointments from mutual friends.

"I'll tell you when you get here."

We sat sipping martinis in the buttery leather chairs of the Clock Bar in the Hotel St. Francis. Frankie revealed that a "client" had flown her to San Francisco and booked her into the hotel until Monday when she would cross the Bay Bridge to Berkeley, hired by a woman there to enact a "scene" she was to script for her.

"A scene?" I asked. "So you're now a playwright?"

"Sorta," she winked.

Over the intervening years, Frankie had metamorphosed into a dominatrix with, according to her, a national coterie of steady clients, both men and women, who paid her well to dominate them sexually.

"Beats teaching!" she laughed.

I glanced down to take in with a new appreciation her knee-high buckle-strapped boots, black leather with solid chrome stiletto heels.

A "scene," she explained, is a choreographed sexual encounter that a dominatrix scripts for a client according to a preliminary video interview detailing the fantasies, kinks, roles, fetishes, perversions—and safe words—required to sexually satisfy.

"This is a new client," Frankie added. "She's paying for a scene to last 90 minutes. I've got it mostly worked out, but I need to shop for a few things in the Castro."

"Details!" I demanded. "And I think we should try a couple of S/M shops South of Market."

"How's about I act out my scene for you? I could use someone to practice on."

"How's about you practice with a bolster pillow and let me critique your performance from a discrete distance, kind of like a drama critic?"

After a liquored-up late dinner in the paneled Oak Room of the St. Francis—her client, Frankie assured me, was paying her handsomely—we staggered up to a gleaming white room overlooking Union Square. I left my clothes in a heap on the floor and fell into one of the two queen-sized beds. Frankie crawled into the other one.

"Lu," she whispered, "why don't you get your butt on over here and get in bed with me?"

"Aw, no, Frankie," I demurred. "I'm not into women anymore."

"Oh, I know all that," she sighed impatiently. "I just thought we could have some fun. You know—for old time's sake?"

"Well, okay," I said. I slid into bed beside her. When we both seemed ready for what I expected to happen next, Frankie excused herself and went into the bathroom.

"Don't move," she said. "Keep it up. I'll be right back."

When she emerged from the bathroom but before she could switch off the light, I saw that she had strapped around her naked waist a wide harness contraption of black leather from which protruded a prodigious dildo. One hand smacked a short horse whisk into the palm of the other.

"Whoa!" I started back and jumped out of her bed.

"Well," Frankie snorted, "you didn't think you were going to fuck me, did you?"

"But you said this was going to be 'for old time's sake,'" I protested. "I think I'd better be heading on home."

"Nonsense!" Frankie laughed. "Let's just go to sleep. I need you in the morning."

I awoke to Frankie grazing my cheek with the dildo. "Last chance!" she leered. "I'm sorting out my props to see what else I need."

Spread out on a desk in the room were a pair of metal-studded cuffs; wrist restraints; a pair of alligator-toothed tit clamps; a leather dog collar and a chain leash; a riding crop; a red-leather fringe flogger; a paddle; leather straps laid out according to varying widths, girths, and lengths; a black-leather halter; a whip; a blindfold; leather gloves; several ball-gags; a neoprene sheet folded to a square; and, of course, the horse whisk and the black-leather harness and dildo.

After brunch in the Castro, we hunted up some S/M leather shops. Frankie had what she called her "titillation list." She selected a black-leather corset or bustier, black vinyl pants, a set of stainless-steel butt plugs, a rope of pearlized rubber anal beads, a pair of handcuffs, and a smart black-leather case, like a business woman's clutch purse.

"What's in the case?" I asked.

Frankie unzipped it to reveal a set of stainless-steel razors and scalpels, German-honed and gleaming in the store's neon glare. "Blood scenes are my specialty," she purred. "It's an aesthetic experience for the client—for me too—the way I slice in patterns so the blood seeps in pleasing figures and designs. It's especially dramatic when I cut by candlelight: the skin glows golden and the blood laces almost black against it!"

I went wobbly in the knees.

Frankie headed for the dressing room to try on the bustier. She called me in to cinch her up.

"Oof!" she panted. "I knew I shouldn't have ordered that breakfast burrito. Tighter!"

"How will you get into this contraption when you meet your client? Who'll cinch it up for you?"

"Once this bitch is laced tight, I can open it with these hidden latches in the front. See?" She unclasped the front of the bustier to free her large breasts which had been splaying over the top, then hooked the corset closed again.

Frankie slithered into the pair of gleaming black-vinyl pants, so form-fitting that it looked as if she had waded in crude oil up to her waist.

"How do I look?" she asked.

"Like an Amazon," I said. "Like a Valkyrie."

"Not good enough. I need to look like Athena rearing up ominous from red hell, armed to the tits and glowering with menace."

"Nailed it!"

An admiring clerk, multiply pierced and densely tattooed, totaled up Frankie's purchases, which amounted to close to a thousand dollars. Frankie seemed relieved that her credit card was good for it.

I helped Frankie lug her loot back to the hotel.

"Now get lost until we meet at 6:00 for cocktails in the bar," she demanded. "I need the afternoon to fine-tune my scene and work this new stuff in."

I left the hotel early the next morning, dropping Frankie off at a car-rental agency.

"Good luck in Berkeley," I said at parting. "Let me know how it goes."

I never heard from Frankie again. None of our friends can now locate her.

XIII

Almost a year after this adventure with Frankie, I received a call from the long-ago Boston boyfriend, Owen. "I have never been able to stop thinking about you or that enchanted summer we shared in Boston," he said. "I have to see you!"

"Where are you now?" I asked. "Are you still married?"

"I'm still in Baltimore," he said, "and of course I'm still married. But I'm on the job market. The bastards here didn't grant me tenure. I'm suing the fucks. I really need to see you."

Our rendezvous took place in Owen's home, his wife again away on a research trip. We made their Shaker-style bed heave and groan like a timbered sloop in a tempest. In the mornings, all the skewed prints on the bedroom walls had to be put to rights.

"Though my marriage has nothing at all to do with you, I want to tell you about it anyway—just this once, in case you have ratcheted up any puritanical qualms about your connection with me." Owen and I are lounging in his back garden, icy martinis glinting in the shifting light of a coy moon spying on us through a black fringe of mimosa leaves.

"My wife and I (Owen never disclosed his wife's name) both want to be married. Marriage is stability, an anchoring and a rootedness in something solid. I suppose we both see marriage as a shore against a cosmic loneliness we both intuited would be ours if we remained unattached. Children were never an issue. My wife has never exactly said so in words, but I gather she regards sex as little more than a sweaty, grunting mess. She has no illusions about my erotic tastes—which is one of the reasons you're here now—and she seemed almost relieved when I told her I could not promise to be monogamous. All she wants is for me to be there for her when she needs someone, and I have promised her that. I want the same from her. And, of course, we enjoy each other's company. Now I'm not going to talk about any of this ever again. It works for us. And it doesn't concern you."

"It wouldn't work for me," I sighed, "but I'm the last person to judge." I, who believed in neither love nor marriage, could afford to be generous.

"Typically smug of you," Owen sneered, "and insufferably condescending."

Our days were filled with forays into the blooming countryside and a few night journeys to the gay bars in Washington's Dupont Circle. These excursions gave Owen an opportunity to rehearse his grievances against students who had panned his classes with cruel evaluations and against colleagues who, intimidated, as Owen avowed, by his superior intelligence and stellar publications, had vented their venom by denying him tenure.

Our lubricated evenings always began with martinis and dinner in his candlelit garden. As these evenings progressed, his slurred avowals of love became both more morose and more ardent, always ending in the Shaker bed.

Could I have loved this man? Could Owen have introduced me into those amorous mysteries as he had earlier introduced me into a thrilling sexuality? I did not believe such love existed. I liked Owen, loved him even in a companionable way, but his matrimonial encumbrance, which I knew then he would never free himself from, supplied a sufficient impediment to prevent me from even considering the possibility of romantic love for him.

This first adulterous adventure was repeated the following summer when Owen secured a research fellowship at the University of Chicago. Before he moved into university faculty lodgings, we took a room at the Four Seasons where I fucked him, teetering on a wide inside window ledge on the tenth floor, the Ferris Wheel at the Navy Pier glimmering below in blue neon, my face, reflective like a revenant, poised just above his on the glass. We spent our days touring the Frank Lloyd Wright houses in Oak Park and driving up to Racine, Wisconsin to view Wright's Johnson Wax Headquarters and his Wingspread Retreat Center. On another night we boarded a train to Ravinia for a picnic and a starlit Liszt piano concerto featuring Andre Watts.

Owen and I arranged many clandestine meetings over many years in many locations, depending on where Owen ended up after being denied tenure again and again at various universities. His field was then in academic high demand, its professionals deemed "hard to hire" because they could earn so much more in the private sector than in academe. So Owen continued to secure professorships from faculties impressed by his credentials and his publications but soon disillusioned by his sense of superiority and his inability to suppress his contempt for those he deemed fools, particularly if they were his students. His positions—in Maryland, New Jersey, Indiana, Tennessee, and Florida—usually lasted three, at the most four years. Given our academic schedules, we could often be together for weeks at a time.

While separated on these various jobs from a wife who did not seem to mind his absences over much, Owen

135

indulged in all manner of wayward predilections. He explored the leather scene, though without Frankie's dedication or talent for it. Dry-marooned on a rural campus in the great hush of Indiana, he would buckle on his leather livery on weekends with no one to strut before, ogling leather porn in the square beige living room of his standard rented apartment. Is it any wonder he was eager for me to join him?

We enjoyed an uproarious interlude on one of my visits, chortling and swaggering around in all the leather appurtenances ordered up online from New York S/M shops. When, predictably, Owen failed to earn tenure in Indiana, he boxed up all his leather frippery and his porn tapes and Fed-Exed them to me for safe keeping in California before returning to his wife. Soon, however, he had landed yet another university position and demanded that I return the leather and the porn, still stashed in the boxes he had sent them in. I simply exchanged the shipping labels.

On one occasion, I met Owen in Rome for a month. In a contentious settlement aimed at averting the lawsuits Owen was adept at lodging against the tenure-deniers, his disaffected colleagues had cobbled together a grudging severance package including a semester's teaching position in the college's international program—anything to get rid of Owen without a fuss. In Rome, Owen had an apartment overlooking the Tiber. I had a sabbatical.

If I had believed in love or had ever expected it to befall me, Rome was the place to have fallen in love with Owen. I savored being with him—most of the time. I felt more alive when with him, my body leveraging a thrilling sexual amperage, my mind a spirited enthusiasm. Long term, however, I, like his many former colleagues, would have flinched from Owen's arrogance.

In the Galleria Borghese one gloriously lucid early Spring afternoon, Owen stood rapt before Bernini's sculpture *The Rape of Proserpina*, pointing out to me its Mannerist gestural extravagances.

"What's 'Mannerism'?" I asked.

Owen exhaled forcefully through his nose and pivoted a deep scowl in my direction: "Are you really such a rube?"

That night we drank merry and made the bed creak and groan as if I had fielded no insult.

Several days later, we had agreed to meet for drinks near the Castel Sant' Angelo at our favorite taverna with its leafy, lively terrace overlooking the Tiber. Meeting times meant nothing to Owen. He expected me to wait for him however long it took for him to arrive. On this day, he was over two hours late. I swiveled around from the river view every time I heard the terrace door shush open. Finally I had had enough: I took the tram back to the apartment, poured myself a glass of Nebbiolo, fierce enough to match my mood, and sat down to pout. When Owen keyed the apartment door and let himself in several hours later, he was relieved but livid on finding me in the apartment, my mood wine-moderated. I was stirring anchovies into a puttanesca sauce.

"I didn't know whether to rush over to the hospital, call the police, or drop by the morgue!" he exploded. "Why the hell didn't you wait for me? I know what an idiot you are about directions and finding your way around."

I mollified Owen with several martinis, the promise of a blow job, and a fiery pasta puttanesca. Though both of us were woozy, the postprandial sexual armistice was lively nonetheless.

We were awakened too early the next morning by the daily matitutinal clanking up of an antiquated lift and the arrival of an elderly woman at her friend's apartment down the hall: loud smacking on the solid door with the flat of a hand, then a screeching "Bina! Bina! Ciao Bina!" A bit hung over, Owen delayed rising to put the espresso pot on the burner. Yawning and stretching, he asked me to describe my house in Sacramento.

I loved my house, its Asian screens and sleek white furniture, its reversed room arrangement—bedrooms downstairs, public rooms upstairs to offer a view from a grape-arbored veranda of the American River fringed in willow and honey locust. Owen suddenly silenced me with a raised hand: "I'd <u>hate</u> your house!" he hissed and rolled over me and out of the bed on my side.

Several days later, I left Rome. Owen skipped his classes to ride the train with me to Fiumicino Airport to see me off. We both cried on saying good-bye.

Though Owen and I still frequently email, the last time I saw him was at our house in Palm Springs several years ago. He called me one evening from Los Angeles where he was doing research. He was staying at the Beverly Hills Hotel on Sunset. He insisted that I join him there. "You've got to <u>see</u> this place," he snorted.

"I told you," I started, though with some hesitation, "that if I ever got into a committed relationship...."

"Oh, I know, I know," he cut me off, "but I thought you'd enjoy the pool here, maybe a drink at the Chateau Marmont later? Since you've been married to Bud for nine years, wouldn't you enjoy a discrete little carnal vacation?"

I was tempted.

I relayed to Bud the terms of this invitation. He indicated that he would not mind if Owen visited us instead. A pause preceded Owen's saying he would come to Palm Springs a couple days later. "I'll be there around 8:00 tonight," he said on the morning of the day he said he would arrive. "Don't hold dinner for me."

At 10:30, I called to ask if he still intended to visit us. No answer. At midnight, Owen called: "Am I still welcome?"

"Where the hell are you," I asked, furious. Bud had given up and gone to bed.

"In your driveway."

I do not think I could ever have lived with Owen for long, even after I had finally learned by heart that romantic love was real, even for gay men. I would have found it difficult to tolerate Owen's intermittent arrogance, the blade of animus he could slash with, or his countering insecurity. When with Owen, I whirred and spun with an electrical charge, galvanized, but that thrill was not enough. What elusive, alchemical tincture makes attraction and affection blaze into love, like flame dazzles black coal into diamond flare? That tincture did not flash for me, however alive I was when with Owen, however great the gratitude and deep affection, tilted towards love, I feel for him still for having opened my life for me.

XIV

In my book *Losing Time*, I chronicle my progress from initial sexual attraction to infatuation and at last into an awareness—sudden and illuminating—that I could regard another man, Dore Tanner, as important to my happiness. The book chronicles the belated epiphany that I could love a man—deeply, richly, with abandon—and that I could extend that love to another after the too-early death from AIDS of the man who taught me that love was one of life's wonders.

When Dore died, my heart stopped. In my disordered thinking at that sad time, I saw Dore's death as dark karma for my feckless promiscuity. I had found love after having disclaimed its reality for so long: love denied was thus denied me. I recognize now that the universe does not work in that way.

I soon returned to my libidinous ways after Dore died, bedding as many desirable men as I could lure between my sheets. However, now susceptible to love after my illuminating experience with Dore, I desired that love intensity again, that orchidaceous daze that softened the world's sharp edges for the new lover while leaving him eager and alert to all of life's rich sensations. Now, each sexual encounter seeded the possibility that love might be discovered in lust's retinue. I did, however, miss my former sexual insouciance, lust evanescent without reverberation after its satisfactions.

In January 2000, a post-coital acquaintance, not at all lover material, was exploring a move from Sacramento to Palm Springs and, thinking to share hotel expenses with me there, asked if I would consider accompanying him while he looked for a job, and if employment seemed promising, a place to live.

I had heard that Palm Springs was paradise for gay men, a resort of lubricious ease. We flew out early from Sacramento, cold and curtained dark with rain, and arrived in Palm Springs on a late morning shocked with translucence, the air caressing and buoyant, the atmosphere that which must have invigorated prelapsarian Eden.

While my friend was job hunting, I set out on an afternoon jog, a lark through neighborhoods indistinguishable from gardens, interrupted by my stopping to filch tangelos from trees overhanging the sidewalks. I wafted through pliant breezes. Mid-run, I tarried at an outdoor palapa-bar to sip a margarita, served me in a fishbowl goblet under gently rustling palm trees. On my finishing it, the bartender encouraged me to have another:

"Margaritas," he flashed a flirty smile, "are like breasts: one is too few; three are too many."

Attempting to stand after that second margarita, I caught my running shoe on the rim of the bar stool and clattered down to the adobe pavers, the bar stool straddling me like a clumsy lover. Back at the hotel, I found my friend in close conference with a realtor, eminently doable but all business while negotiating a possible sale. Within half an hour, the realtor noticed that I was more interested than my friend in the property spec-sheets he was offering. The realtor showed us a number of properties before opening a door into a two-bedroom, two-bath condo unit in a walled development of sixteen units staggered around a shimmering turquoise pool. Price: $48,000. Palm Springs was again in the midst of one of its cyclical real-estate busts.

To the realtor's annoyance, I immediately dubbed the unit "the granny pavilion": an elderly couple had for many years been escaping to it from the stiff, raw winters in Alberta, but the old lady had recently miss-stepped a curb on a downtown Palm Springs street and had broken a hip. They had immediately decamped for Canada on her release from the hospital.

The "granny pavilion" featured a scallop-backed blue and pink floral chintz couch, its ruffled skirt brushing the sea-blue carpet it squatted on. A number of sun-bleached Thomas Kinkade prints of impossible cottages in far-fetched gardens imposed themselves on walls tinted a murky green. Blue and pink faience irises twined up squat blue lamp bases topped with tatty fringed shades. Funereal beige curtains swagged the large windows like the folds and tucks found on casket drapery. The owners were offering it "turn-key" and wanted a quick escrow. I bought it on the spot.

Two weeks later, I flew down to Palm Springs to take possession of the "granny pavilion." Not only had the owners abandoned all their furniture, as agreed on, but they had left their clothes on hangers in the closets as well as moldy cheese and spoiled food in the refrigerator and stale crackers and out-of-date canned goods in the cupboards, stuff quickly dispatched or expedited to Good Will.

While this purging progressed, my new next-door neighbor appeared in the doorway wearing a sweeping caftan aswirl in garish Caribbean colors. He introduced himself as Garland Weary, an amiable Black man with a booming laugh and a swishy gait. Gay, of course. He was not laughing at the time. An electrician I had called in to replace a breaker earlier that morning had made the mistake of telling Garland that he liked Garland's "house dress."

"That man is ign'rant," Garland fumed. "He don't know this a <u>dashiki</u>!"

Garland and I became fast friends. Soon after learning that I had earned a Ph.D., Garland began referring to himself as "Dr. Weary," declaring that he had earned his Ph.D. in "life experience" and was now entitled to that distinction as an "elder" in the community.

One morning a trick staying overnight with me in the condo answered a 7:00 A.M. doorbell while I was shaving. I heard him talking with Garland. After a moment or two, my bedmate came down the hall bearing a plate of muffins: "Aunt Jemima, she be bakin'," he quipped. Garland and I cherished our friendship until his death of a heart attack one day while walking to the grocery. We had enjoyed a gossip over a cup of coffee together by the pool only an hour or so before.

I transformed the "granny pavilion" into a desirable property during the eleven years I owned it. I looked forward to spending a month there during Christmas breaks, fugitive long weekends during the semesters, and almost three months each summer. I found it easy to meet men in Palm

Springs, lust ever tinged with an openness to something more—the orchidaceous daze....

Each summer I connected with a different man, a "summer boyfriend," with occasional adventures on the side. One "summer boyfriend" served as a project manager for a developer; one was a real estate agent who had been a singer/dancer on cruise ships for 23 years; another worked for a condo management firm; yet another was a bartender at a nudist resort who could not fathom my preference for remaining clothed while we ate dinner or watched television during the hot summer evenings we shared. For me, disrobing was a sexual preamble; for him, it was an existential state of being. With some of these congenial men, a friendship developed; for none of them did the sexual attraction incandesce into love.

Love, I concluded, was no longer available to me. I had expended my life's share. I was wrong: A friend introduced me to Bud in a leather bar in Sacramento nearly ten years after Dore died, and the orchidaceous daze softened the world again. (See my account of this romance toward the end of my 2019 book *Losing Time.*) As of this writing, Bud and I have been together for nearly sixteen years, married for fourteen. We now reside in Palm Springs full time in the house we bought together after our retirements.

XV

In spite of my love-conversion with Dore, in spite of my marriage to Bud, I was still accosted by self-anointed heralds from the straight world who made known to me that gay love was a poisonous perversion, noxious to one's soul and pernicious in its effects on the family and, consequently, on the whole of society.

One such messenger materialized on the Halloween after Bud and I had married in September 2008 while living in the little 1849 gold-rush town of Grass Valley, California in the foothills of the Sierra. We were rigging ourselves out in our costumes before the second of our two annual Halloween dress-up parties, the previous night's being the grand gala for the Nevada County gay and lesbian coalition. We had entertained over 60 revelers. Tonight's was to be a smaller Halloween costume gathering, about 30 straight friends from the 8:00 church service we attended.

I was inserting the studs into my tuxedo shirt while Bud was laboring to squeeze into a wedding gown we had bought for $15 at a thrift store, a big girl's cast-off dream dress, blanched in a blizzard of bows, rick-rack, lace, gauzy roses, and plastic pearls. Apparently this bride had not tripped fantastic down the flowery path into the flourishing future she had foreseen and been promised.

We had each tried the gown on in the dressing room, laughing convulsively and carrying on outrageously, unaware of the reactions, ranging from amusement to disapproval, of other shoppers we did not realize were in the store with us. "You guys were having a little party in the dressing room, were you?" frowned the clerk who rang up our purchase.

We always planned our Halloween get-ups to parody an accomplishment completed during the preceding year. The Halloween before, Bud had hitched himself into overalls like those worn by the farmer in Grant Wood's painting *American Gothic* to commemorate our having laid out 265 square feet of raised vegetable beds in our backyard in Grass Valley. That left me as "the butt-ugly farmer's daughter" in the painting, as Bud dubbed me. I cannot say that this sobriquet was misattributed.

While I was attempting to winch up the zipper on Bud's wedding dress in our front room—"Exhale, Bud! Bend your shoulders back!"—the doorbell rang. Bud beat a hasty retreat down the hall.

I opened the door to the neighbor across the street, a retired cop. Bud and I had made friendly overtures to him and his wife on our first moving into the neighborhood, but they had remained glacial for years. He now felt called upon to confront us on this evening, apparently by his standing as a former enforcer of the law. He complained about having to view the sign staked in our front yard opposing California Proposition 8, which, if passed, would have abrogated the recent California Supreme Court ruling permitting same-sex marriage and would have restricted marriages in the California Constitution to those between a man and a woman. Apparently, someone, on leaving our LGBTQ party of the evening before, had lifted his own sign supporting Proposition 8 and had driven off with it. He had seen them do it.

But his mission was broader. He had to bring God into it. He was there to inform us how affronted he and certain of our other fundy neighbors were by what he termed as our attempt to pass ourselves off as married, that biblically they used to stone people like us, that our coupling was an abomination, a scandal.

This retired cop then launched into the lame witticism that God had created Adam and Eve, not Adam and Steve. I cut him off with a raised hand, disappointing him in disallowing his conclusion to a quip he thought both incontestable and comically clever.

"When I was a cop in Los Angeles in the 70s," he said, "you people were skulking about in filthy back alleys, hiding out and fornicating behind the garbage bins. Now you flaunt it. Marriage!" he spat. "You want everything these days."

"The skulking is finished for good," I said, "and the sex is now more sanitary. But you're wrong: we don't want everything. We'll settle for all the rights you now enjoy. And, whether you like it or not, Bud and I are as married as you and your wife are." I fluttered some cash in his direction: "Now here's 10 bucks to replace your sign." And I shut the door on him.

Bud was spewing with rage, taxing the already swelling seams of his dress. He sputtered disbelief that anyone would consign us to the foul L. A. alleys gay men had been forced into while facing the moral and legal opprobrium and physical threats from cops like this neighbor. For this mustered-out old cop and all his bigot buddies on the force and on the block, gay sex could never be anything other than vermin-lust.

All my life, I absorbed such messages like gamma radiation. Marriage for gay people assumed that we could love. For most people, lust alone was allotted as our portion, something I had consequently also long believed.

We had come to expect these denunciations from the Evangelical Christians who sometimes appeared on our doorstep uninvited to share with us the "Good News" that they, like their God, "loved" gay people but hated our sinful lust which was destined to blaze up like pitch in the fiery pit where we would be blistered without reprieve if we did not subscribe to their creed then and there. And we could expect added accelerant to be spilled on that inferno if we dared to blaspheme by contracting a sacrilegious "gay marriage." On these occasions, when I could summon the patience, I enjoyed announcing to them that God did indeed love gay people, not in spite of, but because we were gay. I would then ream them out for being so ill-bred as to stand on my own doorstep, relishing their bad news that I was soon to be spitted at the great bonfire down below for all time. I would

146

denounce their arrogant self-assurance that they alone had penetrated the incomprehensible mystery of the divine. And I liked to throw in a few castigations for good measure about their sending their blonde teenagers, decked out in Izod polo shirts, khaki cargo shorts, and Sperry Top-siders, all purchased at Nordstrom's, to venture from their posh Caribbean resorts to convert impoverished Hispanic Catholics in their tin-roofed hovels to their version of a middle-class American Christianity without providing them any means of actually entering the middle class themselves.

Occasionally these gay-bashing denunciations dropped down on us like acid rain from unexpected sources.

Before I met him, Bud regularly attended the 8:00 Sunday service at a small church his partner of 24 years had gone to. After the death of his partner, the congregation had befriended Bud, alone and grieving on his isolated 89-acre Keystone Ranch deep in the Sierra Nevada foothills, approached at the end of a rutted two-mile dirt road, literally at the end of the earth.

Coming from a long ancestral line of Presbyterian ministers, Bud had thrown all that over and been born again as an atheist, though he enjoyed his church's social aspect— its horizontal dimension, as he termed it—eschewing any truck with the church's vertical dimension—its theological trappings and its purported commerce with a nebulous Divine. Bud reasoned that if a god existed, it must flourish in far other inaccessible dimensions than the 3 ½ dimensions we are consigned to.

Bud and I wed during the marriage-permitting "window-period" of 2008 in California before that window was slammed shut by the narrow passage of Proposition 8— regardless of our front-yard sign opposing it. Soon after he became aware of our nuptials, the rector of Bud's church asked if we would be open to a pastoral visit. On arriving, he announced that he was wrestling with the issue of gay marriage, a fierce contest, like Jacob with the angel at the foot of the ladder but without the blessing that Jacob extorted. We assured him that we felt no need for any ritual or sacramental validation of our marriage from him or his church, but we would not disguise our marriage from the congregation either.

That compromise made, I joined Bud in attending the 8:00 service. We knew we had made a devil's bargain, settling for a grudging tolerance on the rector's part, allowing him to disregard our marriage while ritually celebrating the marriages of his straight congregation.

Following his sermon at each Sunday service, the rector invited people observing a birthday, an anniversary, or a special event or achievement to come up for the congregation's acknowledgement and congratulations. This communal custom in no way constituted a church-sanctioned ritual or religious observance. Our fourth wedding anniversary happened to fall on a Sunday in 2012, and, as the rector had been tipped off, we intended to go up at the call for the communal acknowledgement. This would in no way violate the compromise we had earlier reached.

"Before I invite anyone up before the congregation," the rector intoned after that Sunday's sermon, "I want to extend a few remarks. First, I will never engage in what my priestly predecessors in the history of our church have deemed to be intrinsically wrong: I will never officiate at or recognize a same-sex 'marriage' (here he inserted a raised two-fingered air-quote dismissal) as a legitimate sacrament—even though current leadership in our church seems determined to do so. Now, in no way does this mean that I do not support gay people socially, nor would I favor denying them any of their hard-won legal rights."

"Listen," he continued, "I understand gay people. I myself have only ever been sexually attracted to brunette women, never to blondes or red-heads, so I understand the force of particular sexual attraction and that same-sex desire is not open to alteration, just as my preference for brunettes is immutable. Sacramental marriage, however, is built on more than preference or even sexual desire: it has always been defined by the church as valid in joining one man and one woman as one flesh in a mutuality and a coherence that includes sexuality but is so much more. Thus, societal re-definitions of marriage as possible between same-sex couples are irrelevant in church law."

The rector should have shut up at this point, having implied that homosexual connections are determined by lust alone, but he chose to blunder on: "I feel sympathy for gay people, I truly do. My wife's gay uncle entertained a man on most weekends for close to 15 years. He never knew the man's last name or how to contact him. It was simply a standing assignation, which our uncle allowed nothing to interrupt. These meetings were secretive and, my wife and I suspected, unworthy because we were certain this man was married and cheating on his wife. Then suddenly, with no warning or explanation, the man stopped coming. My wife's uncle never heard from him again, never found out if he was alive or dead. Now our uncle is in his 80s, a sad, lonely, desperate old man."

"I went into all this," the rector concluded, "because I want you all to know where I stand on same-sex 'marriage'."

A few people in the back pews applauded.

"Now," the rector beamed, "are there any of you celebrating a birthday, an anniversary, or some other occasion with claims on our notice? If so, you're welcome to come up."

149

Bud and I sat on our hands. I was fizzing with rage, face smoldering, eyes darting murderous.

"What do you want to do?" I hissed.

Bud looked ashen. "We'll leave at Communion."

"No one?" the rector asked again, glancing at us, growing uncomfortable, his smile fading.

After making our way out of the church against the surge of parishioners approaching the Communion rail, we met a friend out front who had hosted a wedding reception for us four years before and who had come running out after us: "My hair is on fire!" she spluttered. "I am just furious!"

"Let's talk later," Bud sighed.

We heard that after the service, our friend stormed up to the rector as he was shaking hands with the parishioners at the church door: "I am resigning from the parish council. And I will not keep my monetary pledge. However, this is MY church. I was here before you came, and, by God, I will not be leaving it. But you can no longer count on my support or my husband's."

Later that morning, other sympathetic friends from the congregation dropped by our house. "What should we do?" they asked. "We're thinking of attending the Methodist service next Sunday."

I wrote a letter to the rector indicating that few of his "priestly predecessors" had had the courage or maturity of faith to protest against slavery either, putting themselves, like him and his stance on homosexuality, on the wrong side of history and of an evolving spirituality. I also protested his demeaning equation of a preference for brunette women with the same-sex orientation of gay men. I reminded him that his predilection for brown tresses carried with it no social, political, legal, moral, or attitudinal consequences for him, the kind of consequences that shaped gay lives. I accused him of betraying the compromise I now regretted agreeing to during his earlier pastoral visit. At that visit, I reminded him, I had warned him against making his tone-deaf analogy between gay sexual desire and his preference for dark hair, reasoning that his penchant for brunettes could easily be satisfied with a bottle of Clairol hair dye in the hands of a salon stylist, opening wide to him any woman who could stand him.

This episode reaffirmed for us that even liberal religious denominations were frequently unwilling to credit the existence, let alone the worthiness, of gay love, refusing to honor it with the same canonical approbation accorded to the love of straight couples. To them, our sexuality remained an intrinsically disordered descent into lust, one of the seven deadly sins whose voluptuaries were to be whisked around in the searing whirlwinds of one of Dante's infernal tiers.

XVI

The journey traced in these pages was mapped by societal, legal, and religious road signs, pressures, and directional signals negating gay people as acceptable and honorable and their love as a value to be cherished and celebrated. These negations underlay the libidinous gay life I have lived, relished, and certainly never regretted. I require no absolution for the way my life has gone. I feel neither guilt nor contrition—and certainly no shame. And that is exactly where I need to be: at self affirmation and a radical self acceptance. As I have learned the hard way, all love starts with love of self before it can branch and tendril and leaf out to enfold others.

I now wonder if I have indeed lived my whole life devoid of love. Was lust really the sole polestar that guided my journey? Certainly I must have loved, in my way, all those I have lingered with along my path—the two women who were such valued parts of my early adult life for so long; Frankie and Owen, who both played such significant roles in my eventual happiness. Though my love for them all stumbled as unrealized and uncertain, often selfish, certainly dented and bungled, it must have been love all the same. Beyond question, it was a deep and abiding affection. I sense the upsurge of that affection, that love even now, so it must always have been there. This recognition of my love for them does not stem from an aging man's need to appease his conscience for wrongs committed against them. Mine is an affection, a love for them more solid than the sentimental self-delusions often brought into view by the amending spectacles that age fits us with when we peer into the past.

I do not think I deceive myself in also sensing now some degree of love, at least affection, that coincided with my lust for all the tricks and one-night affairs and fuck-buddies that caromed through my promiscuous years—all the turgid tendernesses, the ribald vigors, the shared carnal ardors. There existed then a concomitant intimacy, however temporary; a real affection, however fleeting. Gay love manifested in this way need not endure to be love. Affection need not be stable or fixed. But it can be an approximation, a version of love all the same.

What are we but creatures of clay lightened by a shimmer some call spirit: spirit levitating clay, clay grounding spirit. Is it not possible to satisfy the demands of both clay and spirit without making any durable commitment to the co-participant in acts that produce that satisfaction? Mutuality is the gleaming key to sexual morality.

Lust turns dark when coercion of any kind is resorted to, when one partner exercises an un-negotiated power over an unwilling partner, when sex is not completely consensual, when one partner uses deception or exploitation or drugs or alcoholic incapacitation or force or trickery or undue influence or lying or any other strategy that denies the other partner full knowledge and consent to the sex act. There is, I believe, such a thing as sexual sin. That term has, however, been co-opted by puritanical Evangelical Christians who have lost all authority to condemn it in their avid support for a lying, abusive, adulterous has-been President who bragged about his sexual assaults on women by "grabbing their pussies" and then doing whatever he wanted to them, protected from their lawsuits by his wealth and later by his corrupt political power. But in spite of the collusion of many Christian churches in such behavior, all such actions are reprehensible nonetheless. These hypocritical churches join in condemning ALL homosexual acts, though, no matter how consensual and life affirming they are to those who engage in them.

When shared with full consent and for mutual pleasure, lust glides into sacred fulfillment. Then, lust is illuminated by the holy. Lust then arcs two distinct lines into a circle embracing both partners, regardless of its duration. This orb is a haven against isolation and alienating detachment. It is a form of love.

For those whose love for me was more mature and selfless than any love I was then capable of extending to them, I own now that their love seeded in me a corresponding love that ripened in time, allowing me to extend it to others. Nearing 50, I fell in love—fully and beyond doubt—for the first time. I was struck down from my wanton high horse, a Damascene conversion. Since then, I have purged myself of those forces that earlier poisoned me with the toxic message that love—in all its degrees, manifestations, and expressions—was an Edenic garden party gay men were denied access to by so many forces wielding flaming swords.

The gay sexual history recorded here, unmuted by euphemism or evasion, outlines the effects on me of those forces—both external and internalized—that would debase, discredit, and anathematize gay love and the sexual expression of it. These forces have led me and so many other gay men to attune ourselves only to the lust that our bodies unerringly disclosed to us early on.

I now acknowledge that it must have been love all along that kept covert company with my lust and intensified its pleasures. I just was not taught to recognize it at the time or to credit the existence of love. I know now that love is the heart's clamoring to fill its chambers with something more vital than blood. The heart purposes more than merely to sustain the body, salt fluids coursing mechanically through a lumbering flesh bag. Love is my heart's need, tired at last of its own echoes. And I know now that I can love and be loved—in my own gay way and on my own gay terms.

MY GRANDFATHERS

I

I knew one of my grandfathers. The other died before I was born.

My Italian grandfather was grafted tight to his home and vegetable garden in the small Mississippi River town of White Castle, Louisiana, just upstream from New Orleans and named for the largest antebellum plantation mansion in the South, an ornate white Italianate confection called Nottoway House, located just outside of the town. My German grandfather was a nomad who, for the most part, had no home, a wanderer seemingly deficient in any need for a stable domestic life.

Were I to graph the lives of my two grandfathers on a Venn diagram, the inner convergence would define my own alloy. Like my Italian grandfather, I would never be content as a drifter. I look upon homeless people as among the most unfortunate of human beings. But like my German grandfather, I acknowledge a zest for roving, manifested in me from early childhood when I would range about the neighborhood to the consternation of my parents who were forever searching for me, fearful that I was lost or had gone off with someone. Unlike my siblings, I was eager to stay overnight with anyone who would invite me. During several summers, I was the only kid in my child-crowded neighborhood who would venture for a week to a free, city-run camp set up with cabins in the woods. I elected to go away to school when I was fourteen and stayed there for two years. Fortunate in a career that afforded me generous amounts of free time, I have traveled the world, and, after retirement, I have goaded my husband into journeying with me to all corners of six continents. But always home draws me back, the domestic siren song irresistible.

Writing about my two grandfathers is, then, a way of reading myself.

II

My Italian grandfather was born on March 16, 1889 in Gibellina, a town in Trapani Province, Sicily, not far distant from Palermo. His life in the Sicily of his day was constrained by unscrupulous barons, corrupt police, venal judges, and brutal Mafiosi. A landless peasant, he faced bare-subsistence poverty, the periodic droughts that parched the countryside, burdensome taxation, enforced army conscription for up to seven years, and organized banditry. My grandfather and others like him lacked the power to improve their hard condition, their hopelessness impelling a mass migration from Sicily to the Americas.

Though the majority of Sicilian immigrants sailed for the Northeastern cities of the United States to take industrial jobs, nearly 70,000 Italian immigrants, mostly Sicilians, arrived in the Port of New Orleans between 1898 and 1929. Many were attracted by agricultural work in the sugar cane and cotton plantations of Louisiana where the demand for farm laborers was heightened by the migration of Black workers out of the repressive South to northern cities like New York, Chicago, and Philadelphia.

My grandfather's brother Giacomo, born in 1884, preceded my grandfather, arriving alone in New Orleans at the age of 19 on the ship <u>La Massilia</u> on October 14, 1903. Chain migration was a common practice at the time. After emigrating, relatives who had come over before would scrape together enough money to pay the passage of the next relative to come over. His brother paid my grandfather's passage on the final voyage of the <u>Vincenzo Florio</u>, which docked in New Orleans on May 14, 1906. My grandfather was 17.

My grandfather had been warned by earlier immigrants that Americans liked to play practical jokes on gullible recent arrivals. Accordingly, he was vigilant. After his ship had anchored in New Orleans but before the immigrants had been processed, several women from a local church were allowed on board bearing great baskets of fruit to hand out to passengers who had been sailing for close to a month without access to fresh produce. One of these women handed my grandfather a banana. He had never seen one before. It was ripe, bright yellow, and deliciously aromatic. As he watched other passengers bite into their apples, peaches, and pears, he too took a large bite out of the banana, not knowing that he needed to peel it first. Furious at the trick he thought had been played on him, he heaved the remainder of the banana into the river.

Once processed at immigration—weighed, examined for physical deformities or obvious illness, and given tests for mental acuity—he was released on the dock where he expected to meet his brother. Apparently the ship had arrived earlier than scheduled, so my grandfather sat alone on the dock for hours with his ragged cloth valise at his feet, fumes swirling around him from the hard cheeses he had brought from home as a gift for his brother. As he recalled it, he spied a Black man sauntering idly in his direction. Though my grandfather had never seen a Black man before, he <u>had</u> seen a ferocious devil rendered in black on a fresco of the Last Judgment covering a wall in his parish church in Gibellina. Terrified, he took up his valise in a panic and ran for blocks, getting lost in the narrow streets of the French Quarter. Sweating, filthy, hungry, and afraid, he stole into a back alley after dark, dumped the water out of a horse trough, filled it with the moldering hay he raked up off the cobblestones with his fingers, and spent his first fitful night in the New World.

His immigration journey was the one great adventure in the quiet, secluded life my grandfather would go on to establish for himself.

Unlike most of their fellow émigrés, both my grandfather and his brother had come over with a trade, dutifully entered in their ships' manifests. They had both been apprenticed to the village cobbler in Gibellina who had taught them his occupation in exchange for several years of their free labor in his shop. This profession gave both brothers an advantage over the many unskilled laborers who had sailed with them.

After a few weeks at his brother's lodgings trying to accustom himself to this foreign world he had entered, my grandfather was hired out as a leather worker and cobbler at a harness, saddle, and shoe repair concern in Mississippi, paid a pittance and provided with a damp, mosquito-droning room and meager board in town. He labored from dawn to dusk in a workshop built onto the back of the company business office, repairing saddles and horse gear and re-soling the heavy boots of those men doing local agricultural work and laboring in lumber mills. In addition, he mended the workmen's heavy leather gloves and stitched up the tears in their leather aprons, chaps, and leggings. I have a photograph of him clad in a white shirt, tie, and vest, covered from upper chest to near his ankles in a canvas apron and standing, arms akimbo, next to the stern-looking owner of the saddle shop and another laborer not nearly so nattily attired as he.

His workshop had one small window and a warped door that would not close all the way. There my grandfather toiled under a roof that alternately let in streaks of sunlight and streams of rainwater. For the first several days of his work there, he would look up suddenly to see men and an occasional woman staring at him through the window or peering furtively around the door. On his meeting their gaze, they would dart away.

My grandfather asked a fellow laborer there why he was being stared at as he worked. "Because," said the man, "the foreman is telling everyone he has a savage wild Dago chained up, and if you ever broke loose, you would work mayhem in the streets or, after dark, in the workers' sleep sheds." My grandfather's sojourn in Mississippi was brief.

I was never told how my grandfather made it to White Castle, Louisiana, where he was to spend the remainder of his long life. I suspect he chose White Castle because his brother had settled in the small adjacent town of Plaquemine.

Work was plentiful in White Castle: during the sugar-cane harvest from October to January, the cane cutters brought their heavy, mud-caked boots for my grandfather to clean, repair, and waterproof at 50 cents a pair, returning for the same service during the cotton harvests the following summer. My grandfather supplemented this steady income with shoe repair services for people in the surrounding towns.

He soon eked out enough to pool funds with his brother to send for their younger brother in Gibellina, who, as it turned out, had lost his nerve about immigrating. When he pocketed the money they had sent him, my grandfather would have nothing more to do with his Sicilian family, even when, decades later, they sent plaintive letters begging for relief after having lost what little they had in the devastating Belice earthquake of 1968, which destroyed Gibellina completely..

159

Soon after he arrived in White Castle, my grandfather wooed the young daughter of an immigrant family, the Sciortinos, who had come over in the late 19th Century from Corleone, a village close to Palermo, later made infamous as the originating village of Vito Corleone, Mario Puzo's central character in *The Godfather* on which the Francis Ford Coppola films were based.

The Sciortinos established themselves in the grocery business before branching out into the furniture trade, over time acquiring considerable rental property. Several later went into the saloon business. They also ran the town's ice house and eventually served as mayors and police chiefs in White Castle.

My grandmother, Lucy, was born on July 11, 1898 into this relatively affluent family. She was nine years younger than my grandfather, who contracted an engagement with her when she was sixteen or seventeen. Her family must have considered this a less-than-brilliant match, my grandfather only recently off the boat and without significant prospects.

Their engagement did not run smoothly. At one point, the Sciortinos broke it off for reasons my cousin and I agree on, though our versions of the story differ considerably in details: On a pre-nuptial trip to New Orleans where my grandmother's parents were to buy her trousseau, my grandfather groped his teen-aged intended, nuzzled her neck, and stole a kiss as they were going upstairs to their rooms. She giggled and scampered up the hotel stairway, all in full view of the proper and disapproving people sitting in the lobby below. My grandmother's parents viewed these indiscrete liberties in a mirror at the top of the stairs. Early the next morning, my grandfather woke to find that the Sciortinos had taken the first train back to White Castle. They left a letter blustering about the dishonor done them and breaking the engagement. When my grandfather returned to White Castle on the next train, my grandmother's brother was waiting for him. Along with a few insults, he handed my grandfather a bag containing the gold coins and trinkets he had, by custom, distributed to various members of my grandmother's family. A year or so of my grandfather's petitioning through the parish priest re-knit the rupture.

I must have heard this version of the story from someone gifted with the Italian penchant for embellishing mundane memory with invented details and nuances. I am uncertain how much this accretion resulted from the tricks of my own memory.

My grandmother apparently refused other suitors, and, after cooling off, the Sciortinos relented, understandably desiring to get this pining, morose girl out of their house. For their wedding gift, the Sciortinos gave my grandparents the house where they raised their family. They probably married in 1916 because my father was born in 1917. My grandmother would have been about 18 when they married, my grandfather nearly 27. They were married for over 60 years.

I suspect the Sciortinos, themselves a contentious lot, never really liked my grandfather. Perhaps they never forgave him for the dishonor they felt he had done them in the episode on the hotel stairway. When my grandmother's parents died, my grandmother and several others of her older siblings were left out of the will, apparently at the instigation of my grandmother's younger siblings who persuaded the old people to leave them the bulk of their estate.

My grandfather, in league with my grandmother and her dispossessed siblings, sued the estate, incurring staggering legal fees and acquiring a fairer distribution of the property but provoking familial hard feelings. This

Sciortino family strife soon escalated, their squabbles occasioning much bemused gossip in White Castle. On one occasion, my grandmother apparently cracked one of her brothers over the head with a split log of stove wood during an argument over a radio antenna wire she claimed he had cut down out of meanness. On another occasion, one fratricidal Sciortino gunned down one of his brothers. The victim survived his wound. The Sheriff, closely allied with the family, spirited the intended murderer aboard a night train for Los Angeles where he settled, rarely heard from again.

The citizens of White Castle apparently held long memories of these Sciortino family fracases. On a visit to my grandparents as a young man, I stopped in a store to buy a pack of cigarettes. "You're Tony Agosta's boy, aren't you?" the clerk asked. "I'll bet you're glad your name doesn't end in 'Sciortino'."

For most of my childhood, I could never understand anything my grandfather said to me, so thick was his Italian accent. When he addressed me, I stood there and stared at him, mouth gaping. I would frown and tilt my head to one side like the RCA dog, trying to affix meaning to what he was saying and backing away from his fine spray of spittle. In exasperation at this, he would sometimes turn to my grandmother, hook a thumb in my direction, and shrug as if to ask, "E stupido?" It is difficult to feel anything but uneasy around someone one is afraid to speak to and whose attempts at communication so persistently failed.

In spite of this, my memories of my grandfather are vivid ones. He was a short, wiry man with wavy, iron-colored hair and small, squinty eyes. He emitted a peculiar odor, perhaps from the leather with which he mended shoes on machinery that whirred stitchers and sanders and polishers on a byzantine Rube Goldberg system of belts and wheels and pulleys. His shop was built onto the front of his house. Next to a stove topped with a flue that rose through the high ceiling of the shop was a work counter strewn with awls and curved knives and stretchers and balls of dirty wax bristling with long needles threaded with yellow twine. On occasion, he tried to engage his grandchildren by folding sheets of newspaper into strange Robin Hood-like hats or crafted kites that never made it into the air.

Andrew Agosta, Lucy Sciortino Agosta, her brother and his son, two unidentified customers in the Agosta Shoe Store, White Castle, LA

My grandfather presided over his cobbler's last, his lips pursed around the nails he used to attach heels or soles to shoes he was repairing. He wore a stained apron of blue-striped mattress ticking. The shop smelled of soaked leather, shoe polish, glue, and an indescribable odor emanating from the long shelves of new and mended shoes lining the walls, ready for pick-up or for sale. The door and window of the shop had solid wooden shutters slammed shut at the end of his work days.

In old age, my grandfather continued to walk to the 6:00 A M mass at Our Lady of Prompt Succor Church on Sunday mornings, having sometimes to stop to rest on someone's front porch on his way back, startling residents who had come out in their robes to get their newspapers. He read the local and the Italian papers from New Orleans every day, first fishing around in a drawer full of cheap magnifying eyeglasses he bought in the five-and-dime. After every supper, he loaded leftovers onto a tin plate and served them up to a skittish herd of feral cats. Once a week, he stoked a fire in a dented, rusty oil barrel at his back fence to burn garbage, its acrid stench allied with the same reek emanating from other yards.

My grandparents were little more than accepted presences in my life. I did not feel any particularly strong attachment to them. Added to the difficulties I had as a young child communicating with my grandfather was my early perception that my grandmother was largely indifferent to us. She never seemed to really enjoy the company of her grandchildren, never baked cookies with or for us, never cooed over us or treated us to sleepovers, did not seem particularly interested in our games or occupations. As a child, I would enter my grandmother's kitchen where she usually sat sipping a demitasse of black coffee so potent that I wondered why the tiny spoon she stirred it with did not corrode. I would plant a light kiss on her cheek. Then she would flutter her hands: "Go play in the yard now." She warned us to stay within the confines of her fence lest the "Black Hand" nab us. I thought at the time that she was inventing some childhood terror to frighten us into obeying her. I discovered later that she, like her Sicilian relatives, still feared the Mafia, known in New Orleans by a designation derived from their leaving the imprint of a black hand on the walls of those they had harmed or whom they wished to terrify or intimidate.

In spite of my largely indifferent regard for my grandparents, I never carped when it came time for my family's frequent visits to White Castle. A scant 35 miles from Baton Rouge, White Castle was a strange, alternate world, determinedly unlike the linear, antiseptic, secure urban environment my parents had constructed for us in Baton Rouge. After the scouring and purging of World War II, my parents essentially broke with their European roots, appalled by a blood-stained continent where over 100 million people had been massacred or made refugees during the grim period between 1900 and 1945.

My parents' enthusiasm and optimism in the post-war American years led them to bear five children in a little over seven years, their own baby boom. They determined to do life right. They subscribed to Dr. Spock's method of child-rearing. My mother looked on breast-feeding as primitive and unsanitary. They insisted that we bathe with fresh towels and don newly laundered clothes every single day without fail. Our house was new and clean, our yard, like every other yard on our open and safe street, mowed and trimmed.

The world of my grandparents was foreign and estranging, beginning with our journey to them. We usually had to wait for a ferry to take us across the Mississippi River. We would park in a winding line of cars along a white clamshell road up the levee. An old Black evangelist baptizer stalked the line clad in a white sheet tied at one shoulder, pulled up between his legs, and cinched in a rope at his waist. He leaned on a crooked staff and carried a hand-lettered sign offering to save any soul he could persuade that a dunking in the muddy brown river water would cleanse them sufficiently to enter the gleaming City of Paradise.

Once over the river, we would drive through fields of sugar cane, their ribbons razor-sharp and brilliant green during the summer, dimming to a purple-gray just before harvest. When the mills at the sugar plantations stoked their boilers, bittersweet clouds of steam belched up from roiling syrup crushed from canes hewn by men whose boots my grandfather had serviced.

My grandparents lived in a double-barreled shotgun house, so called because all the rooms had doors in the middle of their walls, making halls unnecessary. One could shoot a gun all the way through the rooms from front to back on both sides of the house. Their dark rooms smelled of old cypress boards, furniture polish, moth balls, coffee, and Dove soap. The shadowy room my grandparents shared glimmered with a red votive candle my grandmother kept burning before a statue of the Virgin.

Faded gray-tinged roses bloomed against a murky ground in the living and dining room wallpaper pasted above dark-green wainscoting, so different from the off-white walls of our house. Their walls were hung with hand-tinted photographs of relatives from the old country, lugubrious in their convex oval frames as if peering out through the glass of old-fashioned coffins. Over the sideboard in the dining room hung a faded print of da Vinci's <u>Last Supper</u>, seemingly required in all Italian homes.

In an added-on back porch, my grandparents had a washer and dryer installed after the Black women they once hired to do their laundry in a tub on a gas ring in a back shed left them for less arduous and more lucrative employment. For some reason, my grandparents emptied boxes of detergent into a bucket they kept with a measuring cup by the washer, a tempting target for a delinquent cousin of mine who took it into his head to stir handfuls of ground coffee into this detergent. Undeterred by a spanking before the brown clothes he had dyed, on his next visit he buried under the dirty clothes already in the washer a pair of my grandmother's patent-leather pumps.

My grandfather's garden exuded the subterranean earthy scent of the black river soil which nourished every conceivable vegetable needed for the Sicilian cuisine my grandparents subsisted on. Between the garden rows erupted crumbly crawfish chimneys. The yard featured several sheds aged a silvery gray where braids of curing garlic hung from the rafters. At the back of the yard was an old outhouse my grandfather still used and which he referred to as a "brickousa." As with almost everything he said, I did not understand his joking allusion until I was older.

Sometimes when we were visiting, a battered old panel truck would cough to a stop outside the shop. Emerging from it was a tiny man not much taller than I was at seven. He wore a diminutive black suit, a sloppily tied black bow at his neck, and pointy black shoes. He had crinkly red-orange hair like the celluloid tangle capping the Barbie my sister and I occasionally fought over. He made weekend deliveries of imported Italian foods to immigrant families up river from New Orleans. He would creak open the shadowy back compartment of his truck to reveal pendulous globes of cheeses suspended like pale moons from loose nets, long salamis dangling like withered arms, barrels of black olives covered with salt-crusted wooden slat tops, glass vats of anchovies and sardines glinting silver through their amber brine, cans stuffed with caponata, jars filled with shimmering limoncello, and dozens of bottles of chianti nestled together, corks to straw fiascos.

While my grandfather haggled over the prices of the cheeses and olives in Italian, the little man would throw up his hands, turn to my brother and me (I still remember how disconcerting it was to meet a grown man's gaze eye-level with my own), and hand us sesame cakes so bone-hard that all we could do was gnaw on them, their seedy sides soon sliming with our saliva and pocking with tooth-grooves.

My last visit to my grandfather occurred during the early summer of 1977 after I had just earned my Ph.D. I went alone on this visit to say goodbye before I moved to my first teaching job in Kansas. My grandfather was then 88 and, though he kept his cobbler shop open, he had very little work. The sugar plantations had mostly closed by then, and those that were left harvested cane by machine now. People in White Castle were buying inexpensive shoes and, when they wore out, they threw them away rather than having them repaired and incurring my grandfather's scorn for their "cheap plastic shoes."

During this visit, my grandfather, recognizing that I was just venturing on my career, lamented that he was not also a young man making his way in a new, modern America now offering so many more opportunities than were available to him on his arrival seven decades earlier. Weeping openly, he avowed that America was the greatest nation on earth, that it offered his grandchildren unlimited possibilities he wished he had had.

At the end of our visit, he walked me out to my car. He had never embraced me, and he did not then either. We always concluded our visits with a handshake. "See you in the funny papers," he would add, with a heavy accentual spin. As I was getting into the car, he plucked a sprig of basil he always grew along his oyster-shell driveway and thrust it into my shirt pocket, a custom he followed himself before going anywhere. He claimed that the scent was more enticing than any cologne.

I never saw my grandfather again. Later that summer, he was struck by a train, an ironic emblem of the travel he so adamantly eschewed, and thrown 50 feet. His house and shop were on Railroad Avenue, aptly named for the wide set of tracks running down the middle of the street. It was his habit to dart out of the shop on first hearing the warning whistle as the morning train approached the town, hurry across the tracks, and walk downtown to do his banking and shopping. On hearing the train whistle that fatal morning, he had dashed out of the shop and had narrowly missed being hit by a car. This had apparently so disoriented him that he failed to realize that he had not crossed all of the tracks. He turned to wave to his three grandchildren playing at the front of the shop. Horrified, they screamed for him to get off the tracks. They witnessed the accident.

Shortly before my grandfather's death, he reported having dreamed of his deceased brother Giacomo, whom we called "Uncle Jake." He had told my grandfather he would be seeing him soon, that they had shared a great adventure in their immigration and that he should get ready for his final one.

After my grandfather's funeral, my grandmother had the shop torn down and the front of the house restored preparatory to selling it. She moved in with my aunt in Baton Rouge, but soon after that, she suffered a paralyzing stroke. When I visited my grandmother, I often found her weeping. We had little to say to each other. When awkward silences would settle, she would tell me to go call the "red puttana" in the kitchen. On other visits, it would be the "blue" or "yellow puttana." When I asked my aunt who these colorful prostitutes were, she would laugh and point to herself: the whorish colors were coordinated with the tint of the blouse she was wearing that day. Apparently this was a joke the two women had constructed to amuse themselves.

On parting from my infrequent visits to my grandmother on her sickbed, I would plant the customary farewell kiss on her cheek. "Don't follow bad company," she would frown by way of dismissal.

My grandmother survived nine years after her stroke, her left arm shriveled, her hand frozen in a fist, her mind often stumbling through dark delusions that my grandfather had gone back to Italy without her or had left her for another woman. Toward the end, she seemed to wander aimlessly among memories that brought her little comfort.

With regret hollow in his voice, my father would often recall the harshness of his own childhood with a stern father and a mother he deemed "mean," adding that "You children never had real grandparents." This judgment I came to understand only after I had left childhood. My father was right if by grandparents one meant a typical older American couple whose rough corners have been smoothed by their years, who are indulgent and affectionate and amused by children, who, themselves tending to the amorphous in physical form and grown tolerant in mental scope, delight in the yet unformed lives and behaviors of their grandchildren.

III

I did not know my mother's parents, and my mother rarely spoke of them. Their deaths before they could know my mother's children exonerated them from the burdens and joys of grandparentage.

My grandmother, Rose Kalt Landes (1873-1924), died suddenly of a stroke on the day following a particularly joyous Christmas. That sad history was first related to me in explanation of the puzzling fact that my two maiden aunts, my mother's sisters, never put up a Christmas tree in their house. During my childhood, I imagined my mother's sudden bereavement: a twelve-year-old girl in a white nightgown, her empty hands dangling by her sides, her mother suddenly taken from her as she sipped hot chocolate on the other side of the breakfast table from my mother. My mother's uncle, called home from work, had pitched their decorated Christmas tree down into the cellar in his grief along with other signs of the festive holiday. My grandmother's wake was to take place in the house. I envision my mother peering down at the wreckage of Christmas in that dark cellar, one detached silver ornament having escaped destruction to roll slowly into a dim corner, describing a glimmering arc in the darkness before coming to rest in a stillness it helped to define.

Of this grandmother, I know next to nothing. She was born in Springfield, Ohio, to immigrants from a Catholic region of Germany. Her father was a tailor and her mother, my great-grandmother, a housewife who long outlived her daughter, serving as a surrogate parent to my own mother, helped by my mother's unmarried aunt and uncle who shared the house. How my grandmother met my grandfather or any real details of their marriage I never learned.

My mother's father, too, I know only through foxed, sepia-toned photographs. There are several before me now, one of my grandfather in a slouch hat and round spectacles peering up at a huge parrot perched on his left forefingers and another of his flock of white cockatoos, the "Hjlan Wonder Birds," staggered in formation up a tiny ladder, each sporting a spangled satin vest and gripping a miniature American flag in its curved beak, a nod at patriotism by an immigrant whose first job in this country was as a saloon keeper before he took to the road as a lion tamer and roustabout in a carnival. Soon, he was traveling the Vaudeville circuits with his bird act, journeying during Vaudeville's off season all over the world to capture and export exotic animals and birds to populate the cages of circuses and zoos during the great American zoo movement of the early 20th Century. He was away from home through most of the American involvement in World War I, having been placed under house arrest when unlucky enough to be visiting his family in Germany when the United States entered the war. My mother recalled anti-German mobs storming through the immigrant neighborhood where she lived in Springfield, Ohio, hurling rocks and execrations through their windows as she cowered under a bed.

Fritz Landes (1866-1947)

My mother was more generous to the memory of her father than were her older sisters who apparently resented him for what they saw as his abandoning his family of four children. After the death of my grandmother, my grandfather only occasionally returned home, leaving his children to be cared for by his dead wife's relatives and irregularly sending money to them.

Besides the photographs, all I have of my grandfather are a few memories of him provided by my mother, a few references to him in her letters, and a number of newspaper advertisements and reviews for his Vaudeville engagements. My maternal grandfather, then, is to me like an object seen under water, characterized by shifts of perspective, swerves of light, glimmers of surge and shadow. I have had to piece together a life I know only in outline, but this construction helps me to place my grandfather, somehow to steady him in vision.

My maternal grandfather was born Friedrich Landes on April 1, 1866 to a solidly middle-class family of cigar importers and tobacco merchants in Eichtersheim, Rhein-Neckar-Kreis, Baden-Wurttemberg, Germany. I assume his immigration to the United States was motivated less by economic necessity than by a sense of wanderlust, though there seem to have been other members of his family who immigrated to Cuba and parts of Latin America, perhaps in furtherance of the family cigar trade. I do not know when he immigrated to the United States, where he landed, how he made his way to Springfield, Ohio, or how he came to woo and wed my grandmother. Their eldest child, a son they named Alphonse, was born in 1899, so my grandparents must have married in the late 1890s. My mother, their fourth and last child, was born in 1911.

After immigrating, my grandfather was never known as "Friedrich," using the name "Fritz Landes" professionally and exclusively. That is the name on his tombstone. His Vaudeville act was billed as the "Hjlan Wonder Birds: Cockatoos at Their Best." "Hjlan" (pronounced "Highlan") is an anagram formed from the first letters of his children's names: Helen, Josephine, Louise, and Alphonse, with the final "n" tagged onto the "la" section to stand for the family surname—Landes. His successful Vaudeville act was on the road for years. He toured with various Vaudeville circuits, the most significant ones being the Keith (primarily touring in the Eastern U. S.) and the Orpheum (with offerings primarily in the West). He also toured with the Pantages circuit which at one time controlled 60 theaters.

Performers who played these three circuits were considered to be playing the "big time" or, at the least, "medium time" as opposed to "small time," circuits which booked acts in two-bit towns where the "theaters" might be church basements, school gymnasiums, Elks' lodges, or park band gazebos. The "orchestras" were hastily convened after the town's butchers and plumbers and carpenters slipped out of their work clothes, grabbed their fiddles and trumpets, and gathered for an evening of off-key tunes to an irregular beat.

From his bookings, my grandfather mostly ranked at "medium time" as a Vaudeville performer: his act did not attract the critical attention, large audiences, or the high salaries of such "big time" Vaudeville sensations as Fanny Brice, Sophie Tucker, Bill "Bojangles" Robinson, Al Jolson, and others of their widespread fame. Nonetheless, my grandfather pursued a lucrative career in a difficult business where one had to fight for bookings and please individual theater managers who could object to content or talent for any reason and dismiss a performer at whim, earning that performer a black mark with the circuit bosses, making it difficult to continue to play respectable houses.

Though my grandfather had been traveling the circuits for years before, the earliest newspaper advertisement I could locate for his act appeared in The Janesville, Wisconsin <u>Daily Gazette</u> (October 14, 1922) followed soon after by a notice in the Sheboygan <u>Press</u> (October 27) where the writer credits this "novelty bird act" to one "Frank Landes" who "proves what wonderful intelligence birds possess when carefully and properly trained." Each following year showed my grandfather's steady bookings, with a promotional notice in the June 30, 1925 San Francisco <u>Examiner</u>. Playing San Francisco was the "big time" in Vaudeville.

The year 1926 featured newspaper notices of my grandfather's appearances in towns across the West, probably while he was traveling the Pantages circuit: Modesto, San Pedro, and Santa Ana, CA; Cochise and Phoenix, AZ; Medford and Salem, OR; and Great Falls and Anaconda, MT. Though some managers of theaters in these towns advertised their Vaudeville offerings in their local newspapers, most theater managers simply posted names of the featured acts on their theater marquees instead so as to save advertising expenses. Occasionally, a manager would authorize a full review of my grandfather's act, such as the following one which appeared in several newspapers in 1926:

An unusual offering, one that appeals to old and young alike, is the educated flock of cockatoos known as Hjlan's Wonder Birds. The gold-crested white birds perform acrobatic tricks, dance and do other stunts almost without command. The birds are truly wonderful in their exhibition of tricks, and the act is more remarkable from the fact that trained

birds—which really do show some intelligence—
are a great rarity on any stage.

Unlike Vaudeville singers, dancers, jugglers, and musicians, my grandfather had the expense and encumbrance of carting around fragile birds consigned to baggage boxcars. Thus, he had to perform in towns in geographical proximity or break up his journeys so as to tend to his cockatoos every few hours.

When my grandfather was off the road, he occasionally visited his family in Springfield, Ohio, birds in tow and often accompanied by midgets and dwarfs and jugglers and singers and magicians and other Vaudeville performers also on leave from bookings nearby. Once, according to my mother, he brought home to dine a well-known pair of bejeweled Siamese twins who played double piano and danced in aqua chiffon evening gowns with men from the audience in hilarious attempts to maneuver a coordinated four-person fox trot. These rare evenings delighted my teen-aged mother; it is difficult to imagine the same level of enthusiasm in her relatives who supported her.

The year 1927 saw my grandfather on the Keith Circuit, playing houses in the eastern section of the country: Atlanta, GA; Louisville, KY; Cincinnati and Dayton, OH; Wilmington, DE; Harrisburg and Altoona, PA; and Bridgeport, CT. The Atlanta, Georgia <u>Constitution</u> on September 6 noted that "The Hjlan Birds are the best-trained feathered pets exhibited in Atlanta in many a day," and the Bridgeport, Connecticut <u>Telegram</u> noted on December 31 that "The Hjlan Birds introduces a flock of wise old cockatoos and their trainer Fritz Landes."

On September 13, 1927, my grandfather was in Los Angeles to film his bird act for the Vitaphone Company. According to Edwin M. Bradley in his study of these

Vitaphone disks, *American Film Short Subjects*, one of the first shorts the prolific Vitaphone director Bryan Foy filmed in Hollywood—No. 2110 in an irregularly numbered series—was "Hjlan Birds, Cockatoos at Their Best." Bradley described the short as "a bird act, accompanied by instrumental music; the cockatoos danced and performed to 'La Paloma,' 'School Days,' 'Yankee Doodle,' and 'Sewanee River'." My grandfather was paid $350 for the film, a handsome sum for a single performance.

Many Vaudeville performers like my grandfather agreed to have their acts filmed by the Vitaphone Company for one-time payoffs, not realizing that they were thereby inadvertently hastening the death of Vaudeville. As a consequence of the wide availability of these Vitaphone shorts, even "small time" theaters could present "big time" performers on screen for a fraction of the cost of booking a full Vaudeville performance. And the subjects of these shorts received no income from residuals, though the films were shown widely throughout the country and even internationally. Vaudeville was essentially wiped out within five years of the prevalence of these Vitaphone shorts.

Though listed in every filmography chronicling the hundreds of Vitaphone shorts produced at the end of the 1920s, the entry for the film of my grandfather's act has a disappointing appended note: "Disk exists (either in archives or private hands) but currently no picture element is known." As early as November 19, 1927, a scant two months after the Hollywood Vitaphone filming of the act, the Dayton, Ohio Herald noted that the Hjlan Birds "will be a touch of the novel on this Vitaphone bill" being shown at a local Vaudeville house. My mother recounts an evening out at a movie theater with high-school friends when she was startled to see her father appear before her on the screen, larger than life, with the bird act she had only ever seen live at local Vaudeville theaters. She had not known of the Vitaphone recording used as a short before the feature film.

Sometime after this, my grandfather was traveling with the Wonder Birds to a Vaudeville booking in the Midwest. As usual, the cockatoos were in a baggage car; he was in coach. For some reason, another train commandeered the right of way. The passenger cars of my grandfather's train were uncoupled from the baggage car, which was shunted off to a side rail, and the passenger cars were coupled with the other train and proceeded onward. On arriving, my frantic grandfather demanded the immediate return of the Wonder Birds. They were returned the next day. Most had suffocated in the hot car, lacking food and water, their wings stretched out in a death rigor. The few still clinging to life had to be euthanized. My grandfather had assumed that these cockatoos, which live in captivity an average of 40-70 years, would see him into retirement.

My grandfather was able to engage a lawyer willing to represent him in a lawsuit against the railroad, but, with his German gutturals, his "Vunder Birts," and his dubious U. S. citizenship, the case was thrown out, the railroad claiming it was following orders from the government and was not responsible for civilian losses.

The next newspaper reference I could find to my grandfather appeared in the Dunedin, New Zealand Evening Star for November 23, 1929. I assume he was in that country to replenish his cockatoo flock and had trained them sufficiently to mount performances in New Zealand and Australia. But the days of Vaudeville, at least for "medium time" performers like my grandfather, were all but over in America by then.

During the 1930s, my grandfather disappeared from public notice, and I am forced to construct a picture of his remaining years from memory fragments shared with me by my mother. After Vaudeville ended for him, apparently my grandfather ventured on fulltime travel to Africa, South America, and Asia under commission to export animal and bird specimens for American circuses, zoos, and research laboratories. Successful in this career, he would occasionally return to his family in Springfield. Once he brought home an anteater for my mother and a shrieking spider monkey for her older sister, who would have nothing to do with it. My mother walked her anteater around her neighborhood on a leash for the amusement of her neighbors, but, of course, she had no intention of keeping it. Once again, my grandfather's in-laws resented him for feeding steak to some of these captured beasts while they were making do at their table with meatloaf and fish sticks.

My grandfather apparently lived a random and, according to my aunts, a disorderly life. They noted that he would send home to them boxes of greengage plums he claimed were from lands he had bought in Oregon or bushels of pineapples and coconuts from Hawaii when my mother's family in Springfield had little left over each month after paying their rent and grocery bills.

My grandfather's peripatetic life continued until age began to slow him down. In his 70s, he returned to Los Angeles. It is inconceivable that he would want to return to or be welcomed back by his family in Springfield, now consisting of my mother, her two unmarried sisters, and their unmarried maternal aunt, all stitching a living together in their side of a duplex they had been renting for well over thirty years. His only son, felled earlier by a stroke, the family curse, was languishing in a nursing home.

In Los Angeles, my grandfather applied at the film studios for work as an animal handler, but few were making animal pictures other than those using dogs for movies or horses for cowboy features, animals my grandfather had little experience with. Neither circuses nor zoos were hiring men of his age and declining physical strength, and the war put an end to his travels. His eyesight, never strong, was failing him as well.

Attempting to unload unprofitable speculations in land sold him by unscrupulous hucksters in Montana and Wyoming and Oregon in his earlier, improvident years and depleting whatever assets he had managed to save, he continued to live in Los Angeles, picking up occasional odd jobs when animal acts returned to home base after lackluster runs in the few Vaudeville theaters still managing to bring in increasingly meager audiences.

Finally, he ended up in a retired actor's hotel in Hollywood, having wisely maintained his membership in a union for actors, entertainers, and superannuated Vaudevillians. There, blind, alone, and in increasing ill health, he died of a stroke at the age of 81 in 1947. My aunts paid to have his body shipped back to Ohio on the very railroad he had earlier sued. In addition, my aunts had to pay passage for a transient to accompany the body on its last journey. My mother, then in Louisiana and pregnant with my older brother, could not return to Ohio for the funeral.

Like my German grandfather, I have also settled at last in California. My post-mortem fate will differ considerably from his, however. I have directed that my ashes be scattered among the San Jacinto Mountains surrounding Palm Springs. The genius loci in this desert region is a particularly bright and luminous spirit—stern and forbidding in summer, genial and beneficent in winter. The light is spectacular here in the desert, with colors so lucid and saturated they seem to levitate around the objects they tether to. Shadows anchor a rich blue-black. My father, on hearing of my final plans, desired that I be at least remembered in our family burial place. Accordingly, he had a bronze marker made for me that is already laid among my family's graves. All it needs now is my date of departure.

My grandfather, a lukewarm Lutheran who nevertheless politely rejected the Catholic priest sent him by his daughters toward the end, was buried in the unhallowed ground of the Protestant section of the Catholic cemetery next to his son Alphonse, who had left the Church after marrying a divorced woman, much to his sisters' dismay. Their tombs are thus at a distance from the rest of their family's graves—in death as in life.

IV

In my two grandfathers, then, I trace the tension in my own nature: my insistent hunger for new places far from home, new sexual encounters with new people, new adventures in life, all countered by my desire for stability and settled comfort, for one person to concentrate all my affection on.

THIRTEEN WAYS OF
LOOKING AT A RACIST PAST

I

I was born in 1948 in Donaldsonville, Louisiana, a withered little river town butted up against high earthen levees restraining the roiling flow of the silty Mississippi when at full spate. Donaldsonville, a mere ten miles from White Castle, the town where my father grew up and his parents still lived, was home to Cajun French, Creole, Southern Italian, and Black families, with a smattering of Anglos who had arrived to work in the petrochemical plants surrounding the town and poisoning its air and the river where Donaldsonville siphoned off its drinking water. The Choctaw and Chittamacha Indians, original inhabitants of this land, had all been driven out long since.

The ancestors of the Black citizens had been kidnapped from Africa a few centuries back and brought over in duress to be bought and sold as slaves to labor in the sugar cane and cotton plantations lining the river, largely owned by prosperous French and Creole families, early settlers in the region. The Italians, almost all of them recent immigrants from Sicily, were the latest to arrive in Donaldsonville, having drifted upriver from their debarkations in New Orleans around the turn of the century. The stretch of little river towns straggling up from New Orleans to Baton Rouge was sometimes referred to as "the Italian coast."

By the time I was born, mass emigration of Sicilians into the area had ceased. Consequently, the animosity, social disfavor, and xenophobic insults these Sicilian immigrants had initially met with had dissipated, for the most part. The Sicilians were no longer tagged by slurs like "wop," "dago," "eyetie," "guido," "gumbah," "greaser," or "guinea"—at least not to their faces.

Their memories of the earlier prejudicial reception they had met with had, however, proven of so short a duration that by the time I was born, these Sicilian immigrants and their families had assumed the prejudices and outright racism that they themselves had been subjected to when they had arrived in large emigration masses.

By 1948, a scant fifty or so years after their own immigration, Sicilian racism and disparagement of Blacks was indistinguishable from that of their French, Creole, and Cracker neighbors, if not even more pronounced. Ironically, these Sicilians had earlier been designated by "old-stock Americans" as "the niggers of Europe."

II

My Sicilian grandfather arrived in New Orleans penniless during the first decade of the 20th Century, staggered by the city he sighted from the ship he sailed in on up the Mississippi River. Apprenticed as a boy to a cobbler in the old country, he parlayed his occupation as cobbler and shoe repairman into a level of middle-class prosperity that astonished him all his long life, especially given the low level of his education and his lack of proficiency in speaking English. It had not hampered his success in life that he had married a woman whose Sicilian immigrant parents had arrived in Louisiana several decades before him and had amassed some modest real-estate holdings and other assets in the little river town of White Castle.

My grandfather often said that Blacks in White Castle, though not enjoying the standard of living maintained by Whites, were nevertheless living comfortably enough and should have had little to complain of. He saw Black living conditions as leagues better than those he had fled from in Sicily where entire families were crammed together into one or two rooms directly over lower-level stables housing a few scrawny chickens, maybe a goat or two, a donkey, if they were lucky.

Black families, on the other hand, could afford to rent the levee "nigger shacks" that he had acquired as part of my grandmother's dowry—narrow shotgun houses with bare electric light bulbs hanging by their cords from the ceilings and plenty of tap water flowing from rain-collection cisterns. Each of these houses came with private insulated outhouses adjacent to the back doors. My grandfather provided his Black tenants with far better housing than anything his own family and all their neighbors had inhabited in Sicily.

My grandfather observed Blacks driving their own cars and shopping for their food at the grocery stores owned by his in-laws. He, on the other hand, remembered digging around in rock-scrabble fields, desperate to coax a few wilted tomatoes, some dried-out eggplant and gaunt zucchini, and a couple of parched figs from a thin soil exhausted by centuries of peasants germinating what little they could from their barren land. He recalled stumbling home as a little boy with leather buckets of water filled at the village pump, spilling much of the water because the buckets were too heavy for him to lug home. In short, my grandfather could never understand what Black people could possibly want for, even if most were not living as well as their more affluent neighbors in the Whites-only sections of town.

My grandfather believed that something inherently lacking in Black people must explain their failure to thrive as well as he had managed to through hard work, thrift, and agile planning. He accused Black people of taking it easy in

185

life, apparently blind to the straining of the Black women my grandmother hired to wring out by hand and then hang up water-heavy sheets, towels, and work clothes on the clothes lines that crossed the back yard, or the hard labor under a broiling sun of Black sugar cane harvesters, razor-sharp leaf-ribbons slicing their flesh wherever bared as they slogged through muddy fields slithery with water moccasins.

He accused Black people of not striving as strenuously as he had in a country where opportunity hung like golden apples in easy reach. Blacks did not save their money, he claimed, trifling it away on gambling, dancing, and getting drunk in juke joints like the local Blue Heaven Bar and Dance Hall, which made my grandmother's sister and her husband wealthy.

Blacks were improvident, my grandfather maintained. They did not value the educational opportunities available to them, advantages he never had. They lacked ambition. Consequently, they deserved their lot in life, which, after all, was still better than anything his relatives back in Sicily were experiencing. If he, born with no opportunities, no education, no status, and no assets, could wrest for himself and his family a comfortable place in life, then what possible reason could there be that Blacks could not do the same?

My grandfather repeatedly contrasted his abysmal beginnings with the comparative advantages in general living conditions that Blacks began their lives in America with. His own life trajectory was so steep that he could never fathom why Blacks, born in a country offering advantages that would have caused him to remain in Sicily were he possessed of them there, could not rise to the levels that he, starting with nothing, was able to arrive at.

My grandfather just could not get it through his head that he could accomplish what he had in life because he was White.

III

My father, born in 1917 in White Castle, Louisiana, held as his highest values fairness and equitable dealing for all people and in all matters. He was more educated than most people he lived among, having earned his B.S. degree from Louisiana State University in the late 1930s. He was drafted soon after and stationed at posts in Ohio before being shipped overseas during the war.

As an Italian-American from Louisiana drafted into the Army Air Corps, my father met with a bias against Southerners, but a particularly strong prejudice against Italians stemming from left-over American anti-immigrant sentiment as well as hostility towards Italy, then allied with Hitler's Germany and thus at war with the United States. Having himself felt the sting of Italian disparagement, my father was especially sensitive to the denigration of Blacks and the unequal treatment that conditioned their lives.

Consequently, never did I ever hear my father utter the word "nigger," though it was the only term for Blacks used by most people he lived among. My mother was as adamant as my father in forbidding her children ever to employ this slur. This denigration was as distasteful to my parents as cursing, lewd language, or any other utterance they considered ill-bred. I grew up thinking this forbidden term was a "cuss word." In spite of this, my parents could not insulate us and were not themselves immune to the pervasive racism that tainted the Louisiana environment which nurtured us during the 1950s and 60s. My parents, however, suffered a milder infection from that racism than their neighbors and most of their family.

My father's residual racism could manifest itself in casual and unselfconscious ways. For example, in a letter my mother wrote to her sisters in Ohio on February 3, 1947, she noted that my father was overly sensitive and at times had difficulty maintaining control over his emotions. She quotes him as telling her that "Funerals always affect me, even if it's only for a colored person." Though the second clause in this sentence is dismaying, his reported use of the word "only" is particularly so.

On the other hand, my father recognized that the racist culture he was a part of could at times interfere with his own wishes and the general well-being of the family my parents were planning. In his letter to my mother's sisters of March 18, 1946, he complained that reliable family physicians were difficult to engage in the small town of Donaldsonville after the war. Good doctors were attracted by higher earnings in larger cities that afforded them greater opportunities.

A new doctor had recently established a practice in Donaldsonville, however, whose credentials and reputation had impressed my father. But, as he noted in his letter, "This doctor is a colored doctor and he couldn't be our family physician for that reason." Apparently, this Black doctor was understandably reluctant to take on any White patients, particularly White women. In addition, he obviously wanted to avoid providing separate White and Black waiting and examining rooms as expected of doctors practicing in the community. He also may have feared being perceived as "uppity" by Whites, a perception potentially dangerous for him.

My father's letter makes clear that his inability to consult this doctor was not through his own decision but was due to attitudes prevalent in "the South in general." He concluded his letter with the assertion that "this situation here is changing daily, and I am glad of it." My father's optimism that racism was waning in the South in the 1940s seems credulous and naïve today. It would take decades before the stranglehold of Southern racism would even begin to loosen.

A case in point: In about 1955, when I was seven or so and after we had moved from Donaldsonville to Baton Rouge, my father invited our neighbor, whom we called "Mr. Chuck," over for dinner because he was alone after his wife and children had gone to stay for a while with her ailing mother in Laurel, Mississippi. Relaxed and enjoying another snort of bourbon after supper, Mr. Chuck, with a twinkle in his eye, asked if my father had heard of the "Nigra" who had tried to register to vote in the parish. He was told by the voter registrar that only those who could read a newspaper were eligible for the ballot. The Black applicant was then handed a newspaper—in Chinese.

"Can you read that now, Uncle?" the registrar had asked.

"Hmmm, lemme see," said the Black man: "It say here ain't no niggahs in Looziana gon' vote in this election."

Mr. Chuck erupted in a loud guffaw.

My mother frowned and rose to clear the table. My father's lips compressed into a thin line before saying in a low, even tone: "Chuck, there are young children here listening to this."

Mr. Chuck seemed puzzled by the distinct chill that had suddenly descended after a dinner he had found convivial.

IV

My mother, reared in Ohio in a tightly knit German immigrant community, had little close contact with Black people. She was initially unsettled by the overt racism she met with after her marriage and move to Louisiana where the interaction between the two races was an everyday occurrence. Her new connections in the South had inherited a deeply ingrained racism along with their bayou inflections and their tolerance for the sticky humidity they slow-walked through. My mother was a woman of her time, influenced by the new culture she met with in Louisiana. Thus, she did not escape entirely the taint of racism prevalent in her environment.

A hint of her racial condescension is evidenced in my mother's letter to her sisters written on Mardi Gras Day, February 11, 1948: "The colored people had a parade which I saw from our balcony through my field glasses, a rather pathetic attempt of a down-trodden race to do a little something." My mother did not go out to see this parade, spying on it from a cultural and privileged racial distance through her "field glasses," as if regarding an exotic species.

Nowhere do my mother's racial prejudices show themselves more clearly than in her exasperated attempts to hire a "colored maid" in Donaldsonville to clean, do laundry, iron, and generally help her around the house preparatory to the birth of her second child in little over a year. She begins her search on May 26, 1948 with the optimistic news, conveyed in a letter to her sisters, that the wonderfully named "Alce Dee Billy," the "colored girl" who had worked for them for a short period the year before "seemed pleased to work for us again this season."

After a few days, however, Alce Dee went AWOL. On inquiring, my mother was told by Alce Dee's mother that Alce Dee needed a rest. Besides, Mrs. Billy added, Alce Dee "was doing ironing" for another White woman and earning "more a half day than for two days of housework" at my parents' house. Alce Dee's mother suggested that my parents go to Alce Dee and offer her more money, but my mother, as she noted in her letter, "said no, Alce Dee wasn't to be depended on, and I'd be afraid to rely on what she said."

My father then asked the janitor from his workplace if he might send someone over from the Black section of town, quaintly referred to as "Froggie Moor." Accordingly, on June 20, 1948, Jannie showed up. She was "black-black and not too prepossessing in appearance but seemed nice and was eager for the work." Jannie was "in her late forties," my mother noted approvingly in a letter to her sisters, "and should not be so flip as a younger person and more experienced." My mother felt that Jannie would be grateful for the job she offered her because her previous employer, owner of a local eatery called the Royal Café, had expected Jannie to arrive every morning no later than 5:30 AM to lug their heavy garbage cans around the property to collect the evening's trash. My mother termed this "a man's job" foisted on Jannie because "some people think colored persons can do anything, no matter how heavy." Noting to her sisters that the Royal Café "was a very clean place," my mother "felt Jannie must be pretty clean too."

In spite of this promising beginning, a scant three days later, on June 23, Jannie sent "two colored girls," her nieces, to inform my mother that Jannie "had to go to Charity Hospital for 10 days to receive further treatment for an industrial accident received during the war." Her nieces were there to fill in for Jannie until she could return to work. Noting in a letter that "one can't help but like Jannie, who is a good worker—frank and funny and easy going," my mother agreed to take on these temporary substitutes until Jannie returned.

The arrangement did not work out. Three days after the nieces arrived, my mother noted in another letter that the older of the two "was an old hand at housework and consequently felt her importance" while the younger one "was very nervous. I had to show her how to do everything and am quite convinced that she had never seen an inside bathroom before." The next day, the older niece informed my mother that her younger sister was needed at home. My mother disapproved of this older niece's attitude: "She was very superior and informed me that she was a fast worker and knew just how much there was to be done in a day" and "if she deemed a certain amount of work was enough, the rest would have to wait till next day."

That this woman expressed herself so frankly did not go over well. "I could feel the hackles rising," my mother noted, "and when she finished, I dressed her down," telling her "that I neither over-worked anyone nor asked them to do more than I myself could do." Furthermore, my mother avowed, "I would not tolerate being dictated to in my own house." In this interchange my mother reminds this "colored maid" where the power lies and who could legitimately exercise it.

Following this berating, this putting this "colored maid" in her proper place, my mother notes that "she became tame as a cat and all that day was very respectful." My mother seemed surprised when, the next day, the older niece failed to appear. My mother concluded this episode with an exasperated sigh: "Have we ever had a time with our colored help!"

My mother seemed not to have expected this degree of autonomy among the Black women she was attempting to employ. She seemed not to have considered that these women would assert their right to seek opportunities congenial to them and that would remunerate them appropriately. My mother seems to have thought that if she had a job to offer, there should be ready takers without the power-jockeying she was experiencing from those she had deemed to be less powerful than she.

My mother may have been exasperated, but she remained undaunted. A day or so after Jannie's niece had decamped, another "colored girl" showed up, but several days later she too did not report. On July 1, my mother noted in a letter to her sisters that she "called the last name on my list of possible maids this morning," and a 20-year-old arrived. She "makes a very clean appearance and spoke very nicely." My mother's initial assessment of these potential hires always focused on two aspects: their cleanliness and their respectful address to her.

In spite of my mother's favorable first impression, this young woman's mother arrived the next day to inform my mother that her daughter had suffered a sinus attack and that she had come in her place until her daughter could recover. After one day with this substitute, my mother concluded that the arrangement would not work: "Is she ever independent! She thinks she knows how to do everything and refuses to be told anything. She says exactly what she thinks too. It seems as if we're getting all the characters in town, and paying them as well as anyone too!" This woman's lack of subservience, her independent frankness, and her assumption of domestic authority failed to please my mother, a woman accustomed to the dominance expected by her class, social position, and White privilege.

In her letter of July 1, 1948, my mother complains that she would have written to her sisters in Ohio "more often had it not been for training five colored people in a week and a half." And, in a condescending addition to this complaint, she notes that "The Southern Negro is a fearful and a wonderful thing, and I'll never be able to understand what makes them tick."

My mother did not give up her search for adequate help, even as her pregnancy neared its term. The next woman to make her appearance was Evalina: "She has a nice personality," my mother writes on July 6, four days before going into labor with me, "and goes about her work quietly and cheerfully so far, and tries to please. She doesn't get on one's nerves and seems well bred." These positive traits are ones exhibited by the docile and obedient Negro, pleasant, non-confrontational, and subservient.

Several weeks later, however, my mother's high initial assessment of Evalina as a worker was under revision: "We have a very nice ('servant' they say down here but I never say it) girl who does what she does well but is slow as a tortoise both in movement and at grasping anything. She's certainly not one to go ahead and take hold, but I'm glad she's not forward." Here my mother complains of Evalina's lack of self-assertion, the very quality that had displeased her when exercised by previous maids.

A week later, my mother continues to complain about Evalina: "My dusky handmaiden is so s-l-o-w. She takes constant supervision, and she's too timid to do anything on her own. She's so very nice, however, that much can be forgiven her." My mother concludes her letter by taking a brighter view: "I'd rather have a slow one who's clean and willing rather than a smart-aleck who rushes through the work and can't wait to leave."

My mother's approval of Evalina approaches the proprietary, growing increasingly patronizing. By August 2, she comments that "Our Evalina is so very nice. She has a nice way about her" and is "very well bred." This breeding is manifest in her being "an old timer" who "calls me Miss Louise and Tony Mister Tony, really knows her place, and is refined." "She sings spirituals and has a sweet voice," my mother concludes approvingly before penning a final sentence on Evalina: "The young ones don't sing like that, and I enjoy hearing her." A woman of her time, my mother approves of Blacks "who know their place" is subservient to hers. Influenced by her new Southern environment, she values Blacks who exhibit the stereotypical traits of plantation Negroes.

On August 11, my mother recorded in a letter to her sisters that she was wearing a red print pinafore apron one of her sisters had designed and sewn for her when Evalina, "in a bold manner entirely foreign to her," said "Look lak you'd give that apron to me case hit's too loud for you." When my mother protested that she liked the apron as well, Evalina responded, in a way "very unlike herself": "You go on and tell your sister to make me a apron." Evalina's "liberties" may indicate a growing sense of connectedness to my mother and to the household—or it may have been my mother's invention at Evalina's expense aimed at complimenting her sister on her sewing skills.

By September 7, the connection with Evalina had frayed. Evalina did not show up one Saturday but appeared during the afternoon of the following Monday, citing as her excuse the rough winds blowing in from a distant hurricane in the Gulf: "Miss Louise," she explained, "the storm had me bound." My mother concluded that this "was just an excuse for a day off." When Evalina failed to show up the following day, my father, who had finally had enough of this drama of women traipsing in and out of the house, took it upon himself to bring home a wringer for their washing machine, anticipating that Evalina, who had struggled to wring out the heavy sheets, towels, diapers, and clothes with her own strength, would quit her job.

Five days later, September 12, Evalina was history and my father had mostly taken on her tasks. My mother had decided that since my father would "cheerfully sweep, dust, wash, and make beds, but <u>detests</u> dishes and only offers on rare occasions to do them," she could dispense with a maid. My parents worked out a suitable division of labor, and there was no more talk of hiring "dusky handmaidens."

A final mention of Black people occurred in my mother's letter to her sisters of October 5, 1948. My parents were awakened in the wee hours by a Black woman screaming on their porch and pounding on their door, begging to be let in, a man slapping her around and ordering her to come home with him. My father called through the door, demanding that they leave, but my mother, against my father's advice, insisted on calling the police to protect the woman: "I guess," she noted, knowing all too well White attitudes to their Black neighbors, "nobody cares what happens to colored people."

V

I must have been about four years old when my mother took me grocery shopping with her one day at the Piggly Wiggly, promising to let me ride the little mechanized pony out front if I was good. While she was making small talk with the butcher who was carving some pork chops for her off of a glistening slab of pink meat, I wandered over to a water fountain to take a sip. When I stood on tip-toes to try to reach the water jet, I heard a horrified gasp behind me and a woman's frantic voice: "Ma'am! Ma'am! Pay attention! Tend to your child! Pay attention!"

When my mother, alarmed, pivoted from the butcher's counter and saw where I was, her shoulders sagged in relief.

"Oh, for Heaven's sake," my mother fumed. "I thought he was in some kind of danger."

"But just look at what he was about to do!" the woman exclaimed.

My mother called me over to her.

"Mind your own business, not mine," she hissed through clenched teeth and under her breath so the woman would not hear her.

"Drink at the other fountain," my mother told me, pointing to a fountain a little ways down the aisle, "not at this one."

"But why?" I whined, my face a crumple preparatory to crying, fearful that the pony ride would be denied me now.

"You didn't do anything wrong," my mother soothed, "but some people don't like it if you drink at this fountain. See? There's a little sign above it which tells you that only colored people drink water there."

"But why?" I asked, confused. "That fountain over there looks just like this one. Why do colored people have to drink water here?"

"It's just the way it is," my mother sighed.

VI

I did not know my mother's family. Both of her parents had died before I was born. Thus, they were to me people of hearsay, of story, enshrined in a nebulous sphere, close to me in blood relationship, far removed in any real connection. They seemed perfected beings, haloed in a vague mist of someone else's memory, to be spoken of in hushed tones.

However, I did know my mother's two sisters, both spinsters, who moved down to Louisiana from Ohio when I was five or so to join the only family remaining to them. They brought with them old family photo albums which fascinated me with their thick black pages thronged with colorless photographs captured and held in place by four white triangles at their corners.

I remember a set of photographs that puzzled me—one, a close-up of my aunts in black face, and several others of them in a group of people, also in black face, surrounding a pretty lady in a white hoop skirt tiered like a wedding cake. She twirled a lace parasol shading the long platinum ringlets dripping down like icicles on each side of her pale, simpering face.

The men in black face were draped in loose, shabby coats and wore crumpled pork-pie hats or dented derbies, white gloves, and huge floppy shoes like clowns wear. The women had wigs on with short pigtails pointing out in all directions or their hair was tied up in bandannas. They lifted long print dresses with white aprons between thumbs and forefingers as if they were dancing. The eyes and lips of both the men and the women were widely ringed in white before the black grease paint was applied. They all seemed to be rolling their eyes and puckering out their lips, especially two men in top-hats and long frock coats with large brass buttons, hands in white gloves distended to frame the white lady with the lace parasol as if shouting "Ta-Da!"

"Who is that lady?" I asked my aunts. "And what is she doing surrounded by all those people?"

"That's our friend Gert with the parasol," my Aunt Helen laughed. "And there's your Aunt Jo. I'm over here. Weren't we funny?"

"But why are you dressed like that?"

"We were putting on a Minstrel show for our church bazaar. We all sang Doo-Dah songs and tap-danced around Gert like darkies down on the Dixie plantations. We had such fun!"

As I peered at the photographs of my aunts in black face, I said, "But you don't really look like colored ladies."

"Call them 'colored women,'" one of my aunts replied. "Colored women are not ladies."

VII

My mother had five children rather late in her child-bearing years: she was 36 when her first child was born, 43 when she bore her last. She needed help with this demanding brood so close in age, so when we were all still small, Pearlene came into our home. My mother, now living in Baton Rouge, had better luck in hiring Pearlene than in her previous attempts to hire "colored help" in Donaldsonville, where she had given up in despair at finding someone she considered suitable to help with the housekeeping.

I never knew Pearlene's last name or where in town she lived, though my mother must have found that out. I was fascinated when I overheard Pearlene tell my mother about her husband: he was in Louisiana's infamous Angola State Prison serving a life term for having knifed a man to death in a juke joint in the Black section of town. Though I was avid for the grisly details, my mother had forbidden us to ask Pearlene anything about what my mother assumed must be a painful subject for her. I do not know if Pearlene had children of her own, but she sometimes brought her dour, silent mother with her to work. Pearlene's mother came when my mother had extra cleaning to do at the change of seasons when she turned the house inside out, scrubbing every surface and changing out the curtains and rugs and bed coverings for seasonably appropriate ones.

Pearlene arrived on the bus each morning. Neat, slender, her hair usually tied up in some kind of fabric, Pearlene was the color of café au lait, what in Louisiana was called "high yellow." I do not know how old she was—children are never good at guessing the age of adults—but she must have been in her mid-to-late 30s, possibly younger. On arriving at about 8:00 each morning, she changed out of the neat skirt and blouse or sun dress she wore on the bus to a simple light-blue dress buttoned all the way down to the hem, which she carried in a canvas tote. She always smelled of ivory soap and the light almond of Jergens lotion. At around 3:00, she changed back into what we called her "bus clothes," snapped her purse shut on the $3.00 my mother gave her each day, and bade us goodbye.

My mother and Pearlene chatted amiably and often laughed together as they worked alongside each other at their tasks. They sat at the breakfast table to share coffee on their breaks and discussed *The Guiding Light* they listened to together on the radio. Pearlene ate at the table with us the lunch my mother prepared.

We were never allowed to sass Pearlene or to show her any disrespect. We were cautioned to obey her when she told us to do something or corrected our behavior when we grew rambunctious. She called us by our first names as we did her, unlike my parents' friends whom we called "Mr. Chuck" or "Miss Gloria." There was never any question about her being able to use the house bathroom when she needed one.

From what I recall of Pearlene's many years of working in our house, my mother and Pearlene shared a mutual regard for each other. I do not think, however, that either considered the other a friend. It would never have occurred to my mother to visit Pearlene in her home or to invite Pearlene or any member of her family to sit as guests at our dinner table.

We as children in our own home were spared the more virulent forms of racism that we witnessed around us. There were, however, more subtle forms of our racism. Pearlene, for example: Though affectionately regarded, Pearlene was to us a very different order of being from our own family and our friends and neighbors.

VIII

Hands down, my favorite book as a young child was a dog-eared, taped-together copy of *Little Black Sambo* by Helen Bannerman. When I would present it for a nightly reading, my father would groan and my mother would try to tempt me with other options. But no—for months on end, preceding both daytime nap and bedtime reading, it had to be *Little Black Sambo*. And my parents could not get away with reading it only once. I would beg and plead and cry for several readings at a go—or until I relieved my parents by falling asleep at last.

In my tattered edition of the book, Little Black Sambo was depicted as a pickaninny. There was no mistaking him for the Dravidian boy from Southern India originally envisioned by Bannerman in her 1899 first edition of the work. No, my Sambo had migrated from India to the American South: Black as soot, he had distended, pillowy red lips, a bushy thicket of wiry hair, and eyes always gaping wide as if he had just seen a spook. I remember the caricatures of Black Jumbo, Sambo's father, and Black Mumbo, his mother, who clad him in what he termed his "fine clothes," which he was so proud of and which the three ferocious tigers forced him to hand over to them for a time.

I suppose that one of the reasons I found *Little Black Sambo* so absorbing was because of Sambo's unlikely victory over the mean tigers and his treat of buttery pancakes served up by Black Mumbo to celebrate Sambo's triumphant return, again splendidly clad. Sambo's success provided me the vicarious satisfaction all children experience when smaller, weaker heroes—stand-ins for vulnerable child readers themselves—prevail over larger, more powerful forces that threaten them.

But my fascination with *Little Black Sambo* went far beyond this. In my edition of the book, Sambo wore a brilliant scarlet coat with large golden buttons, gorgeous deep-indigo trousers, and crimson-lined satiny purple shoes with their toe-tips curled up into elegant coils. His ears jutted out wide, each pinned with a gleaming golden hoop, inspiring me with the novel notion that boys too could wear jewelry. To top off Sambo's sartorial splendor, he brandished against the sun a jade umbrella with a jeweled handle he had bought in a bazaar. Was he not grand! I was dazzled by his costume and powerfully identified with the pride Sambo took in his gay attire. This early admiration for Sambo's splendid dress undoubtedly inspired me to conjure up my own sumptuous dress-up box and to employ it for opulent cross-dressing shortly after I had consigned my beloved Sambo to the museum of forgotten childhood passions.

My aunts used to laugh about a time when they were baby-sitting for my older brother and me. When it was time for them to give me my bath, one of my aunts went to undress me. I batted her hands away: "Don't take off all my fine clothes!" I screamed, echoing what Sambo told the tigers. At that moment, I <u>was</u> Little Black Sambo, resisting a superior force taking from me, albeit temporarily, possessions I did not then wish to relinquish.

That response may be indicative of why I loved *Little Black Sambo* so ardently: Like Sambo, I too was possessive of my "fine clothes," always wishing to be noticed for what I wore. Even as a young child, I pitched howling fits when I was denied what I thought sartorially exceptional or was forced to wear hand-me-downs I thought ugly in style or drab in color. I understood Little Black Sambo temperamentally and very personally.

Still do! I have never abandoned my penchant for "fine clothes": I alternate get-ups from my adult dress-up box harboring silver-stitched Japanese coats, Chinese damask jackets, Vietnamese silk sport coats in flower patterns, and paisley shirts flocked in black velvet to wear to dinner and cocktail parties and special occasions, flaunting them like the Beau Brummel fop that Sambo and I both are. I am, of course, coerced to select more sober garb for everyday wear, like the plain khakis and button-down shirts I wore on teaching days, my "schoolmarm drag."

At the time I was so passionately absorbed in Sambo's story, I was utterly unaware of the book's racist images, and I was not cognizant enough of the racist caricatures in my edition of the book to take exception to them. One day, I was alone in my bedroom when Pearlene came in to change the sheets on the beds. I held out *Little Black Sambo* to her and asked her to read it to me. She frowned, cocked her head to one side, and said: "Honey, not <u>that</u> book I ain't."

IX

My two aunts did not cook. When they got off of work, they usually took their dinners at what they termed "The Supper Club," a loose confederation of other single ladies and a few retired married couples. None of these people seemed acquainted with the culinary arts, so they drifted together nightly at a cafeteria downtown called "The Piccadilly." "The Pic," as my aunts called it, was a more tastefully decorated cafeteria than one would expect of the genre. The Pic's mirrored walls bore gleaming crystal sconces. The large dining room was defined by tall pillars lit to accent their crisp art-deco plaster capitals. The lighting was soft and subdued, the music low and soothing, the white table cloths immaculate, and the tall palms throughout the room gently swaying a luxuriant deep green beneath the air-conditioning vents that my aunts never wanted to sit under.

In other ways, though, the Piccadilly was a typical cafeteria: one pushed a tray down a ribbed stainless-steel counter, passing various enticing food stations, from salads to desserts. Generally, the main-course options were plated by a team of Black women in hairnets and clad in identical blue dresses fronted by white aprons, starched and spotless.

"Soive ya?" they called out as one made one's way down the line, peering at the offerings through the glass extensions separating one from direct contact with the food. At the end of the line, a White cashier totaled up one's bill, which one paid to another White cashier on exiting the cafeteria.

"Carry that for ya, Miz Helen?" asked one of the Black men in white coats lined up behind the cashier. My aunts knew all of these men by their first names.

"How are you tonight, Homer?" my aunt would ask.

"Cain't complain much," Homer always answered. "Don't never do nothin' good for me to complain, now do it?"

When my aunts treated us to dinner at the Piccadilly, we too had our trays carried for us. My aunts gave each of us a dime to tip the man who carried a tray for us.

"Why can't I just carry my own tray?" I asked one night. "I can do it."

"Of course you can," my aunt whispered, "but that's a job for Homer and the other boys. We have to help support them."

X

My father was repelled by overt racism. He possessed an innate sense of fairness and a strong empathy for others, especially those he considered unjustly treated. When he was newly married, my father worked as the office manager of a furniture and appliance store owned by an older Sicilian immigrant who considered my father more reliable and responsible than his own relatives.

One Saturday my father was working late. Dusk was sifting in, but the store's lights were not yet turned on. My father stood at a plate-glass window at the front of the store, next to a propped-open door, peering out at the darkening street. In the window was a large sign advertising a bar-be-cue to be held the following afternoon at a city park to benefit the Kiwanis Club.

An obese Black man wearing a chef's toque and white tunic leered out from the sign, his red tongue licking enormous lips distended in a huge grin: "Sho-NUFF good, dem ribs," he says in a white balloon floating above his head. "Wisht I had me some for my l'il pickaninnys." There followed information about time and location for the event. At the bottom of the sign appeared in commanding letters: "WHITES ONLY."

Two Black men, walking down the sidewalk in front of the store, stopped in front of the sign. They did not see my father standing at the window. My father could hear them through the open door.

"Look how they do us on this sign," one of the men said to the other. "Makin' us out like dumb animals, like fools. My son axed me the other night why dem ofays got to be so all the time mean."

"Cain't get us no breaks," said the other man. "That White man I'm working for make me go to his house first thing every morning to pick up his huntin' dogs' turds before I shows up at his gas station to pump gas. Don't pay me nuthin' for the turd pickup neither. And don't it beat all: I gots to go on down to Calvin's barbershop to use the toilet. Won't let me use the one at the station."

"Aw, dammit if I ain't fed up with all this," said the first man.

The two men turned away from the window and continued down the street. My father told of over-hearing this conversation many times, including just after watching with me on television Martin Luther King's "I Have a Dream" speech before the Lincoln Memorial in 1963.

"It's terrible to have to live like the Negroes," he concluded. "It's only fair that they get their rights, and I'm all for it. But I'm just afraid they're trying to move too fast. They need to get more education first and more standard living skills before they can really benefit from full equality. I just don't think they're ready for it yet."

I was 15 years old in 1963 and did not know then how to counter this opinion.

XI

After the Civil Rights Act of 1964 had passed and the South abandoned the Democratic Party for good because its standard bearer, Lyndon Johnson, "betrayed Dixie" by signing it into law, Pearlene decided to retire. She was surprised to discover, on her mother's death, that her mother had been paying for years for a sizable life-insurance policy with Pearlene as its sole beneficiary. Pearlene now no longer needed to work. And she found out soon after her mother died that her husband, incarcerated in Angola Prison, was getting out on "compassionate release" after being maimed while working on a prison-chain-gang project to build roads in one of the state's rural parishes.

"That just mean the state no longer want to pay his medical bills," Pearlene explained, "so they givin' him back to me now when I don't hardly know the man anymore."

Alice, Pearlene's replacement, was a tall, quiet woman who took over the housekeeping and laundry when my mother returned to work full time. I never heard Alice speak in anything much louder than a whisper.

I was in high school when Alice came into our house. I would come home after school, fix a snack, lie down on the couch, and turn on the television to watch my two favorite programs—"Amos 'n Andy," followed by "Flash Gordon." As Alice busied herself cleaning around me, I was howling at the antics of Lightning and the Kingfish and their dim-witted Black cronies, oblivious to the fact that Alice, who paused occasionally to look at the television screen to gauge why I was laughing so hard, may have been enjoying the program considerably less than I was. After "Amos 'n Andy," I settled in to watch—or lust after—the buff, blond Flash Gordon forever battling his sinister enemy Emperor Ming the Merciless, the gaunt, bald, wispy-bearded Asian villain who kept Flash and the bimbo Dale on their toes. I was clueless as to the offensive Asian stereotype being played out before me.

Having just acquired my driver's license, I was tasked with driving Alice to her house in a Black section of town at the close of her workday. Alice would always sit in the back seat of the car when I drove her. This made me uneasy, especially because I assumed she sat there because she thought I wanted her to. One day I held the door open to the passenger side front seat: "Alice, why don't you sit up front with me? It feels weird you sitting back there all by yourself while I'm sitting up here taking up the whole front seat and having to turn my head around to talk with you when I should be looking at the road."

"Oh no, sir," she said hurriedly. "I cain't. If my neighbors glimpsed me setting up front next to you, they'd take to shaming me for puttin' on airs and actin' like I thought I was a White woman."

XII

Soon after the passage of the Civil Rights Act, the Catholic bishop of the Diocese of Baton Rouge issued a directive desegregating all church congregations and parochial schools in the diocese. This edict was received with minimal direct resistance in Baton Rouge, unlike the defiance mounted against the Archbishop of New Orleans when he issued a similar decree. He had had to excommunicate three socially prominent parishioners who worshipped at the Cathedral. One, a woman, had stood up at Mass, interrupting the Archbishop's homily on parochial school desegregation and denouncing him for his decision to expose innocent White babies to dangerous and corrupting racial influences. Another, in an excoriating editorial published in the *Times-Picayune*, had encouraged New Orleans Catholics to defy the Archbishop by withdrawing their children from parochial schools and enrolling them instead in the numerous private "White-flight academies" then springing up like funguses everywhere in the area in resistance to school desegregation. A third had actually vaulted over the Archbishop's garden wall and accosted him as he walked the grounds praying his rosary after supper.

In my family's parish, Sacred Heart of Jesus, Black congregants worshipped in pews before a side altar set off from the nave, well away from the central pews where the White parishioners knelt. On the Sunday following the issuance of the bishop's edict, our old Maltese monsignor, who had been pastor at Sacred Heart for years, hobbled up into the pulpit to announce in his heavily accented English that "the Negro members of the parish" need no longer sit off to the side of the church, that instead they should stand up right then and there and find places in the main pews of the nave.

I looked over at the Black parishioners in their separate pews and saw them glancing at each other, trying to establish some kind of consensual response to what seemed more a demand than an invitation. After a few moments of confused indecision, the Black parishioners looked down at their hands. No one made a move. Many White members of the congregation sat still, their eyes flashing resentment and resistance. The silence in the church bristled with hostility.

Desegregation of churches and schools was clearly not to happen in a matter of moments or as the result of an awkward command.

Eventually my parish absorbed its Black members into the main pews in the church nave, a Black woman was elected president of the parish council, and Black children donned parochial school uniforms to walk in double lines behind nuns into their classrooms.

But all this took years.

XIII

As I write this chapter during the Covid-19 quarantine of October 2020, I am hearing claims gaining in common usage that we live in a "post-racial age," that the ugly racism of the past is, thankfully, IN the past. The need for a Black Lives Matter Movement would seem to contravene that observation. So would an experience I had not so long ago. Several years past, I returned to Louisiana for a visit with my family. An old childhood friend heard I was in town and invited me to join him at his brother's house out in the country for a crawfish boil.

When we arrived, an elderly Black man named Nero was hoisting up a 50-pound gunny sack bulging with squirming, pincer-clacking crawfish. Nero poured them into a galvanized tin wash tub filled with salt water to make the crawfish excrete the contents of their mud veins. He then changed the water to fresh, poured in half a bottle of Zataran's crab boil, and set the wash tub of crawfish over the flaring propane bottom burner of a cut-down old hot water heater. After finishing this prep work, Nero pocketed a wad of dollars handed him and drove off down the dirt road in a wheezing rat-colored truck.

"That Nero is one of the good ole boys," my friend's brother announced. "Ain't many of them left. I can call on that ole coon to do anything for me."

After we dispatched the boiled crawfish, skimmed out red and steaming onto a ping-pong table covered in newspaper, my friend's brother and his in-laws from north Louisiana went inside and turned on the television to watch an LSU-Alabama basketball game. They sat bunched up together on a long green naugahyde couch, halos from hair pomade blooming on the wallpaper behind, a Confederate battle flag pinned up on the wall near the ceiling.

Alabama's team was trouncing the team playing for LSU. Black players dominated both teams. Each time Alabama scored, loud protests and execrations erupted from the fans on the couch as if they had met with personal affronts. Alabama continued to pound LSU.

Nearly in tears, our host's ten-year-old son suddenly wailed: "They's niggahs is beatin' us's niggahs!" and brought his fist down hard on the coffee table, making all the beer bottles clatter and jump, toppling a few.

DARKNESS

All things give way; nothing remaineth.

--Heraclitus

I

At five years old, I became afraid of the dark. I would like to be able to place the onset of this fear earlier and to know I had conquered it by then, but I was five alright. My mother had had my older brother's white First Communion suit-pants taken up to fit him and the white jacket and shirt laundered. The suit had been worn first by our cousin. She handed me the hanger boning the paper-draped suit fresh from the cleaners and told me to hook it on the doorknob of the closet in the upstairs bedroom my brother and I shared.

I climbed the dark stairs, careful not to trail the suit on the treads or to trip on it. I knew by heart the room I would enter. The overhead light in this bedroom rounded into an opaque globe like those in old schoolhouses. It hung from the bottom of a fan stuck to the ceiling like an enormous moth. One turned this light on by pulling a braided cord hanging down and ending in a wooden acorn. I could not yet reach the cord, though my older brother could. I had a red tin goose-neck lamp by my side of the double bed that I shared with my brother. He had one too. I could turn it off and on, careful not to touch the hot metal cone-shade.

I crossed the room in the dark toward the glimmer of a mirror on the closet door. A few steps into the room, I froze. I stopped dead in my tracks, like a slug flash-frozen on a spinach leaf in a processing plant.

I do not know how long I stood there. I must have been gone a long time. Then I heard my mother calling my name. Each time she called it, her voice rose a couple of notes. Then I heard her footsteps on the stairs, not rapid, not slow. She called my name again, lowering her tone.

Then she walked smack into me. She pulled the braided cord to thaw me in light. She saw me standing there holding the suit. I dropped it in a crinkled heap and began to cry. She knelt on one knee and turned me to face her. She smelled like the onions she had been chopping. She scanned my face quickly, then drew me close.

"What's wrong? Why are you standing here all alone in the dark?" she whispered in my ear. "What's wrong?"

"Nothing," I stammered. I could not word my terror. "Nothing."

She pulled away and held me out before her. Her love for me levitated her lip at one corner, left the other corner level. Her eyes softened. "Is my little boy afraid of the dark?" she asked. "Never was before."

I looked at her.

"That's it, isn't it?"

I looked at her.

"You don't need to be afraid of the dark," she laughed, but in a way that I knew she was not laughing at me. She brought her thumb up to smudge away a tear below my left eye. "The dark is just the dark," she said. "There's nothing there at all."

But that was just it.

II

Every night someone, usually my mother, sometimes my father, occasionally my aunts Helen or Jo who then lived next door, would read a story to my brother and me. My mother would lie in the middle of the double bed and nestle us to her, one on either side, and open a collection of Grimm fairytales in a red buckram binding, or a companion volume of Andersen stories in a green binding.

"See?" she would say, glancing at me after yet another reading of "Hansel and Gretel," my favorite fairytale. "They came out of the dark woods with treasure! They were afraid of the dark at first, but just look at the rubies and emeralds and pearls they found there!"

"Hansel wasn't scared of the dark, and I'm not either," my brother noted.

But the story did not fool me for one moment. You could not eat a house, no matter how hungry you were. Grown-ups could not be tricked as easily as the witch. They always had their way. Dark houses did not fetch up jewels, nor did swans carry you safe on their backs across black water.

My mother would scooch awkwardly between us off the bed at its foot to pull the covers up under our chins and to kiss us both on the nose and then on the forehead. She would leave my red lamp on, returning after we were both asleep to turn it off.

"What a big baby you are," my brother would say and slap me lightly on the forehead where our mother had just kissed me.

No matter how silently she made her way up the stairs, I always woke when my mother returned to extinguish the light. She padded in soft slippers; she smelled of gardenia talc after her bath. I knew it was useless to protest the click-swallow of the tin lamp's light switch and the darkness that then gulped everything down.

I would lie awake in the dark and listen to the soft shift of my mother's slippers retreat across the wood floor and descend the stairs. Then, in the silence that followed, everything unraveled. Things skimmed away into darkness like milkweed puffs on black water. Everything separated. Everything submerged. I would feel sick in my throat at this terrible divorcing, this digesting.

III

One night I sat across the kitchen table from my brother watching him do his first-grade homework.

"What's that word?" I asked, pointing at his primer.

"Skip," he said.

"What's that word?" I asked, leaning on my elbows further across the table to teach myself to read upside down.

"Jump," he said.

"What's that word?" I asked pointing.

"Momma!" he said. "He's bothering me. I'm trying to read my homework."

"Would you like to draw?" my mother asked me, turning around from the sink, the corner of a blue-gingham apron flaring out from her hip like a wing. "You can use your new color pencils. Go into Daddy's office and get some paper from the file cabinet."

I walked to the door of the bedroom my father used as an office and peered in. The room was dark.

My father came down the hall and saw me.

"Just go on in and get the paper," he sighed. "I'll stand here by the door and watch for you. There's nothing to be afraid of. There's nothing there."

I looked up at him. I knew I had to go in. I crept toward the file cabinet by the desk.

"Look out for the bear!" my father yelled from the doorway. "Oh no! He's standing right behind you with his paw raised!"

I iced all over. I knew there was no bear. What terrified me was the fear I heard in my father's voice. I did not then know that one could fake fear or would ever have any reason to do so. My father too was afraid of the dark!

He turned a light on then at the wall switch and walked up behind me. He took the back of my neck between thumb and forefinger and waggled my head. "Come on, boy," he said, and walked me over to the file cabinet.

"That was mean," my mother said to him when we returned to the kitchen together. She flicked her glance away from him as he sat down at the table next to me. My father laughed and poked his finger in my ribs. My mother tilted a coke and downed a few big swallows. Then she filled the top third of the bottle with Wild Turkey, cupped a handful of salted peanuts in to float on top, swirled the bottle.

After a while, my brother slammed his book shut and stuffed it back in his book bag. He came up behind me and plucked the back of my head with a middle finger launched against his thumb.

"What's that supposed to be?" he asked, looking over my shoulder.

"It's a garden," I said. I had outlined flowers—my approximations of daisies and roses and tulips—using each color pencil in the exact order it had been placed in the box. That meant a gray tulip and a chocolate-brown daisy. Each flower had to touch the one next to it. The flowers began to scrunch up against the right margin of the paper because I had to use up all the colors until I got to the yellow pencil, which I needed to draw the sun. The sun's rays stabbed each bloom from above as if strawing up its nectar, everything thus connected in a spoked ascension.

"Only sissies draw flowers, hunh, Daddy?" my brother said.

My mother swirled the last swig in her coke bottle and upended it, but not before I saw her eyes dart up toward the ceiling.

"No," my father said. "No, boys can like flowers." I looked over at him frowning at me.

IV

I took to wandering the house, fearful in the dark. I would trail my hand over things I could not see, over the backs of chairs, the knobs of doors, the shades of lamps, everything I had held together by force of will in the daytime that had now come undone in the dark. I touched and touched each separate thing—the radio dials, though I knew I would get in trouble for twiddling away my mother's daytime program channel; the houses and hotels on the Monopoly game-board left for me to lose at in the morning, as always; the lopsided purple ashtray I had mashed together out of clay at day care. Everything scumbled out of order, relationless. And when my fingers trailed away from an object, it ceased to exist and vanished forever.

I found my way into my parents' room to stand by my mother's side of the bed. After a time, she would whisper into the silence, "Is someone there?" I heard fear in her voice. She was afraid of the dark too! I would not say anything. "Is that you?" she would ask and reach into the darkness.

One Saturday morning, I came into the kitchen while my parents were drinking coffee. "I heard him breathing by the bed again last night," my mother was saying. "I was afraid to open my eyes until I realized it was him. It's gotten to be almost every night now."

My father saw me standing just inside the kitchen door. "You're going to break your fool neck one of these nights," he said. "When we put you to bed, you stay in bed. Quit all this rambling in the dark."

That afternoon my father returned with my brother from the hardware store where they had gone to buy washers to fix the drip in the backyard spigot caused when I climbed up on it to reach a gypsy moth composing its dusk-gray wings on the side of the house. My father presented me with a flashlight. My parents took to closing their bedroom door at night.

"What a baby!" my brother hissed in the dark as I clutched the flashlight under the covers.

V

By the time I was ready for grade school, my childhood fear of the dark, nebulous until then, began to focus: Death intruded its darkness on my awareness and, seduced, I grew both drawn to death and disquieted by it. I found death inescapable, emblems of it defining my environment. My school, Sacred Heart of Jesus, an ark of yeasty-smelling, khaki-clad boys and starchy girls in blue pleated skirts, was sited amid three large cemeteries, circumferenced by acres of flat graves and upright tombs and charnels. And across from one of these cemeteries was an abattoir, a slaughterhouse, a busy animal killing place.

Unaffiliated with these public cemeteries but anchoring them was Sacred Heart of Jesus Church, a large brick promontory directly across the street from my parochial school. Black hearses regularly floated up to the front of this church, buoyant coasters in a flotilla of frequent weekday funerals I spied from the school playground during recess. Black limousines as long as barges attended these hearses, mourners exiting them, bolstered on the arms of those for whom grief was more supportable. Pallbearers slid coffins, lozenges of loss, out of the hearses. I tasted a coppery tang as I paused at play to spy on someone else's grief through the wire diamonds of the chain-link fence I leaned against. Grief to the boy I was then was taken in like air, though edged in a darkness I could not then have named.

[In April 2000, a startling dissolve across time: As I stepped out of the limousine in front of Sacred Heart Church before my mother's funeral, I glanced across the street to spy a single boy, a silent witness, peering through that same chain-link fence at my mother's coffin sliding from the back of the hearse, its crown of white roses nodding. What premonitory darkness caused his lithe body, backgrounded by uniformed children intent on their play, to sag against the fence in simulation of a grief he did not yet discern. He was I, but on the innocent side of knowing.]

The East Baton Rouge Parish School Board would no longer provide school bus rides to parochial school children after they completed sixth grade and were then in junior high school. Consequently, I often walked the nearly three miles from school to my house every afternoon during seventh and eighth grades. Dawdled, more like it. There was much to see.

Siding my school and across the street was Magnolia Cemetery, a city square block of old brick and marble tombs tenanted by the White dead. A black wrought-iron fence enclosed a somber garden of toppling Egyptian needles, Gothic plinths, crumbling charnels, graves marked with crosses, urns, anchors, lambs, finials, angels, all gnawed at by Baton Rouge's acrid air emanating from the large Exxon plant up river.

Magnolia Cemetery had been laid out in the late 19th Century during the vogue of the "garden cemetery." It featured boulevards and avenues, family gardens and individual plots—mapped attempts at order planted in red-berried yew and cypresses dark as smoke. But it takes vigilance to keep grief in bounds. Magnolia Cemetery grew in time to reflect grief's waywardness, morphing into a muddle of tombs and monuments all escaping the founders' neat linear plot outlines.

Even in my childhood, burials in crowded Magnolia were rare, the dead having migrated to the suburban lawn cemeteries which mandated small bronze plaques laid flat on the grass or mausoleum slots where grief could be tucked away tidily.

As an altar boy, I was frequently called on to serve at Catholic obsequies, including several in Magnolia. One in particular remains in memory, sharpening my awareness of how grief found its home in darkness. The father of one of my little brother's classmates had owned and operated a small amusement park. "Wonderland" offered a rickety Ferris Wheel with half of its lights shorted out, a baby boat ride on water brown from rusted hulls, and a cotton candy and weenie concession that my mother cocked one eye at and folded some dollar bills back into her purse. "Family Fun" the sign over the entrance arch buzzed and flashed intermittently. "I didn't think it was much fun," my sister complained after our only visit there.

So, Wonderland went kaput and its owner found himself with his house in foreclosure and his family living with his wife's parents. Shortly thereafter, he had run his car into the buttress of a bridge, to rumors that it had been no accident. My father had read the newspaper obituary to my mother while she was frying bacon for breakfast. "Very dark days for that family," she sighed. "I hope he left some life insurance."

An altar boy summoned to serve at a funeral rarely knows who the dead person is. I knew this time. Carrying the crucifix, I walked into the funeral parlor ahead of the priest. As I approached the open coffin, I could see the rims

219

of a pair of glasses jutting above the coffin edge. I fought hard against a strong impulse to laugh. Standing at the head of the coffin, I looked down at the dead man cushioned in cream satin, a rosary wrapped around his hands like beaded handcuffs. I had expected to see a scarred disfigurement, but he looked as if he would wake up and demand to know why everyone was staring at him.

After the rosary, the priest turned to speak with Ted's mother while the other altar boy and I companionably chatted at an exit. Ted caught my eye, then stalked up to us, his glare unwavering. "What are you two looking at?" he cried. The priest came up at this point and put his hand on Ted's shoulder. He shrugged it away.

Once the coffin had been lowered into the hole at Magnolia Cemetery and everyone was dispersing, Ted strode up to us altar boys, kicking clods of dirt, and hissed his fury: "Don't let me catch either of you. I'll beat your ass." There was no way: Ted was five years younger than we were. I never saw Ted again. What an intrusion we two altar boys must have been at that funeral, gawking at grief, too young and dissociated to feel what Ted now knew in his bones.

Adjacent to Magnolia was the National Cemetery, a fortress buttressed by high concrete walls. The rows of identical white crosses glimpsed through barred gates were as regular as the ticks of a metronome cadencing silence. This cemetery stood at attention, its formal sequence grief's rigid rebuke.

A block away from the National Cemetery was Sweet Olive, a turmoil of tombs, the boneyard of Black folks. Once plotted on the outskirts of town, this old cemetery was now shackled in an urban stranglehold. Those buried here had mingled with White people all their lives, as maids and handymen, mechanics and practical nurses. Now, crowded into their narrow enclosures, all such mingling was forever circumscribed.

Sweet Olive was a confusion, few fictions of order remaining: pathways had become impenetrable mazes, arterials clogged and impassable. In places, loosened bricks were scattered about, the jagged holes they left in the raised tombs disclosing skulls, hip bones, fragments of old coffins. Many of the wooden markers were hand-lettered in white paint, brief epitaphs inventively spelled, letters shrinking toward the right margins. Some crypts, marked by far too many name plaques for the spaces provided, indicated the practice of Louisiana wet-ground charneling: when a new burial was needed, the body longest buried was resurrected, the coffin burned, the bones laid into the charnel pit beneath the tomb to mingle there with those gone long before. Some of these old family charnels had over thirty names registered but only ten crypt slabs. In Sweet Olive, tombs settled and leaned, graves sank, markers listed.

A solitary, musing child, I remember standing in a brown study one day dead center of the steps from the sidewalk up through Sweet Olive's brick retaining wall. There was violence in the upper air, a soughing in the cypress trees. The wind slapped the green canvas of a raised pavilion with the sharp retorts of rifle shots. Birds were blown about, each a knot in a cast net constantly reconfiguring itself. I stood on Sweet Olive's threshold, a still, fearful boy in a dark and reeling world.

Suddenly I realized that the sidewalks around me were filling with Black women in ornate hats, Black men in dark, shiny suits. A huddle swayed toward me, its center a large woman with a veil obliterating her face. When the throng approached the steps I had hastily vacated, the woman shrugged off her bearers to look back at a metal casket borne by six struggling men sporting white carnations in their lapels. She began then to work strange whooping yelps which glazed my hairline in icy waves. Then her body slumped. The knot around her instantly tightened.

"You have somewhere else to be now?" asked a White policeman straddling a motorcycle and balancing it on one olive-drab leg. I stirred in the gathering darkness. And then it began to rain. Dark drops spattered on the sidewalk, large as half dollars. "Shit!" the cop said.

I sometimes headed for the abattoir catercorner across from Sweet Olive after school. I would wander among the condemned animals confined to covered stalls redolent of urine and dung, water troughs scummed over green. Occasionally I got there at slaughtering time. Mute and numb, I watched the butchers, indifferent to the presence of a flinching boy, lead each cow into a slaughtering pen and heft a sledge hammer to smash into a bovine foreskull. The thunks made me wince. Usually, but not always, the animal crumpled.

A chain was then secured to a kicking hind leg, and the animal was hoisted upside down over a concrete channel gouted a dull jasper. The dewlap was slit, blood flisching down, the air heavy with the reek of iron. Things happened quickly after that: the carcass, sometimes still struggling, was flayed, knives nicking over flesh veined blue, glistening with silvery fascia. The cow's skinned head was severed, de-horned, slammed onto a bloody shelf to join other heads, their wide eyes roving frantically, as if intent on gathering every last sight of their world, even though it had led them to this.

Above all this lowing confusion sounded a susurration of wings and the cooing of pigeons, attracted by the undigested grains in the manure, preening and feeding and wooing in the dark rafters in the house of death, oblivious as angels to the fates of the creatures dying in great numbers beneath them.

The pigs were wise in their despair: unlike the cows, they seemed to know what was coming. They screamed and struggled, making their deaths even more brutal. A knife at the throat curdled their high squeals into thick gurgles. Their un-skinned heads went on the shelves too, some grumpy-looking, others quizzical, some smirking, others cocking an eye as if at a bad joke, others winking, some sly or coy, some cynical, as if nothing—not even this dark end of things—could surprise them.

The lambs went easy. They were led, four or five at a time, into a small holding pen, at first hesitant, then bounding in eagerly on spindly legs, their innocence an obscenity. A flick of a silver blade at the throat dispatched them. They fell docilely out of the kneeholds of the butchers and lay in the bloody hay, coughing gently and apologetically as opera ladies do in the middle of an aria.

Twelve years old, I stood witness at killing time in the abattoir. Dying, I learned, was unattended by epiphany, a dark enterprise in this filthy, rough-hewn slaughterhouse reeking of blood and shit and Lysol. There I experienced the dim shimmer of an ever approaching darkness and learned at last what I was afraid of.

VI

My mother was mistrustful of public displays of grief. She was the resilient daughter of German immigrants. To her inbred cultural reserve was admixed the restraint of the Midwest. Springfield, Ohio was grounded in bedrock, its durable strength raying upward into the bones of those who built their brick and stone houses there. Kind and loving, tolerant and empathetic, amused at childish antics, my mother maintained stern views on the etiquette of grieving: one did not intrude one's grief on others. Grieving was a private matter. Ritual was external, there to guide behavior, answer uncertainty, settle doubt. But grief was an inner phenomenon: the body was a perimeter of control, the darkened soul alone the scene of sorrow.

My mother believed that the more a person carried on emotionally in public, the less grief that person probably actually experienced. She saw external manifestations of grief as undignified, an imposition on others, a public assurance of a grief expected but perhaps less than actually felt. I saw my mother cry only one time—in anger and frustration after a rare argument with my father. Never from grief. Grief for my mother was inexpressible, a dumb distress centered in the dark core of her being.

My mother was certainly acquainted with darkness and grief: her mother taken suddenly with a stroke while sipping hot chocolate the morning after Christmas, my mother then twelve; a nurturing grandmother coming out of her coma to call the names of her two dead children; an older brother dying alone of a stroke in a nursing home, bitter at his wife's perfunctory and perfumed visits; the passing of her parent-substitutes, her mother's unmarried brother and sister with whom she lived, one of a stroke while lacing her shoes, the other discovered in his bed by my mother sent to wake him for work; the telegram from a stranger announcing her father's death alone in a retired actor's hotel in Los Angeles, vaudeville kaput, his beloved performing cockatoos asphyxiated in a broiling boxcar sidelined for hours, his last days blind and partially paralyzed, unable to talk on the phone when my mother and her sisters tried to reach him. My mother knew grief—of a dark and stoic kind—and her greatest grief lay before her.

I was accustomed to seeing my Sicilian father weep. His emotions seemed to quiver just below the surface of his skin. His tears were eruptions, lapses in control, made disturbing, not so much by their frequency, but by his unsuccessful struggles to suppress them. His crying always seemed a defeat: he was forced to concede to something he strove against but was overwhelmed by. Oddly, my mother's contempt for outward displays of grief never extended to him. She comforted him by ignoring these lachrymose lapses, though she gentled her voice when she spoke to him when he was so undone. She seemed to accept that that was just the way he was.

On returning from Mass one Sunday morning, my mother opened the front door to mingled sounds of muffled sobbing and chortling glee. She headed to the baby's room: my little brother was standing in his crib, holding onto the railing and leaning out to peer through the open bedroom door.

"Helloooo!" my mother cooed as she gathered him up, his laughter floating over the ominous undertones. I headed to my father's room to find him still in bed, his face a bleary mess. I stood in the doorway staring at how broken he was. My mother edged past me, my baby brother reaching for the combs in her upswept hair. "Go change into your play clothes," she told me. I pieced together during the day that my father's collapse was caused by a telephone call informing him that an uncle had died suddenly during the night. My father seemed acquainted with darkness too.

It is a green spring evening, warm. The doors and windows of our house are all open. My mother is frying veal cutlets. I am reading to her while my little brother is coloring viciously on the floor, some of his strokes arcing off the paper onto the linoleum. My father comes home from work crying. He begins a sentence relatively normally but must then hurry through it as if outracing the tears he gets caught up in. What I hear horrifies me: a family friend, a funny little man with black glasses and a flat top, parked his Studebaker behind the levee and shot himself in the mouth. Such dark desperation shocked me. I went out in the backyard so as not to hear any more. A mockingbird was echoing piano scales. I looked up into the darkening pecan tree, its limbs, just beginning to leaf out, black lace against a violet sky. Terror thrilled through me. After dinner I was afraid to be alone in the bathtub, afraid to be alone in the dark in my bed. I had peered into the vacancy of the human heart when hollowed out by despair.

Shortly after this, my father's business partner, notorious for fast and erratic driving, had lost control one evening and crashed his car into the culvert of a ditch. He had been thrown from the car just before it had careened up the embankment. On its descent, the car had rolled over him.

Italian men always seemed to die before their wives, who then commenced their long, slow fades, half-regarded relics, gray presences in the active life they haunt. But their shining moment is at the wakes of their dead husbands. There all attention is reserved for them, it being considered an impropriety to outdo them in their mourning.

The wife of my father's business partner was a tragic queen of several days' reign, a veritable Niobe. Swathed in black in these pageants, newly minted Italian widows sit center in the front row of carnation-scented funeral parlors before open caskets—I mean WIDE open--flanked by gaudy flower masses on wire stands. My father's business partner's casket was open full length to display him dressed to the nines in his ceremonial 4th-degree Knight of Columbus tails, his plumed black chapeau nestled by the sword at his side, his gleaming patent-leather pumps splayed sideways.

Mourners approach the corpse, crouch down awkwardly onto the provided prie-dieu, cross themselves, peer into the coffin, pause a moment, check out the flowers, then head for the widow before whom they pass in rigid review. Male mourners in black suits incline their heads curtly: "Condolences," they say, one after another. Their wives lean over to embrace the widow, who out-matches the emotional states of these ladies, tear for tear.

At periodic intervals, the widow is expected to approach the corpse for a colloquy with the dead. Her clustering female relatives decide when this is appropriate. They position themselves to prop her up. This begins "the widow's walk." "She's going up! She's going up!" someone whispers loudly in the funeral home vestibule where people are gossiping, sipping coffee, conducting business, their roles as mourners played out. At this summons, people crowd in through every doorway to watch the widow approach the coffin. Here she staggers, chokes out her dead husband's name, bends over him, weeping loudly. There are murmurs of sympathy and satisfaction from the onlookers. I have never seen an Italian widow play her part less than admirably, with precise timing and the expected fractured poise.

The widow is prima donna of distress for the duration of the wake and the funeral week. Then she is dropped like a pair of old gray gloves, shrunken and misshapen. The last time I saw the business partner's widow was in her home over the cold meats following the funeral. My father was bent over her in an agonized attempt to compose himself.

These Italian funerals were foreign and distasteful to my mother. She sat unmoving through the "widow's walk"; her condolences were sincere, gentle, and articulate. She must have been perceived as cold and unfeeling. One time, in confidence, she referred to Italian funerals as "carnival sideshows." For her, they failed in any way to illuminate the darkness where grief endured.

VII

When I first fell in love at nearly fifty years old, I felt I would never again fear the darkness and all its dissolutions. I would never again loathe the dark daytime shadows placed everywhere to remind me that the light is an illusion, that it floats on an immense emptiness like an iridescent oil slick over fathoms of black water. Loving Dore Tanner would always light my way, would always make everything fit together in ways it never had before. In our nights in our bed, I docked my face at his shoulder's solid flesh. My arms held the centering that assured me that all things cohered, even though I could not see them piecing and patterning until the morning.

I felt, when I fell in love with Dore, that nothing terrible could ever happen to me again, that love granted me an impenetrable resilience. I would never really be sad again. Were I ever sorrowing or lonely, I could call Dore at work. I could unlock the double doors of his house in the forlorn late afternoon to stand by his bed and watch him napping, or walk up behind him as he entered the day's stock figures into his computer balance sheets to kiss the nape of his neck. I could waylay him on a June morning as he rolled the lawnmower out of the garage and trudged through the dewy grass, cursing as the clots clogged the grass catcher behind the mower.

But, in spite of everything I could do to stay him, Dore slid into the darkness.

VIII

Several years before I met Dore, I went home to Louisiana for my Aunt Helen's 91st birthday. She was living in a nursing home then. I was sent to pick her up and bring her to my parents' house for dinner as pre-arranged. I entered the television front lobby at 5:45, expecting to find her there waiting, hunched tiny in one of the stained red velour chairs that seemed more attentive to the blaring television set than their occupants were.

The old ladies looked at me hard, their eyes sharp and hooded, brooding like attenuated hawks in some kind of raptor preserve, taloned hands gripping their chair arms, watchful for any gobs of life thrown within reach.

"Are you my son?" cawed one of them.

Aunt Helen was not in the TV room.

"I think I seen Miss Helen go off to bed," said the night aide behind her glass wall. "She takes to bed real early these nights."

I walked into my aunt's room to find her sleeping in pink nylon pajamas. She had one clip earring on. Her bald eyebrows were penciled in dark, arched up as if she had been taken by surprise. Her hair and face and pillow glowed the same white in the dim light from the hall. I watched her sleep for a time.

"Who are you?" she asked into the room's twilight when I called her name gently. "I haven't done anything wrong."

"Happy Birthday, Sweetheart!" I said. "I've come to take you to your party. We're all waiting for you."

"My party was yesterday," she said. "There was a pony, but mother burned the cake."

"One can't have too many birthday parties when one turns 91!" I said. "I've come to fetch you for one more. And there's a beautiful cake waiting for you."

"I'll get her up," said the aide from the doorway behind me. "You wait a minute in the hall."

"I don't want to watch television," my aunt murmured, "unless Ed Sullivan is on."

When I had buckled her into the front passenger seat and was backing the car out of its parking slot, I asked her why she went to bed so early.

"Right after supper!" she said, as if proud of the fact. "I don't like the nights in that place. That's when the crying starts." I decided not to tell my mother this. She felt bad enough as it was for allowing her sister to go into a nursing home, though my mother knew she was far too feeble herself to care for my aunt who had pretty much run out of her money.

Having already eaten at the nursing home, Aunt Helen picked at the dinner I had helped my mother prepare: chicken pot pies in individual ramekins with leaf cut-outs in the crusts. We also made a molded salad of shredded carrots and pineapple bits suspended in orange jello like bright bugs fixed in amber. Aunt Helen drank a celebratory glass of champagne, though.

My aunt's birthday cake had two candles in the shapes of numbers: 91. My sister turned off the lights in the dining room as I carried the lit cake in. Everyone sang in the dark. I set the glowing cake before my aunt.

"All for me?" she asked when the ragged singing ended.

"Make a wish and blow out the candles," I prompted. "Then I'll help you cut the cake."

She whispered the candles into a flicker and then puffed them out, thin gray spirals twining upwards. Everyone clapped.

"I'm afraid to die," my aunt said.

The room fell silent.

My mother reached over the table to her. "Just think how many we love who are waiting for us!" she said. "We need never be lonely or afraid there."

"Will I be able to find them?" my aunt trebled. "Will they remember me?"

"Yes!" my mother cried. "Oh, Darling, yes!"

Their hands tangled on the shadowy tablecloth, black-veined and indistinguishable. Then someone turned the lights back on.

IX

My sister picked me up at the Baton Rouge airport late in the evening several days before Christmas 1999. Once home, I stood by my mother's bed until she woke. My father followed me into her room. She lay in a hospital bed, her hands in white cotton gloves, her wrists loosely tethered by blue cotton thongs to the metal bars of the bed guards. She turned so she could see me and smiled up at me when she realized who I was. Though she moved her lips in the shape of my name, she had mostly stopped talking by then.

I was shocked to see the restraints, though my father had told me earlier in the fall by telephone why they were necessary. One night, my mother had risen in the dark and found her way across the house to the back guest-bedroom. My father woke to find she had glided the twin beds silently across the floor, a heavy bureau into a corner opposite, the night stands with the lamps beside them in a row beneath the window. He found her asleep on an angled rug at the foot of one of the beds, her nose bleeding from her exertions.

After a second episode of this, he had installed a lock on the door of the back bedroom. A week or so later, he woke in the middle of the night to find my mother sitting at the dining room table in the dark. She had taken twelve silver spoons from their case and had arranged them, bowls to scrolled stem tips, in an arabesque. He discovered her poised over her pattern, studying it in the dark, her hand grasping a fat clutch of butter knives.

Several nights later he woke to find her sitting in the dark at the same place at the table. She had dumped a 300-count bottle of aspirins into a pile and was piecing the pills into a star pattern. The front of her flannel gown was drenched in blood, several clotted Kleenex tissues at her feet. She spent the next day in the hospital until they could cauterize the vessels in her nose to stop her hemorrhaging and to adjust her warfarin dosage. My father had a hospital bed moved into her room before she returned, at her doctor's recommendation. At first she protested, squirming against the restraints. She always slept with a light on in her room now.

"What's new?" my father asked me, the two of us standing on either side of the hospital bed, my mother smiling up at me.

"I had a terrible experience two evenings ago," I told them. My mother's brow furrowed briefly, then smoothed. Her smile remained unchanged.

I told them about my being mugged on the bike trail alongside the American River as I was walking home from campus after posting the fall term final grades.

The river had fogged into a gray nocturne spanned by the black tracery of the distant Fair Oaks Bridge. A thin platinum band barely suggested the western horizon. Things were pulling apart in the dusk. "That's blue," I said as I looked down on the road from the top of the levee, not "That's a blue car." I descended the levee on the bike trail into the darkness of Alumni Grove. Among the dark trees, two boys from Sacramento's large Russian immigrant community were waiting for me. One pressed a butcher knife to my throat; the other brandished a wooden club as if he were eager to clobber me with it. I handed over the cash I had just withdrawn from the ATM on campus but refused to give them my wallet. They demanded, in broken English, that I climb the metal bars of the fence bordering the trail and walk down to the river. I climbed it backwards, facing them. When I dropped to the other side of the fence, they ran.

Back in my office, I answered the police officer's questions. She went through the formality of filing a crime report. She scolded me for my dangerous decision not to hand over the wallet immediately. She offered me a ride home.

I did not tell my parents that when I locked my front door behind me, I stood for a long time in the silent darkness of my cold house, trembling because Dore was not there. He was nowhere.

As I now write this, both of my parents, my aunts, and my older brother have all vanished as well into the darkness. Darkness in time ingests everyone and everything. I had been right about the darkness all along.

As I now approach the edge of old age, however, I have come at last to realize that all the moments in the light we are given, dimmed though that light may be at times, are ample recompense for the inevitable darkness that will in time settle over us all when the comet trails of our lives at last flicker out. The illuminated moments I have left help now to allay my lifelong fear of that approaching shadow. I have foundered at life whenever I have squandered any of those too brief luminous moments, have neglected to fill each gleaming one with the highest intensity my physical senses and my mental perceptions could afford me, when I have failed to realize how very precious life is. To the extent that I have filled my moments in the light with intensity, therein lies the level at which I have succeeded in life. Life's brief incandescence is worth the darkness that encircles it, a darkness that forces life itself to flare and dazzle.

AN ARTICULATE COURTSHIP, AN ELOQUENT MARRIAGE

I: Parenting My Parents

My parents met on Easter Sunday, April 8, 1943, in Springfield, Ohio, where my mother grew up. My father, newly drafted into the Army Air Corps from his home in White Castle, Louisiana, was stationed at Wright-Patterson Air Field in Dayton, a scant 26 miles from Springfield. They met on a blind date. My mother, staunchly averse to these kinds of encounters, especially with soldiers, was pressured into that date by her best friend, who, on learning that the man she would eventually marry had gained an unexpected leave and was bringing along my father, a friend of his, dragooned my reluctant mother into joining the two of them on their date, thereby relieving their awkwardness on being accompanied by an unattached soldier.

My mother was then almost 32, my father not yet 26. I surmise that my mother, like her two sisters and the aunt with whom she lived, did not expect to marry. She seemed not to be looking for a husband. Though she dated on occasion, I never heard her tell of having been seriously involved with anyone before she met my father. My mother and father obviously hit it off on that first blind date and on several subsequent dates, at least enough to remain in contact through their letters without seeing each other again for nearly three years following his transfer from Dayton almost immediately after meeting my mother, first for a brief time to New Jersey and then to North Africa and later to Europe. This frail initial introduction led to a spate of letter writing, their entire courtship articulated through the postal service. My mother kept all of my father's wartime letters; he kept none of hers, unable to secure them in the light gear he was required to stow as he was transferred from North Africa into Sicily, up the Italian boot, through France and the low countries, and finally into smoldering Germany itself.

Their earliest letters were from May 1943. They wrote to each other every couple of days, continually chiding each other if they felt they were not receiving the letters due them in a timely way. Reams of these letters came to me after the deaths of my parents. It is unlikely that such a trove of correspondence as this would ever be amassed again in modern times. Thus, this collection represents one of the last manifestations of centuries of letter writing customs where geographically separated people, unconnected by immediate phone access or high-speed internet and ephemeral emails, remained in contact through pen and paper. Yet my parents' letters, focused on the immediacy of their concerns and heavily censored by Army scrutiny, hold little value for the historian in that they do not much reflect on matters of national or international consequence. They are entirely domestic letters in scope, focused as they are on the ordinary daily events in my parents' lives at the time they wrote to each other.

The letters between my mother and father do, however, offer an intensely human portrayal of an articulated courtship during a difficult time. After a long-delayed marriage that followed the war, my mother continued to correspond with her sisters in Ohio from 1946 to 1952. The hundreds of post-war letters my mother wrote after she moved with my father to Louisiana offer moving glimpses of two earnest, well-intentioned people establishing their marriage and creating a family in a new American-dominated post-war world. My mother thus composes in her letters an eloquent marriage, an account in words of the union she so happily entered. As such, these letters bear a personal and, to a lesser extent, a larger cultural relevance. And I think the letters tell an engaging story in their own right.

All children snoop on their parents, trying to discern what they do not know about their parents' alien lives, eavesdropping, spying around corners, carefully attending to their conversations, their quiet morning musings over coffee, their arguments. I now have these letters which permit me as an adult to pry into my parents' affairs. Their letters allow me to know my parents in ways previously closed to me.

As a child, I was an extension of my parents, a part fitted into their lives, having not yet forged an identity of my own separate from theirs. As an adult reading their letters, I relate to them almost as if they were strangers: their relationship, the situations they found themselves in, are now so other to me, so remote, as if I am reading an account recorded by strangers.

I am now in my 70's, more than twice as old as my parents were when they wrote these letters. Mine now is a strange perspective: Like a parent, I watch their lives unfold through their letters with a mingled sense of anticipation and concern, with an anomalous paternal indulgence, an affectionate patience and forbearance with their stumbling and at times naïve falterings as they, so young then, try to find their way through the war and its aftermath where they negotiate their growing love and need for each other and their attempts to construct a future conditioned by global circumstances over which they have little control. Their letters foster in me the same tenderness towards them that parents must feel observing their own children as they frame their futures. I am touched by their innocence and earnestness.

All is nascent for my parents in these letters; all for them is now completed. The future they contemplated in their writing is now far behind them: I know how their lives played out for the 57 years of their connection. This knowledge provides me with an odd double vision, anticipatory and simultaneously conclusive: I see the entire trajectory, the beginning and the ending concurrently, granting me a singular sense of both expectation and inevitable completion. In reading their letters, in knowing what was to come for them, I feel for them now a more complete love than I could feel for them when they were still present in my life, a part of my life's ongoing current. I know them better now. I feel towards them as a parent would, as God, we are told, does, seeing them blindly but ever hopefully staging their futures and cognizant of all those others whom their lives formed and touched. They lived their lives well, with joy, with sorrow at times, with decency, with a devotion to each other and to their children that persisted until their deaths.

My parents' spirits hover lightly over these letters; their insubstantial presences linger over their writing. Reading their letters, I sense their energies, their life forces in a real way. In their written words left behind on these frail pages, they remain so much more alive than my memory alone has the power to resurrect them now that they have been dead for so long. While their letters survive, my parents do not dissolve into the ether, as we all eventually must. Once their letters disappear, as is their inevitable fate, my parents, too, depart for good.

II: How It All Began

My parents' initial letters, begun shortly after my father's transfer from his base in Dayton in late April 1943, seem at times strained, forced, likely because neither was accustomed to flirtations, written or otherwise, and were novices at conducting them. My mother resorts to clichés to twit this man who has unexpectedly entered her life and seems intent on maintaining a connection that began so casually. And my father seems to retreat into some sort of stereotypical male bravado that in no way ever really characterized him.

Drawing upon their different geographical roots, my mother references my father's being a "Rebel" as opposed to the "Yankees" who surround him at the base. My father acknowledges that she is not the only person to comment on this, that having ended up assigned to an Army Air Force squadron based in Ohio, he is ragged about his "Rebel" Louisiana origins, and not only by fellow soldiers: apparently, Black men assigned to the base in the kitchens and maintenance divisions were especially hard on him, returning to a Southerner a modicum of the treatment they had had to endure before they fled Dixie.

My mother kept up this geographical badinage too long because in his letter of August 1, my father responds to a card she had earlier sent which he found to have crossed some kind of line: "To be sincere, I will expect most anything since you sent that card. I do really think at times you are trying to make me angry. Better watch this 'Rebel' if he does get angry." The irony of this raillery about his being a "Rebel" embedded in a nest of "Yankees" is that not a single one of either my father's Italian or my mother's German immigrant genetic stock was in this country—north or south—during the Civil War that ended nearly 80 years before this banter.

My father begins making demands on my mother in his very first letter to her. On May 3, he opens with a mild assurance that "it has been swell knowing you" before making one of two demands: "I expect an answer to my letters when I write them. Need I say more?" His second demand was for a photograph of her: "Of course, in the future when I get a permanent address, I expect to receive a snapshot or picture of you. I am not kidding: I expect to receive the same."

His letter of May 24 expresses his displeasure that no photograph was immediately forthcoming: "I am forced at this time to ask that you send me a picture of yourself when you answer this letter. This is more or less a demand." He goes on in this letter to posture as a "wolf" in New York City where he spends his evenings away from his transition post in New Jersey: "Women walk the streets of New York in dresses, and since I am a wolf (by your estimation) I can't help but become 'overcome' by such. I feel sure you can picture me stretching my neck practically out of its socket just to see some 'lass' pass by." I cannot imagine a person less likely than my father to be ogling women on the streets of Manhattan.

On July 9, he returns to his earlier peremptory tone concerning their correspondence: "By all means, you will continue writing to me and I will to you." Did my father think this uncharacteristic display of male forcefulness, these "demands," this "wolfish" affectation were his male right, that perhaps my mother would expect or be impressed by this male bravado? I suspect my mother must have seen through all this and was content to engage in this role play for a time, attentive to countering evidence of my father's innate sensitivity, even vulnerability, as indicated by his self-conscious acknowledgement that his letters will inevitably reveal certain things about him, consciously admitted or unconsciously revealed, that may trouble her: "I hope you won't be disappointed at anytime" by these revelations, he notes in his last letter of 1943, dated December 29. In their letters after this, they both drop the male posturing and the geographical clichés they relied on in these early, awkward letters.

When my mother at last accedes to his demands and belatedly sends two photographs, he pens a response on November 15 that must have endeared him to her: "I think a lot of those two pictures; in fact, I have placed them on the door of my wall locker facing inside. Whenever I open the locker door, I will always be able to glance at these pictures." On November 26, he notes that when any of his fellow soldiers spy these photos in passing, they ask my father where his girl is from. When he replies from Ohio, they wisecrack that he had to come all the way north to find a pretty girl, there being none in the backward bayous of Louisiana.

My father concludes this last letter of 1943 with "I am constantly thinking of you" and with a gallant coda: "Don't think I wouldn't want to be with you under that mistletoe!"

Though awkward and tentative in their trying on of unaccustomed roles, in meeting what they think each expects of the other, my parents in their early letters of 1943 nevertheless establish a foundation for future correspondence. My father's initial male-posturing is undercut by his vulnerability; my mother, whose letters were not retained, comes across as more self-confident and verbally more sophisticated, my father constantly exclaiming how full and rich her letters are and how short and prosaic his own letters must seem to her by contrast. The letters of 1943 are explorations of discernment, semaphores of mutual interest, signals that they find in each other complements to their needs.

Louise Rosanne Landes and Anthony Alexander Agosta
at the time of their meeting, 1943

III
1944: An Affair from Afar: A Letter-Courier Courtship

In a January 23ʳᵈ letter, my father responds to my mother's request for a list of his "likes and dislikes" and to a lengthy questionnaire she sends, asking for all manner of clothing sizes from shoes to hat in addition to favorite colors, card games, preferred tobacco, and other predilections. Apparently she considered sending him occasional items he might enjoy while overseas. In his letter, he acknowledges that replying to her questionnaire carries some risks and sensitivities and hopes that "you won't be disappointed at any time about what you found out as a result of those answers." At the very top of his list of dislikes was "writing letters," ironic given that he has promised to write to my mother every other day and has thereby launched into a full letter courtship that he knows may very well last for years. Other dislikes were "being criticized too much" and "being bossed around"—this from someone in the Army...

Most interesting in light of how this epistolary courtship turned out were his answers to "likes for the future": "to get married upon leaving the Army, have at least three and not more than four kids [they had five], own a home with necessities, conveniences, and luxuries to insure normal living."

He concludes this early letter of 1944 by sending "my love to you." "P.S.," he adds, "surprised?" She probably would have been, having met him comparatively recently and, as he reminded her, at "just about the time we were ready to leave" Dayton for deployment overseas, having time for only "a few weekends" with my mother in Springfield as noted in his July 7 letter. Indeed, as late as May 8, my mother did not even know my father's full name, mistaking his middle name for "Adrian" rather than "Alexander."

Running like a refrain throughout his letters of 1944 is a request for constant letters from my mother and for photographs of her. On April 1, he writes, "It's been quite a while since I have received mail from you, so you can imagine how anxious I am to hear from you." He scolds her often for not writing to him frequently enough, reminding her that she had promised to respond each time she received a letter from him. He seems to forget the vagaries of the wartime postal service, even when he often received a cache of four or five letters from her all at once.

The demand for letters is understandable: they are courting exclusively by written word after only a few dates. They do not yet know each other. Their words on paper must provide introductions: in them they attempt to dramatize their personalities, display their characters, expose their quirks and foibles, construct selves in three dimensions, and create their relationship along tenuous handwritten lines inscribed on skimpy wartime paper. Their letters exhibit an anxious need for constant affirmations that, in the face of possibly years of absence, only their letters can create. On May 9, my father writes, "I don't really think you can write too often because it's the only time I can feel myself near you."

My father is even more insistent that my mother send him photographs of herself. She, on the other hand, seems reluctant to comply, perhaps because she is not yet sure she wants her image entrusted to someone she barely knows. There is an intimacy about sharing her picture that she seems not ready for yet.

Letters, frequently exchanged, can reveal the inner person—or at least what one wishes to project of it—but physical attraction, a necessary motivator of romance, is maintained by images. One forgets in a short time the exact lineaments of a face and body when absent from a physical presence. Desire and attraction lock a person in one's affections more than words in letters alone can do. "I am very much afraid I won't receive a photo at all," my father complains on April 14. "This brings up another point," he continues, "maybe you will not send a photograph because you think I am insincere when I write these letters, or maybe it's because you don't think enough of me to send the same." Again on July 17, he grouses, "Sometimes I wonder if you're being fair to me. If you won't send me a picture, then I want a sincere answer from you. You have given me your love, dear, and you have mine, so I find it very difficult to figure out why you continue putting off sending your picture." "Unless I get that picture soon, it's going to be terrible for both of us," he thundered on August 3.

My mother seems so protective of her image for several possible reasons. First, she seems to fear that he will show her picture around to his soldier buddies. She even asks him if he has done so with the previous snapshots she has sent him. These photographs did not satisfy my father because they were distant shots or because she was represented surrounded by others he does not know and has no interest in. My father is quick to assure her that he would never share her photographs.

My mother may also have been hesitant to send him photographs because, then in her early 30's, she may have felt that her picture would reveal a more mature woman than the girlfriends of my father's fellow soldiers, themselves mostly in their early to mid-20's with girlfriends even younger.

Further evidence for this comes in my mother's reluctance to provide my father with the date of her birth. He asks for that information several times: "I don't think you gave me the date of your birth," he writes on April 23, but then he seems to think this too forward: "Maybe this request is a little out of order, so don't think anything of my asking." He does not ask her here for the date of her birthday. He apparently knows that. He asks, instead, for the year of her birth, information my mother does not divulge, for he asks for this information again on August 22.

Being over six years older than my father, my mother was always reticent about sharing her age with those she decided had no need to know it, including her children until we became adults. My mother was often older than the mothers of my friends and classmates. As such, she was usually the most poised, the most verbal, the least shy, and the wittiest of those often much younger mothers.

Finally, my mother relents and sends some photographs which my father deems acceptable and which he acknowledges on August 14: "I must admit now with these swell pictures, I am beginning to see what you really look like. Not bad, if you ask me!"

About halfway through the year, my father begins to fill his many letters with passionate protestations of love for my mother. Apparently before she replied in kind, she asked about his romantic availability. On March 28, he admits to having had a girlfriend for eight months and was even engaged at one time before entering the service, but he quickly assures my mother that he terminated "this particular love affair" because he found out "a few things about this young lady that did not measure up to par." Though the details of this "love affair" and its rupture are vague in the extreme, my mother seems satisfied with this guarantee of his freedom from previous amorous involvements.

My father's love-language is tentative at first, as on March 30 he writes, "Believe it or not, when I express love for you, I am very sincere and I expect you to believe me." On May 16, he concludes his letter with "Now I can say I love you so very much," and on August 14, after finally receiving a new, much-delayed photograph, he writes "I have your recent picture before me, dear, and I can't help but realize how much I love you." In little more than a year since meeting her and having seen her only a few times, my father seems certain he is in love, a sentiment shared by my mother.

This is not to say that doubts and questions did not surface, sometimes in surprising juxtapositions with incongruous amorous assertions. As late as April 14, a year into this mail-in courtship, my father could write, "It's very funny, you know, at times I wonder if you're just writing to be writing to a soldier. This, by the way, is very common to soldiers and sailors overseas. You can imagine how grave the situation has become. Let's get down to brass tacks: No doubt you have been going steady and perhaps are so at present. You only have to tell me about it and nothing more will be said."

Since I have only his correspondence, it is impossible to know what triggered this sudden accusation. My father concludes with "I must have your reactions to this letter." My mother's response to this impugning of her integrity and her motives was apparently indignation leading to an icy silence. As late as April 26, my father has had no response, noting that "No doubt something has happened to you." He suspects that her lack of communication is due to "something in one of my recent letters that didn't go over too big." By April 28, two weeks after his offensive letter, he had received her reaction: "Wow!" he exclaims, "You sure can dish it out!"

By May 5 he seems to have resolved his doubts about my mother's sincerity and declared himself satisfied with her response, incensed though it obviously was: "I can readily see now that our love is very true and by all means lasting. You know, before, I never did think you really cared for me. I only thought you wrote to be writing to a soldier you had met previously." My mother's renewed umbrage over this unwise reminder of his offensive letter of April 14 prompts my father on June 9 to apologize once again and to attempt to bring the unhappy matter to a close: "What a heel I was to write that letter some time ago! I can't blame you for taking such an attitude. I am so sorry to disappoint you, and I want you to forget the incident because I have."

My father's letters of 1944 record the dailyness of life in the 19th Depot Supply Squadron as stationed in North Africa and then in Italy. He records the titles of the Hit Parade tunes he listens to as he writes his letters. For example, on July 24 he notes that the song "Louise," my mother's name, is "returning to the Hit Parade. Every time I hear that number, I can't help but think of you, since I love you so much." He notes the operas he attends in Rome, a musical taste he developed in Italy and enjoyed throughout his life. He was also excited about having seen Betty Grable in "Pin-Up Girl."

He records generalized ideas about the conduct and duration of the war, though all of his letters were monitored and passages occasionally blacked out by the varied censors who stamped their seals at the upper left corner of each of his letters. At other times, he laments the passing of his youth while away from the life he wants to be living. On March 29, he notes wistfully that "when an individual spends the latter part of his twenties in the army, those precious years won't come again." "You're not kidding when you wished the war was over," he writes on April 5, "because I can't hardly wait for the end myself." But he is realistic: on June 18, he notes that "the people in the U. S. actually think the war is over with, but personally I don't think it will be over so soon. I can see much hard fighting ahead even though I am not participating in such at present. I wouldn't be too optimistic at this time." He was, of course, right in this prediction.

But mostly the letters lament his deep loneliness. In his letter of April 8, written exactly a year after having first met my mother, he writes: "I want to tell you at this time I never was so lonesome for you since I have been overseas." "I do get so lonesome for you," he notes on August 13, and this loneliness always prompts him to write to her "because it is the only way I can be with you for a few moments." On July 13, he notes that the night before while lying on his cot, "All I did was look at the stars and the moon and think about you." Realizing that he has to explain how this could be, he notes that he shares a tent with three other soldiers. The tent is of a heavy green-drab canvas, stiff and pervaded with a musty odor. The sides roll up to cool the tent and to reveal the dreamy silver of the Italian moonlight and the balmy night's clear stars. At these times, he explains, he muses on my mother, on his longing for her, and on their futures together as the last thoughts of his day.

Of that future, my father shares his dreams with my mother, occasionally with a male decisiveness that contemporary women might find insensitive. He moves from March 6 uncertainty ("Perhaps sometime in the future we will get together") to a greater confidence that such a reconnection will occur, as on May 16, he writes, "Can you picture the two of us spending an afternoon on the beach after the war is over? I can!" On May 21, after returning from a tour of one of the Palladian villas on the Italian coast, he muses that the villa and its gardens "would be an ideal place for a honeymoon." By June 21, he asks my mother, "Do you think you would like to live in the South?" though he concedes he could "be living in the Midwest should the opportunity present itself." By August 22, he indicates that all his plans for after the war "are built up around you," and he follows this in his next letter of August 24 with "It might be interesting to note that I have decided that we will live in Baton Rouge." He softens this in a seeming after-thought: "provided everything is agreeable with you." From what he indicates in a letter dated September 13, my mother agrees to consider making a home with him in Louisiana, thereby holding him to his promise of May 5: "I will be growing old along with you, provided you let me."

In spite of these seeming conclusions about their future together, doubts inevitably creep in. On April 23, my father refers to a concern my mother expressed: "Along about the end of your letter, you mentioned something about our love unfolding so naturally that it made you almost afraid at times." She expressed similar concerns as reflected in my father's letter of May 22: "I wouldn't be afraid of that jealous sort of 'Fate' lurking around you because I do love you so much." My father too worries at times about the strength of their epistolary connection. As late as December 20, he wonders "about our reactions when we do see each other again," but hastens to assure her that "I don't think our reactions will be unfavorable toward each other because, after all, we do love each other and that, in my opinion, is a very good quality to start with."

My mother writes lengthy letters filled with amusing anecdotes about her job, her family and friends, her dog, her neighbors, her occupations and amusements. In one case, she pens a 25-page letter in response to his asking her to describe her family. Of this epistle, my father notes on September 2, "It was just like reading a book. How you did it is beyond me." He also confesses that "I can't quite figure out your father," a lion-taming, safari-organizing, vagabond proprietor of a Vaudeville act titled "The Hjlan Wonder Birds," a troupe of trained cockatoos.

In contrast to my mother's letters, my father's many short, rote "V-mails" to her have about them a predictable sameness. My mother apparently encouraged him to write more descriptive letters, objecting to his mere outline of his tour of Rome which amounted to a simple short-hand list of sights, available in the glossary of any guidebook. She seems to have forgotten that first on the list of dislikes she had earlier prompted from him was "writing letters." "Please don't be disappointed if I write too much about nothing," he

pleads on October 10: "There is nothing to write about."
Again on December 11, he acknowledges that "There is no
doubt in my mind my letters are somewhat boresome at
times," but it is "hard to write often and interesting when
there is very little to write about." This near-constant
complaint indicates how much he found letter writing an
unpleasant obligation, but he doggedly persists "just to say
again I do love you so."

The year ended in an argument. On November 6, my
father wrote that he disliked "being flattered in any way. I
wrote this because I noticed lately your letters have been
more or less on the flattering side; and I don't think that is
necessary if we love each other the way we say we do." My
mother apparently fired off a defensive letter which my
father objected to: "It certainly was not nice of you," my
father complained in his last letter of the year, December 29,
"to send me the air mail letter of November 15 concerning
your various definitions of the word 'flattery.' I thought we
agreed at one time in the past that we would bring up our
little difficulties without being angry at each other." My
mother further stirred his ire by referring to "the flattery and
insincerity of most of the Southern people," a comment sure
to exacerbate his defensiveness about his Southern origins.
To top it off, my mother's later letter of December 17 asked
him bluntly, "Do you now feel differently about me?" To
this, he responded in his letter of December 29: "I guess one
letter was not enough to worry about, I had to receive a
second one!"

My father cannot seem to let go of my mother's anger:
"I don't expect you to be angry at me; and I don't expect
another of your November 15th letters unless you have actual
reasons to write one." His letter of December 29 is the
longest he wrote all year. My mother had asked for a longer
letter from him. She could not have been pleased with

getting one at last, though my father concludes it with "Until next time, Darling, I am sending all my love."

IV
1945: The Return to Civilian Life

The ardor of a courtship depends on a convergence of the outer and inner selves of those involved. Usually, each partner is first attracted by the physical presence of the other, ideally a mutual attraction founded upon physical features, manner of speaking and walking and acting, particulars of dress and style, perhaps even compatible pheromones. To this attraction are accreted inner components, the thoughts, ideas, qualities, and opinions as aired in the conversations and interactions of two people corporeally present to each other.

My parents' courtship diverged from this usual pattern in significant ways. They met only a few times over several weekends, my father having to hitch a ride from his base in Dayton to my mother's hometown of Springfield to meet her. He had to return to his barracks later that night after each of their several dates. My father was shipped out almost immediately after these encounters, but something impelled him to maintain this frail early connection with my mother. Their only recourse was to construct for each other their inner lives and personalities in words, their intimate thoughts and wishes, hopes and opinions, a display of their individual selves fleshed out in their imaginations from static photographs and from the thin handwritten lines of their letters, devoid of a physical meeting for close to three years.

Theirs, then, was an extraordinary courtship. They were unable to build it from any shared experiences. They were unable, for example, to exchange furtive, complicit smiles at

Easter morning Mass when their sightlines to the altar were blocked by a stout lady's enormous Easter hat, tarted up with silk flowers and looking like a fresh grave. Theirs was not to be a sharing of mutual tastes and preferences as they strolled idly together a downtown boulevard, pausing to peer into shop windows to daydream and comment on the wares. Nor were they able to kiss on a porch in a night soft with the scent of gardenias, the porch light turned off, a whir of moths dispelled. Deprived of this food of love, it must have been difficult to assure themselves that their attraction was real. And this assurance became more difficult to maintain the longer they were separated, as their letters of 1945 reveal.

After the strain on their connection at the conclusion of 1944, their epistolary courtship returned to an easy familiarity early in 1945, though not so wholly that my mother could lay her misgivings completely to rest. My father's letter of January 1 attempts to quell any lingering apprehensions my mother might yet be harboring: "I do realize you doubt my love for you at times, but I do love you, darling. I can only send my love in writing at this time, so I do find it very difficult to remove any possible doubt from your mind. Please don't doubt anything about me." Shortly after penning these commitments, he received a letter from my mother indicating that her doubts had been silenced: "It was especially nice to know you have removed the doubt from your mind concerning the different feeling I might have about us," he wrote on January 3.

Many of my father's one-page V-mail posts of early 1945 remain what my father himself termed the same "boresome" letters written in 1944: descriptions of his lonesome bedtime ritual of trying to crank out letters to radio Hit Parade ballads, his going to sleep dreaming of being with my mother, his continuous protestations of love for her, his complaints about letter writing when he is unable to find anything of interest to write about. He indicates he has been transferred to France from Italy and pays a surprise visit to his brother then stationed in Belgium but is prevented from providing any details about his travels because his letters are strictly censored. He writes also of his enjoyment of my mother's long, detailed letters while deflecting her requests for the same from him.

However, towards April, two full years into their connection, his letter writing begins to flag noticeably. He offers lame excuses for their growing infrequency, such as his new preoccupation with developing photographs with a friend during sessions lasting well past midnight. Or that the censors have become so restrictive that almost anything of substance he could write would be blacked out. Or that lately, being transferred throughout Europe as the war waned, he was bogged down with the increased logistical work falling to him as the troops began to move faster and faster toward the German heartland.

My mother, following the progression of the war in Europe, began to ask in her letters when my father thought he might be returning to the States, either on furlough or a hoped-for discharge from the Army Air Corps. In his letter of April 23, he outlined for her the possibilities inherent in his immediate future: "Here are a few of the possible things that might happen: be transferred to the Infantry from the Air Corps, be transferred to the Pacific area direct, or be sent to the U. S. for a short furlough and then be sent to the Pacific. We may be part of the police force to remain in Europe when hostilities cease. One of the four is sure to happen. I don't think this throws too much light on your question, but it is all I know at present."

In his next letter, April 27, he indicates that his correspondence with her will become "irregular for the next two weeks" because of his growing fascination with photography. But a new and more troubling note creeps into this letter. He indicates that my mother's letters are the only real connection to her that he feels now. He goes on to admit that he looks forward to her letters "because I do miss seeing you, so much so that I often wonder how you really look. I can look at your pictures, but these don't appear very natural to me anymore since it has been so long since we have seen each other."

After April, my father's letters are spaced farther and farther apart, dwindling in frequency until on May 19 my father finally pens a farewell letter: "I have been thinking it is almost useless to continue our correspondence as in the past because I find the same is leading to nothing. Our love could continue but I am afraid it would mean nothing because we are spending most of our best times apart and, as a result, I don't want you to be disappointed when and if I return to the U. S. You see, we don't know each other too well, and besides, we are not learning anything about each other as time goes by. It is no easy matter for me to write this letter, but I see no reason why we should continue writing to each other when we don't know what the future holds for us. I trust you can understand why I write this letter." He omits the concluding protestation of love, ending with just his signature.

This letter, certainly dismaying to my mother, is directly connected to the date of its composition, May 19. The war in Europe had ended on VE Day, May 8. Suddenly my father seems to realize that he has entangled himself in an uncertain relationship, that it was one thing to dispel some of his loneliness by writing to a faraway woman who returns his letters and his avowals of affection, to while away those lonely evenings writing to an imagined woman while listening to romantic ballads on the radio as the warm, velvety Italian nights display a moon and stars to set off his romantic reveries. Here, now, reality suddenly intrudes and with it the demands of encountering a real person with only a vague presence based on a few dates a long time ago. Faced with the sudden immediacy of his situation, he seems to have lost his nerve.

His next letter, June 27, over a month after his break-up letter, expresses surprise that my mother decided to answer the May 19 letter at all. He indicates that it was "very hard for me to write that last letter but I just had to." "I must tell you," he continues, "it has been quite some time since we saw each other and, to make matters worse, we didn't know each other too well or too long when I was in the U. S." Then he attempts the magnanimous, pointing out that he may have several more years of enlisted life before the war in the Pacific concludes: "We are both getting along in age and I don't think it's smart for you to wait for me." This reference to aging must have stung, my mother already sensitive to the difference in their ages. He ends this letter with "Best wishes," thereby confirming their separation.

My mother seems not to have given up on the relationship in spite of my father's attempts to end it. By August 2, the connection was tentatively reestablished, my mother having written to my father several times during the long interim since his last letter of June 27. He expresses surprise "to find out you haven't been having dates," and he expresses appreciation "for your love for me, and I want you to know I love you as much." Then this letter reverts to the old round traced in so many previous letters: listening to the radio, nothing much happening so nothing to write about, and concluding with the old formula renewed: "I love you so much, Darling."

This seeming reconciliation was, however, short-lived, for in his next letter, dated September 23, his birthday, my father provides a lengthy explanation of what has happened in the interim when he stopped communicating. He had been redeployed to the Pacific, but "when we were halfway across the ocean, we found out the Pacific war had come to an end" and so the ship pivoted in its voyage and returned to the U. S. He expected an honorable discharge from the Air Corps by October 1.

In this letter, he explains why he sent the two letters ending their connection, and he suggests again that their relationship should, in fact, conclude. First, he suggests in a tantalizingly vague manner that neither his physical nor his mental health is robust, that he "will have to spend part of my savings for treatment in the very near future" (an early sign of the hypochondria my father exhibited all his life). Another reason offered for this new attempt to end things is that my mother obviously failed to realize "what type of person I am. The same is true for me because I don't really understand you." He notes that gleanings from their long correspondence have provided him with "the impression you would dislike doing some of the things I would perhaps like to do." This leads him to conclude that 'I really don't think we could get along well enough to live a very happy life together at the conclusion of the war."

Though he seems to have decided that all was over between them, he, paradoxically, wants her "to continue writing to me (even though your love for me has come to an end). I really don't expect to hear from you again, and if such is the case, I am really sorry and ashamed of myself." He concludes this letter with the baffling "As ever."

My mother apparently interpreted my father's waffling and confusion as resulting from years of regimented Army routine during which he lacked the freedom to make any real decisions regarding his future. He seems overwhelmed by the new post-war vista opening before him with all its possibilities and inchoate prospects. He confesses as much in his letter of October 29 wherein he indicates that since his honorable discharge on October 6, "I haven't been able to hold onto myself. I mean by this I am somewhat lost." In a romantic aside, he notes that in the midst of his confusion "I always think about you." "It seems," he continues, "that I must see you sometime soon." He worries that these assertions, following so soon on others that these so starkly contradict, will cause her "to think I am completely nuts" and "perhaps I am and that it may not be a fault of my own."

My mother was not a silent receptor of my father's confused and erratic attempts to right himself. She wrote to him after receiving his several separation letters, cautioning him that, as he quotes her in this October 29 letter, "love was not a faucet that could be turned on or off at any one time if love was ever present." He agrees with this and adds that since being home, "I have had a few dates but find it almost impossible to have a good time," remembering instead "the good times that you and I had together." He continues: "It is these things and many other thoughts that come to my mind that make me realize I still love you." Though suspecting he might be "wasting my time," he nevertheless asks for her telephone number and a time when he might call her. "I will be anxiously waiting to receive an answer from you," he concludes, appending a "Best wishes" above his signature.

His next letter, November 25, reveals my father's mounting confusion, tantamount to some kind of nervous breakdown. It is a sad, uncertain letter, a rudderless floundering disorientation. Clearly, he is suffering some sort of post-war psychological distress, traumatized by what he had witnessed during the war. (He would carry that trauma through a lifetime of nightmare-haunted and often sleepless nights.) In this letter, he acknowledges receipt of two letters from my mother but can offer her no reasons for not answering them: "I did not resent anything you wrote in either of your letters. I am not angry at you, and I don't think I could ever be angry at you," feelings my mother apparently attributed to him as reasons for his silence. He then proceeds to the crux of his difficulties: "During the time I have been home, I have been dissatisfied with just about everything I have come in contact with." He hastens to assure her that "I don't think I am going crazy or anything like it," but, in spite of a good job with the U. S. Employment Service helping returning G.I.'s secure jobs in the shaky post-war economy, "I can't settle down and realize what I have. I am so undecided about everything, at times I do think my best bet is to get married and attempt to settle down."

This desperate solution to my father's distress could not have persuaded my mother of the wisdom of committing to such a tenuous marital proposition, especially because he soon follows the rash idea of marriage as a way out of his difficulties with an even more desperate solution: "I seem to have so many worries on my mind and yet when I attempt to solve some of these worries, I find I have nothing to worry about." (This tendency of excessive worrying was to devil my father throughout his long life.) So great is his distress and resulting desperation that he comes to believe "the best place for me is the Army, and yet with the job I have, I couldn't possibly do that because it would hurt my mother so much." This pull-push quandary leaves him cast adrift, grasping at any conceivable resolution which will serve to anchor him, including impetuously returning to the Army life he was so eager to free himself from.

My father protests a continuing love for my mother in this desperate letter: "I do love you even though we are far apart and I do believe I could love you more and more when it will be possible for me to see you personally." He acknowledges that my mother's letters to him at this time were "hard ones," which "I can't blame you for writing. I wouldn't want to hurt you in any way, believe me." He concludes with hoping this letter of November 25 will help her to "realize I need help and, if you can offer any suggestions, please do and I will try to follow them if at all possible. It seems that I can't forget you even when I am most upset." He ends this letter with a simple "I love you."

My mother, ever the ardent Catholic, offers him as sure staff and prop a religious medal and a Novena booklet outlining nine days of prayer and devotional practices in order to attain a goal or desire. In his letter of December 6, he professes to be happy to have received her encouraging letter and indicates that "before long I will realize what a swell person you are, and I am beginning to realize I can't do without you." Then, with a sense of urgency and seemingly out of the blue, he proposes that she spend the upcoming Christmas holidays with him. He suggests that she travel to Louisiana "to spend your accumulated leave with me," because it "is hard for me to try and explain in writing what I want to tell you."

As he warms to this plan, his tone grows increasingly animated, almost feverish: he offers her several possible arrival dates and train schedules, commits to paying all her expenses, promises to occupy her entire visit with entertaining options, assures her that his family is eager to meet her, suggests that she might consider traveling by airplane instead of the train to give them more time together, pleads for her to consider this invitation favorably, explains that he has no accumulated leave yet on his new job so cannot join her in Ohio, and pledges his love for her. Apparently my father envisioned this projected visit as a remedy for his post-war malaise and indecisiveness. The plans for it galvanize him into an energy and animation he has been unable to muster since leaving the Air Corps.

My mother accepts this spirited invitation, though she decides to remain with her family for Christmas, proposing to come South for New Year's instead. My father's exuberance seems to grow, as evidenced in his letter of December 13: "You can't imagine how happy I was to receive your letter this evening. I can't help but look forward to the day when I will meet you at the train. I can hardly wait! I don't think you should worry about the mood you might find me in because I will be so happy to see you!" Over two and a half years had elapsed since they had last seen each other. Both must have been wary of time's transformations and revisions to their increasingly nebulous memories of each other and to the few static photographs they exchanged over that lengthy time.

This letter of December 13 is exuberant with plans for her visit, especially a projected sojourn in New Orleans for New Year's Eve and Day. He has invited a friend from his squadron to join them, apparently as chaperone. This New Orleans trip did not materialize: my father forgot that the Sugar Bowl was played in New Orleans over New Year's and hotel accommodations were impossible to secure. Perhaps my father mentions the presence of his friend to blunt the force of his amorous overtures. He will not, he says, "be able to sleep at all while you're here with me. This is not a threat, Darling, so don't be alarmed." This is, of course, sexual banter, and more followed: in a postscript to this letter, my father adds that "it will be wonderful <u>to love you and love you</u> during these cold holiday nights," for it is on cold nights that "I would like to love you best."

In a letter of December 17, he confesses that he stays up "half the night thinking about you and the few times I saw you in Springfield and the fun we had those few times." He promises to spend her entire visit "loving you up." These assertions seem odd liberties given that the wreck of their relationship had only very recently been righted, and tenuously at that. My mother's feeble attempts to douse this unexpected ardor are reflected in my father's final letter of 1945, December 21, where he refers to my mother's "threat" to "put ice down my neck." Surely, he concludes, "you're trying to tease me."

This letter ends with his concern that they will not recognize each other at the train station. He describes for her what he will be wearing and prepares her that his hair, longer now and wavier, makes him look different from the soldier she first met so long ago.

V
1946: The Post-War World

My mother's visit to Louisiana over the 1946 New Year holiday occasioned several outcomes. Most importantly, it rekindled the love for each other that my parents had been shaping in the many letters ranging back and forth for years between Europe and the U. S. and, more recently, between Louisiana and Ohio. This confirmation of romantic interest was by no means a certainty. They had not seen each other for close to three years, a long span of time to nurture a love affair devoid of kisses, embraces, dates, shared experiences, or any of the other necessary incitements to love. And, too, my father had broken up with my mother in May 1945 before his honorable discharge from the Army.

A second outcome of my mother's visit was to introduce her to the alien world she contemplated entering. Coming from a middle-class German immigrant family from the Midwest, she must have seen my father's middle-class Italian immigrant family as exotic, especially framed as it was in a land of bayous, oysters, alligators, and cypress swamps, a Southern Louisiana Mediterranean gumbo of

French, Italian, Creole, Black, and Cajun cultures. She clearly understood that she was venturing into this strange land out of the conservative Midwest and her own particular background populated by two sisters, aunts and uncles, friends, priests, and nuns, almost all of whom were devout Catholic celibates. (I have excluded from this group her Lutheran Vaudeville vagabond father who was rarely ever around his family.)

Finally, my mother's visit revealed what my father and his family judged in her to be objectionable traits and behaviors, which my father was quick to point out but which he considered correctable. My mother was at a clear disadvantage on this initial visit: she knew little about my father or his family, largely uneducated and provincial, confined to a small backwater Italian-immigrant village on the Mississippi River between Baton Rouge and New Orleans but having little commerce with either urban center. These Italian immigrants had engaged in one great journey in their lifetimes away from the rock-scrabble farms of Sicily to an insignificant river town in Louisiana. There they stuck, evincing little further interest in engaging with the larger world.

My mother, on the other hand, was from a mid-sized industrial Ohio city in a heavily populated urban center near Dayton, Cincinnati, and Columbus, cities frequented by my mother and her family and friends. Consequently, she was more worldly, more cosmopolitan and sophisticated. She presented herself in that way to my father's insular family and community with her long ivory cigarette holder and Lucky Strikes, her brimming liquor flask she kept in her purse and her penchant for mixing and enjoying the day's popular cocktails with the silver-plated shaker she brought with her, her tailored suits and rakish hats, her seamed hose and smart-ass pumps, and her open and forthright personality, all features my father's family deemed forward, even femininely unsuitable in the world she entered without sufficient knowledge or preparation.

Though my father in his letter of January 2 relayed to my mother several tepid compliments extended to her by his acquaintances, she quickly learned that my father's family was uncertain of her suitability for him. Their more vocal objections were that she smoked too much and drank too freely, talked too easily and too volubly, and was generally more socially outgoing and genially familiar than they were comfortable with or could approve of. They judged her too worldly-wise, too sophisticated, a woman who "had been around" and would find little to satisfy her in the small-town world my father could offer her. They let my father know they thought her too old for him. They were suspicious of her German and Midwestern roots and her irregular family life. In short, her visit occasioned much discussion as to her ability to inhabit their world happily, both for herself and for them. Though they eventually reconciled themselves to my father's choice of wife, and though my mother always maintained cordial connections with them, she never forgot their early response to her.

My father's family soon communicated their reservations to my father, who was quick to address them in the letter he penned to my mother immediately on her return to Ohio. After several perfunctory inquiries about her journey home by crowded post-holiday train, my father launched into those habits and traits of my mother's he did not approve of. On January 12, just over a week after her return to Ohio, he prepares her for his complaints by reminding her that "we decided to hold nothing back from each other, no matter how personal it might be." "Since you have been away," he continues, "I have been thinking about two things that I personally want you to make every possible attempt to break. The first thing I want you to start working on is to try and stop smoking." He condescends to admit that she is "old enough to know what you want to do" and that he has "no right to ask such of you." He assures her that he "wouldn't ask this of anyone I really didn't love."

The second "habit" concerned her "alcoholic drinking" which apparently she evinced too great a fondness for while visiting in White Castle and on their dates at "Mike's Roadhouse" and at the "Pirate Room" in Baton Rouge: "I am asking you, darling, how much do you drink when at home? Be sincere when you write your next letter and please don't be angry with me because what I have written has certainly not changed my love for you." Rather than ask her directly if she is a lush, he asks her to imagine their sitting together holding hands as they have this conversation. He wants "to know if you think your drinking is just something I shouldn't be concerned about" and "if you think you could see these things in the same light as I see them," and, he fails to add, as his family sees them as well. My father blunts the sharp edges of these disapproving criticisms with continual hopes that he has "not hurt your feelings in any way."

Apparently my father worries he has gone too far in his letter of January 12 because he follows it on January 14 wherein he returns to the smoking and drinking issues, citing his resolve not to keep matters like these to himself "because we may be married someday, provided you agree to such an occasion, and I think these things should be settled." He also worries that her affable familiarity and her social openness will need some reining in were she to move to Louisiana: "You will have to adjust yourself to a different type of living and possibly a different type of social life." He assures her he does not mean she "will suffer physically [!], socially, or otherwise because I will devote myself to making you happy in every possible way," but nonetheless "these adjustments will have to be made if you have to live in the South." He worries that these behavioral modifications he is calling upon her to make "might result in causing you much unhappiness in the future." Should they be married, he struggles to clarify, he wants "to be sure you want to make these changes" in the frank and artless familiarity which will set her apart in the sober backwater she would be entering. He broaches these issues because, he assures her, "I will have to know you're happy because otherwise our possible marriage might be a failure and I certainly don't want this to happen to me because I feel I don't deserve it." The egocentrism of this last assertion did not seem to faze my mother, though her responses to these letters have not been retained.

My father cannot seem to let well-enough alone, returning again to these issues in a letter penned the next day, January 15. He begins by assuring my mother that "I don't have anything to tear into you about at this time" and desires her, in the interest of fair play, to be equally candid about any issues she feels that he needs to address, "knowing I am not perfect." He worries he might be "trying to enter into your personal life before time" but assures her he addresses these issues early on because "I want you to be the ideal that I would have for a wife."

His concerns seem to subside in his letter of January 21, where he professes himself satisfied with my mother's responses to his earlier letters: "I don't think you could have answered my letters in a better way. Your answers are fair enough and I will hold you to them at the proper time, particularly the smoking." But then he cannot refrain from getting in one last caution concerning my mother's drinking, warning her that consuming too much alcohol "can become harmful at sometime in the future."

He concludes this letter by promising to leave these criticisms behind so as to assure her "how much I love you in spite of the fact you mentioned you almost felt sure I couldn't return the love you had for me." My mother cleverly responds to these complaints by putting my father on the defensive: "You continue to think," he notes, that "I am holding back on my love for you whereas I am not." "I have no one else in mind," he continues, and he conjectures that he "won't be able to prove how much I love you till we're actually together."

My mother acknowledges her misjudging of the social expectations she fails to meet during her visit. My father cites a passage from one of her letters: "Now I understand how others must have felt about me and how clumsily and cruelly I must have treated them because I didn't understand and couldn't return their feeling." This puzzling self-abnegation was extreme, as my father hastens to assure her on January 21: "I can think of only one way to measure our love and that is to get married, at which time I will devote all in my power to making you happy." This letter concludes with his commending my mother on her growing "conception of a small-town housewife" and assures her that if in that role "you think you could be happy, then you have solved a problem and have made me even more sure of myself."

But he has not yet put his concerns to rest. On February 3, he references again her "flaws," as he calls them: "Very much pleased to find out you're doing so well with your campaign against those two vices—cigarettes and liquor." He continues to interrogate her as to her progress in eradicating these two "vices" throughout his pre-nuptial letters to her, including in his letter of June 23, written after they have become formally engaged. In answer to my mother's owning up to still smoking "a little," he writes

"When we are married, I expect you to stop altogether," though he amends this demanding tone with the assurance that "We will be happy together, darling, I am sure of this!"

In addition to concerns about my mother's smoking, drinking, and adaptability to life in the South was my mother's age. Born in 1911, she was only thirteen years younger than my father's mother, who was born in 1898. My mother was self-conscious about the age difference with my father, born in 1917, and did not take it well when my father indicated in his letter of June 20 that he has forgotten "the date of your birth," and "you had better send the year too!" He realizes he has cut too close to the quick here and attempts to salve the wound: "I can see you now, I am mean, darling, and I hope you won't be angry and don't you worry, I love you with all my heart regardless." He promises never to mention her age again: "Please don't feel angry and please don't think anything will happen. It won't, I promise, because I love you."

My mother responded negatively to this attempted levity over what she perceived as a real concern for my father and his family, so my father assures her on June 30 that he will not forget her birthday—day and year—again: "I had no motive in asking for your birthday," he assures her, but then callously twits her further: "I will publish it, in fact I am having it put in the form of a news release in the local papers. Angry?—better not be because I am kidding and besides I wouldn't tell anyone because it wouldn't concern them." He concludes: "I love you, darling, regardless of what your thoughts are concerning our birthdays." This matter seems to end with this letter, and by then, they were already engaged.

Their engagement occurred during my father's visit to my mother in Springfield, Ohio, in May. Before he could bring himself to offer this proposal, however, he had to satisfy himself on one other important matter: vetting her on her previous connections with other men. He clearly asks if she is a virgin in his letter of March 2: "I want to ask you certain questions that may sound personal." They are indeed personal: "In your past life, darling, did you ever have any affair with any man that you would be ashamed or afraid to tell me about? Perhaps these things are trivial to you but to me they are important." He acknowledges with relief her "frank" but "sharp" response to this question in his letter of March 9, admitting that he did not know "if my love would have stood the test had you admitted a 'previous indiscretion.'" Clearly my mother asked in her "sharp" response if his professed love for her was dependent on her being a virgin and expressed displeasure with the implications of his possible answer. According to my mother, both of them were virgins on their wedding night as my father seems to admit in this letter: "I think I have lived a real clean and normal life, and I wouldn't be afraid to compare it with any other man's past life. I am happy and proud to have lived such a life."

Other considerations had to be addressed. For instance, my father questioned my mother's commitment to a serious Catholicism. He makes a virtual date with her to listen together to Bishop Fulton J. Sheen on radio's Catholic Hour: "Did you carry out your part of our date, darling?" he asks on February 17. Sheen had addressed the issue of birth control, "Something that really concerns us in our future lives," as my father adds. He goes on to say how emphatically opposed to birth control his parish priest is, as evidenced by that morning's sermon at Mass in which the priest "does not hold back" and "does not hesitate to call anyone down." My mother concurred with him. In their married life they did not use artificial birth control, preferring the Catholic-approved "Rhythm Method," which my mother claimed worked for them, a claim belied by the actual sequencing of their children and by assertions to the contrary in my mother's later letters announcing her pregnancies.

Another important consideration surfaced when my mother questioned whether or not she would be able to continue in her career as a medical records librarian in a hospital after their marriage. In his letter of February 24, he responds: "I am almost totally against working wives unless the husband possesses a disability whereas the family might suffer. For young couples I am totally against it." He acknowledges that as a supervisor for the U. S. Employment Service, he has to place both men and women equally in jobs, though the only "placing" he is interested in with my mother is "placing you in my arms, kissing you, and holding you tight!" In his follow-up letter on this issue, he does ask about my mother's spending habits, cautioning her that "you may have to budget our, or my, salary," an uneasy admission that they will have to economize on only one paycheck.

This attitude against working wives persisted in their early marriage, with the exception of my mother's taking dictation for letters and insurance invoices from several local doctors in her home for a little extra income. Later, when faced with considerable tuition obligations with five children in parochial schools, my mother returned to work at an area hospital.

Though ever optimistic, my mother must have had her own concerns about the connection she found herself encouraging. In his letter of February 8, my father confesses to being "upset" and feeling that everything is "out of place": "I seem to be so dissatisfied with everything, even little things." He is unhappy living with his parents and unhappy with his work, blaming "my recent Army career" for these general dissatisfactions. He notes that "As far as I can figure, my solution is being with you." This assertion must have both confirmed the solidity of their connection and, at the same time, set off alarms for my mother as she realized that no one without training can help to solve psychological problems like these for another. Clearly my father's adjustment to life after the war did not progress smoothly.

In addition to his persistent anxiety and clearly related to it, my father was suffering near continuous gastric distress, which he referred to as "nervous stomach," and was under a doctor's care. This doctor had been prescribing various medications with minimal results. In his letter of February 19, my father acknowledged that he "was under the impression this medicine was for the stomach disorder," only to find out "the medicine was not for my stomach but for my nerves." On March 11, he announced his diagnosis: "I have a very nervous stomach, in fact, extremely nervous." (These stomach complaints plagued my father for the remainder of his long life, as did his "nerve issues.")

On March 8, my father complains of things "not going my way for some reason or another" and that "so many small problems come up daily that I have to deal with" that he thinks "about the Army and how we didn't worry about many of these small things." In this same letter, he acknowledges that his stomach doctor told him that he "was having a tough time getting adjusted to civilian life" and that "it was taking a bit longer than most other individuals." In his letter of March 21, he attempts to settle the doubts that understandably arose in my mother as she read with dismay of his multiple dissatisfactions: "Darling, nothing is troubling me concerning you in such a way that I doubt anything about you." "Oh," he continues on March 24, "if you only knew how much I love you, darling, you would never doubt me or anything I wrote or did." As late as July

19, after they had become engaged, he seems to think his marriage will immediately and completely right things for him: "I keep telling myself you will be the one to help me. I can't help but think you will bring me happiness and also can't help but think we will both be happy."

My father's recent breakup with my mother, his "dissatisfactions with everything," his wistful reminiscences of how easy Army life was, his complaints about her "vices" and his family's initial coolness concerning her, his persistent anxiety and "nervous stomach" problems, and his seeming to see being with her as a panacea for all his unhappiness made my mother uneasy—with good reason— especially as the time set for their marriage was fast approaching. She needed regular assurances of his love for her. In his letter of January 21, he refers to an assertion she penned in a previous letter that she felt my father was unable to return in equal measure the love she felt for him. He accuses her of continuing "to think I am holding back on my love for you whereas I am not!" She clearly made this assertion and others like it to gain the assurances she needed to proceed. He was quick to provide them. Each of his letters is filled with passionate proclamations of his love for her. On January 21, he repeats a total of fourteen times that he loves her, misses her, needs her, that he looks forward to the day they will be together, apparently believing incessant repetitions like these would establish a rock-founded certainty for my mother. He contemplates their marriage, "at which time I will devote all in my power to making you happy." Each letter is loaded with a cannonade of assurances of his love, apparently well-received and equally returned by my mother. In his letter of April 12, he vows that "I will love you all the days of my life, and I will be happy!"

My father traveled on the train with his sister to visit my mother in Ohio from May 14 to May 21. While there, he proposed to her and was accepted. They had been corresponding by then for over three years, during which time they had actually been together only a few times. While on this trip, he had had a "gastric attack." He noted on May 24, several days after his return to Louisiana, that "I guess it was about the worst attack I ever had." I cannot think this report would have been particularly encouraging to my mother, following so soon after his proposal. When my father informed his family of his engagement on June 10, "No one had anything to say against it. I had to be pleased because I had to live with you." Again, this tepid response of my father's family to their engagement could not have assuaged my mother's doubts about the step she was taking.

In my father's letter of August 13, he reflects on my mother's paradoxical assertion that she is saddened "by being so happy," that this happiness frightens her. He assures her that he thinks of her "as a person with every quality that I would want you to have." He cannot fathom why "you have mentioned about being frightened some three or four times" and wonders if "there is something about me that is worrying you now or will maybe in the future." He seems not to take into account that he has been itemizing for her the real problems he has been facing. He also seems to have forgotten the cool reception she endured on her first and only visit to Louisiana, made conscious then of how different her personality, tastes, habits, background, values, and upbringing were from those of everyone she met there. On August 29, my father seems to grow more aware of the reasons for my mother's hesitancy. He cautions her not to "worry about how people will react towards you because I am quite sure that won't be a problem. We won't have a bit of trouble with anyone, darling."

In spite of these assurances, my mother's understanding of what her life would be like in Louisiana was in many

273

ways naïve. She seems to have dismissed as excessive my father's constant worry about locating a suitable home for them to live in after their honeymoon. He tries to find an apartment for months with no success during the severe housing shortage following the return of thousands of servicemen from the war. Finally, after nearly giving up hope, he locates a filthy apartment in an old house in Donaldsonville, Louisiana, where the employment service has transferred him. He describes this apartment as fitted out with splintery wooden floors, drafty windows swagged in rotting curtains, sagging wallpaper, and stained, sat-out furniture. The unit was essentially a one-room studio, though it had its own kitchen with a shared refrigerator in a neutral space back of the apartment. When he reports this desperate find to my mother, she naively responds that he must immediately engage a tasteful interior decorator (with appropriate testimonials), a skilled furniture maker, a vetted upholsterer, and, because she fears bedbugs, an exterminator!

I can only imagine my father's reaction to these spectacularly unrealistic suggestions, though he offers her, without further comment, the more practical solutions of new curtains, fresh paint and wallpaper, a replacement of all the old furniture with new, and a vigorous scrubbing and re-finishing of every surface in the place. For some reason, my mother asks my father to buy "Hollywood twin-size beds," perhaps influenced by the decorating magazines she has been perusing. My father wryly suggests he will nail the two beds together. For the entirety of their long marriage, they slept in the twin beds he bought at her urging, for, as my father wrote resignedly on June 25, "I will love you as much in a single bed as in a double bed."

The remainder of my father's letters of 1946 are concerned with practical matters regarding his upcoming wedding: rings; travel schedules for arriving in Ohio with his mother, brother, and sister (his father refused to leave his home in White Castle); itinerary for their honeymoon in New Orleans and the Mississippi Gulf Coast; getting a blood test and a copy of his birth certificate; fretting about the livability of the shabby apartment he has reserved. My mother too is busy planning her wedding—getting her Victorian ivory-velvet gown made, complete with bustle and flowered muff; locating and renting the cutaway morning suits my father cannot find in Louisiana (and was so completely unfamiliar with that he asks my mother to have someone at the ready on his wedding morning to help him put it on correctly); ordering flowers; and arranging for the nuptial Mass and the breakfast at the Hotel Shawnee to follow. My father's mother was scandalized that my mother planned to walk down the aisle before the ceremony on the arm of my father, in lieu of her gadabout father and eschewing the usual custom of the groom seeing the bride for the first time at the foot of the altar.

My parents were married by a close family friend, Father William Shine, at St. Bernard's Church in Springfield, Ohio, on Wednesday, September 11, 1946 at 8:30 in the morning. The music played in the church and during the following breakfast reception was supplied by a close family friend, Pat Miller. My mother requested her favorite song to end the breakfast: "Kiss Me Once, Kiss Me Twice, Kiss Me Once Again." For the remainder of their lives together, whenever one or the other of them left their house, they gave each other three quick kisses. My father kissed my mother like this for the last time when she lay in her coffin, the wedding ring placed on her finger 54 years before and never once taken off, now permanently encircling her 88-year-old ring finger turned into a talon by arthritis.

My parents on their wedding day, September 11, 1946

VI
1946: Letters of a New Bride

With their marriage, my father was relieved from letter-writing, a task he repeatedly indicated he found an odious duty. My mother took over, writing to her sisters Helen and

Josephine Landes and her Tanta Anna at home in Ohio. Unlike my father, who never retained letters sent to him, my aunts were as assiduous in preserving the letters they received as my mother had been. My mother's letters are buoyant, imbued with enthusiasm, seasoned with stylistic animation. She proves herself a skillful correspondent with an eye for vivid detail and an ear for lively phrasing. One longs for the discarded letters she had earlier written to my father. My father's letters, on the other hand, are stolid and businesslike, except for their incursions into love language. In stark contrast, my mother's letters are breezy, light, and specific.

Her post-marriage letters begin with expressions of gratitude to her sisters for their parts in helping her orchestrate the ideal wedding. She describes her first night in Cincinnati as a married woman, their flight the next day to New Orleans, and then, after a few days, their continued honeymoon in Biloxi and the Mississippi Gulf Coast. "The flight," she notes with relief, "was wonderful, and I wasn't the least bit scared."

In her honeymoon letters, she plays tourist, detailing the "foreignness" of New Orleans. Their room at the Hotel Monteleone in the French Quarter featured above the ceiling light "a big white wooden propeller, something like the type seen in meat shops, and it seems very tropical," as she notes on September 13. (Apparently she had never seen a ceiling fan in a residence before.) From their hotel room they could view steamers, tankers, and barges plying the port of New Orleans. They glut on oysters, gumbos, and etoufees at Antoine's, Commander's Palace, and Galatoire's and café au lait and beignets at Café du Monde. Later she delights in the dreaminess of the Hotel Buena Vista in Biloxi and their evenings dining and dancing on music-filled, palm-laced verandas overlooking the moonlit, starry Gulf. She revels in the luxurious slow pace of their lives during a honeymoon she wishes would go on forever, this "glamorous existence" she describes so glowingly on September 17.

She is most eager to tell her sisters what she is discovering about the man she has married. In her letter of September 13, she reveals that her new husband "isn't the man I thought he was when I married him—he's ever so much more fun, a wonderful companion, and more wonderful in every way than I had even thought." She ends by exclaiming, "I'm terribly happy!"

On September 17, the eve of their first week anniversary, she writes that "it seems I've been with Tony a long, long time. I don't feel newly married at all," so natural and comfortable is their connection. On September 18, she notes that she was "really surprised to learn Tony's so humorous. I love everything about him!"

She waits until September 19, the last evening of their honeymoon, to address "what you certainly must have been anxious to know": in their "most intimate relations," she informs her celibate sisters, her husband "is the gentlest of men and has had the utmost patience. At no time has he ever bulled his way through and no matter at what cost to him, has always considered my feelings first." She reports that he has asked her "what he could do to preserve me as long as possible from pregnancy to keep it just us for a while." (Whatever plan they came up with did not work: they married on September 11, 1946; they welcomed my older brother on June 25, 1947, just two weeks over nine months later.)

This letter of September 19 concludes with her assurances that "I haven't felt the least bit ill at ease with Tony, and he's been exceptional about everything. I know that this, more than anything else, must have been in each of your minds, just as naturally it was in the back of my mind all along until I knew for sure." She finds my father "a devoted husband," and she adds that "it is so refreshing" to find that "he is so very clean in all his personal habits." She indicates that this letter is written to relieve any concerns that her sisters might harbor and is for their eyes only, that no one else is to read it, not even the husband whom she "adores."

Louise Landes, her aunt Anna Kalt, her sisters Josephine and Helen Landes

Lucien L. Agosta, Ph.D.

My mother soon recognizes that there are attitudes towards women in the South that she does not share. For example, in her post-honeymoon letter of September 23, she writes that on asking where and how she is to do their laundry while staying temporarily with my father's parents, she is told by my father that "women are fragile and should not do very much manual labor and he wants everything to be the very best for me." He thinks, she continues, that "washing and ironing are too hard on a woman, especially ironing." Her mother-in-law, too, thinks "a woman isn't able to iron physically," she reports on September 26.

My father and his mother fail to see any irony in this claim: my mother begins her letter of September 23 noting that "Lula came early this morning" to do the washing, "and has been hard at it." She notes in subsequent letters that "Lula" and "Delores" and another unnamed "colored girl" come three days a week to do astonishingly large loads of the family laundry in a tub on a gas ring, stirred with a paddle and then wrung out by strong arm in a back shed, returning later to do the ironing. My mother is wryly aware that not <u>all</u> women find such work "too hard."

My mother takes a dim view of this over-protectiveness in her letter of September 26 and decides to do the ironing for my father herself. She recounts her attempts to help Lula by ironing my father's "beautiful new pair of silk pajamas," when, "alas, I couldn't pull the iron away, and finally when it let loose there was a blob of cotton candy on it." That night, "in fear and trembling," she related to my father what had happened and was surprised that he thought it "screamingly funny" and determined to buy "a bolt of cheap material" for her to practice on. Tony, she continues, "is the sweetest thing. Everyone in this town seems to think he's wonderful, and he is!" "It's unbelievable," she adds, "that each day we love each other even more than the day before."

"As pleasant and short as the days are," she concludes, "I live for the time I hear Tony's car in the drive. I've always been happy; all my life I've had good breaks, but I'm so much happier than I had ever looked for so far!"

My mother's ebullient letters of 1946 return again and again to this theme of her happiness, of her increasing appreciation for her husband, of her continuing discovery of his excellent qualities that never fail to surprise and delight her. In her long letter of November 13, she tells her sisters of a wedding gift sent to her late on purpose from a friend who wanted it to arrive after "the first breathless moments of marriage were over." "I'm still breathless," my mother exclaims, "and wonderfully happy!" My father and mother enjoyed a love match from their first married days together.

Two issues, however, shaded this radiant happiness that held them: post-war scarcity and the continuing difficulties in finding a suitable place to live. My mother's letters account for the difficulties of "foraging" for meat, cooking oil, canned goods, sugar (though surrounded by Louisiana sugar plantations), sheets, towels, soap, and laundry detergent. My father's parents, long established in the small village of White Castle, had connections that helped provide some of these necessities, and my mother's sisters, with a readier access to larger markets in the industrial Midwest, were regularly sending them packages of supplies. Early on, my mother had asked them for a speedy delivery of her ration book with its much-desired sugar stamps. In her letter of October 18, my mother describes the paucity in the markets, crowing that she has "found a hitherto undiscovered grocery, and oh joy! they had Philadelphia cream cheese and seedless grapes. Also they had radishes, sorry ones, but I bought them. Fresh things like that are out of the ordinary here."

A more urgent issue for my parents was locating suitable housing. Though my father had engaged an apartment close to his work, my parents had judged it unacceptable. The day after their return from their honeymoon, September 22, my mother notes that they "went to see our apartment, and to say the least, we're discouraged. Tony said each time he goes there it looks worse to him. The possibilities are great—the place is in a large old house, and if it were only real clean, it would be nice to fix up, but the woman hadn't touched the place—it's filthy, and the furniture is awful. If we can get her to move most of it out, we might move in, provided we don't find anything else in the meantime. We won't use the bed or the mattress." They were staying with my father's parents and were eager to move on as soon as possible.

Their problem was resolved at last when their landlady had the place cleaned after moving out all the objectionable furniture, except for a large armoire, there being no closet in the place. My parents then had their own cleaning lady scour the apartment yet again and scrounged around for furniture, difficult to locate. They did some painting and patching and floor refinishing before finally moving into the apartment. In a long letter of November 13, my mother notes that after a month in the apartment, she finds it "quite cozy" and that they are "so used to the place now we even like it." They remained in that apartment for well over a year and brought their first newborn home to it. They spoke of their first apartment with amused nostalgia for the remainder of their long marriage.

At the close of the year, my mother assures her sisters of my father's happiness in his new married state. On December 1, she notes that though he is not much given to expressing himself on such matters, Tony "told me last night how very happy he is. You can tell he's happy, too, in spite of the fact that he worries about every little thing." Of her own feelings at the end of the year, she notes on December 11 that "Tony is really the Ideal Husband, and I'm a lucky girl!" So closes the year of their wedding, an initiation into a marriage of over five decades of devotion to each other.

VII
1947: New Parents

My mother was a happy person, naturally inclined to optimism, as evidenced in her 1947 letters to her sisters. Replete with details, these letters offer accounts of ordinary happenings in an ordinary life, told with a novelist's eye and in a lively style. Rarely do they comment on national or even local issues, their epistolary borders edged by her home and by the specific doings of those in her family circle. These letters, written every other day or so, are essentially diary entries: they open an aperture into a uniquely personal perspective on life and outline a domestic era now long past.

As a new bride, my mother continues to learn much about her husband that further endears him to her. On January 1, on hearing of marital discord endured by one of her friends in Ohio, she writes that "not everyone can be lucky enough to rate a guy like Tony. He has every fine quality you could name, besides being very sweet and considerate and human. The world is a very wonderful place!" On January 30, she discovers how emotional my father was—and I certainly knew him to be so all his life: when he had to inform my mother of a telegram he intercepted indicating her father's sudden death in Los Angeles of a stroke, "he was so sorry that the tears spilled down his cheeks too." She also learns of his affection for children, especially babies. "Tony," she writes on March 23, "was the only one in the room paying any attention to the baby of a friend who had stopped in for a visit." "It's the funniest thing how Tony notices children," she concludes without yet knowing what a fortunate attribute this was, given that they were to have five children of their own, their contributions to the "baby boom" then occurring.

My mother also discovers my father's inherent zaniness. On March 25, she wonders "what our landlady thinks when she hears the ungodly noises issuing from overhead" as my father "goes through all his startling maneuvers, dances, and pantomimes" to amuse her: "It really is a riot!" Their neighbor next door "says he's the only sign of life in this big house," though their landlady "must think we either move the furniture daily or someone is always falling down." She concludes on May 10 that my father "is in excellent spirits and is full of craziness—he keeps me well entertained."

She finds my father to be a close and amiable companion. On April 14, she notes that he "never goes out of the house without me, except to go to work," so fond is he of being with her and so little time he feels he is able to spend with her. On April 24, my mother notes that around the house there is nothing "too small for him to notice and share in. He seems interested in every little thing I do," and on April 27, she describes the pleasure they shared in the simple task of "re-arranging the furniture," my father "having moved the chests and the trunk and the big chair about six times before we were satisfied."

My father made it known to my mother that there was one trait in her that he did not like: her tendency, characterizing her for her entire life and passed on to me, to fall asleep easily, suddenly, and, according to him, inappropriately. She strives to head off her postprandial evening somnolence by napping in the afternoons because she knows this narcoleptic inclination "irks him": "That's the only thing he ever criticizes me for—if it happens out, he's embarrassed, and if it happens too often at home, he thinks I'm bored with him." So the naps "pay big dividends: we both have so much fun when I stay awake." She notes again on March 27 that her early sleepiness is "the <u>only</u> thing that he doesn't like about me and that he wishes I'd correct." More easily ordered than achieved: a number of her letters devolve into a series of scratches, squiggles, and blots as she falls asleep while writing them. One such letter was dated June 1 and, after the erratic smudges of a sleep-guided pen, she concludes: "Honestly, I'm so sleepy that I can't keep my eyes open." Some of these letters diverge into inscrutable scribbles, hastily corrected the next morning before being consigned to the post.

Though my mother pronounced the little towns of White Castle and Donaldsonville "really dead," she claimed on January 8 that "I don't mind it." Her letters reveal the simple amusements that occupied them. My father held memberships in the Lions Club, the American Legion, the Knights of Columbus, the Holy Name Society, the Elks, and the Catholic Veterans, as well as serving on several local planning commissions. He attended meetings of these organizations alone, though my mother accompanied him to their social events. My mother was less inclined to join women's groups, though she felt pressured to join the Ladies Sodality and the Catholic Daughters, but declined memberships in various non-academic sororities.

In addition to these community involvements, they occupied their pre-television time with card games, dominoes, chess, and community bingo, and on rare occasions, they went with friends to dance at the "two so-called night clubs, actually just little roadhouses" around Donaldsonville. My mother adopted the odd avocation of weaving rugs from sock tops on little square, nail-studded looms for gifts and to sell at a local handicraft gift shop. She entered national contests with avidity, hoping to win cash prizes, such as the $7,500 first prize for selecting the winning name for the bull-calf of Elsie and Beauregard, mascots for the Borden Company. They listened to radio programs and went a couple of times a week to the movies, though she notes on January 8 with exasperation that "It's so crazy, but the manager of the white theater in town had a quarrel with MGM, and, as a consequence, he doesn't get any of their pictures, and, of course, they make the best. The colored theater gets all the <u>good</u> shows."

Other pastimes included reading, though my mother lamented that there was no library in the area. They particularly enjoyed shared reading: On June 11, she notes that they have been reading aloud *The Count of Monte Cristo* "every night to each other and we're so fascinated by it we really look forward to evenings, even can hardly wait to get into the book." (It was a simpler time.....)

Because my father did not want her to have a job outside of the home, my mother found an outlet for her creativity in letter-writing. This persistent activity filled up most of her free time. During 1947 alone, she wrote almost 130 letters of considerable length to her sisters in Springfield, addressing them always as "Darlings." Not included in this count were the many letters written to friends in Ohio but not retained. Her letter-writing became for her an obligation: she repeatedly decries not being able to keep up with her correspondence. On March 25, she feels "humiliated" at all the letters she owes: "I'm helplessly bogged down in a mire of unanswered correspondence, and then I have the unmitigated gall to want letters when I go to the P.O." On September 2, she writes: "Time passes by so quickly, and I'm always feeling sorry for not being able to write oftener to you, or to keep up with my other correspondence. Maybe after a time I can apportion my time better."

My mother considers letter-writing a duty and continually castigates herself for failing at it. On October 28, she notes that she had dedicated the entire day to catching up with her correspondence, only to be interrupted and called away from her task, succeeding in writing to only six people in addition to a typed two-page, single-spaced letter to her sisters. At the end of the year, to assuage her guilt at her "irregular letter-writing," she types a four-page, single-spaced Christmas letter on carbon to the numerous recipients of their Christmas cards that year, begging their indulgence with this "general bulletin" as "the one scheme I can devise whereby I can get all the letters I've wished to write crammed into my limited writing time." "Rest assured," she continues, that "this letter is written with each of you individually in mind." Thus she composes an early mass-letter so commonly resorted to in today's Christmas greetings.

Other activities engaged them. Their lives, for example, were firmly anchored by the Catholic Church of the Ascension in Donaldsonville, at which they attended frequent Masses, novenas, Benedictions, and Stations of the Cross as well as cultivating socially the priests stationed at this parish. As she notes on January 8, "the majority of the people are Catholic. It seems everyone you talk to or do business with goes to the same church you do. It's nice!"

Along with church, they spent an inordinate amount of time visiting my father's parents and brother in White Castle and his sisters in Baton Rouge. My father's family accepted my mother as they got to know her better and as she learned to meet their expectations more attentively, but she never quite forgot their initial reception of her.

At least two dozen of my mother's letters to her sisters describe gratefully the contents of the gift boxes they frequently sent my parents. My mother begins her March 28 letter with "<u>Another </u>box! It's such a thrill to get them, but you shouldn't spend all your money on us!" "Living away from home," my mother writes on June 10, "one misses one's home folks—that's the only drawback—but to compensate partially is that when one has folks like mine and good friends like mine, one has so very many Christmases during the year." She comments on each item in these gift boxes in her acknowledgement letters, such as the one on August 11 thanking her sisters for a folding bed table, a full complement of the cosmetics unavailable to her in Louisiana, a bottle of Old South whiskey in a cut-glass decanter, several boxes of stationery, nylons, underwear and bras, dish cloths and towels, gift wraps, cookies, and bubble bath. She concludes with "Believe me, I'm terribly grateful for all you do for us!" These boxes helped to counter the post-war scarcity still confronting them in small-town Louisiana as late as 1947.

In summary, my mother's letters all reveal that she and my father were busy, engaged, and enjoying their lives together in spite of several dark clouds that amassed over them early in 1947. The year began with the January death of my mother's father in a retired actor's home in Los Angeles. My mother did not return to Ohio for his funeral, nor could she travel home for the burial of her beloved Tanta Anna who died suddenly in February. My mother and her sisters made their home with this maiden aunt after their own mother's death when my mother was 12. Still imbued with Victorian attitudes towards mourning, my mother thought it improper to listen to the radio, go to movies, play games, or attend dances for several months following these bereavements. She notes on May 7 that she has seen her first movie since the death of her father five months before. For years, she marked the anniversaries of the deaths of the members of her family with Masses for the repose of their souls.

A further interruption in their genial lives was my father's continuing stomach problems. "Tony has had a worse flare up of his old stomach trouble during the last month," my mother writes on January 27, "and after a year and a half he's not much better." On March 28, my mother laments the blandness of their meals, necessary until "Tony's off his diet. Poor guy, everything's gotten so it tastes the same to him without seasoning, and the doctor keeps cutting out more and more foods." My mother notes on April 3 that my father's doctor has "put him on a most rigid diet" and, after two days on it, he "already feels weak." He begins to lose weight alarmingly.

By April 8, my mother notes that their doctor "has tried everything with Tony and it hasn't helped," so, in desperation, he has recommended a complete gastrointestinal work-up at the well-regarded Ochsner's Clinic in New Orleans where my father checked in on April 15 for a week's battery of tests, staying at a boarding house on St. Charles Avenue, an expensive proposition for my parents. By the end of this week, the doctors diagnose his condition as "nothing serious." By April 27, my mother notes they have received "good reports from the Clinic! It seems that Tony doesn't have a whole lot wrong with his stomach after all." The doctors refer him to what my mother calls a "neurologist," clearly a psychiatrist, who advised my father that his stomach problems were caused psychologically by his nerves. "Tony has been advised to take life easy and not to worry about little things." With that benign diagnosis (and facile advice), my father "has been in high spirits ever since, and is really trying to be carefree."

(My father died in 2011, shortly before his 94th birthday, having been deviled all his life by stomach complaints and professing an aversion to spices, fats, onions, and garlic in his bland food. And he worried about everything. I suspect that his persistent stomach complaints, nightmares, insomnia, and inability to refrain from incessant worrying all resulted from PTSD brought on by a stern childhood, a hyper-sensitivity to slights of any kind, real or imagined, and his wartime experiences in a devastated Europe that he never could put behind him.)

At this time, my father also expressed serious dissatisfaction with his job, which prompted my aunts to strategize with my mother about a possible move to Ohio where they offered to house them until they were settled. My aunts were adamant: on April 10, they wrote "Why doesn't Tony chuck his job and come on up here?" "Tony should look out for himself and let his job go hang," they insisted. My mother was all for this: on April 15, she responded that "Of course you know I'd jump at the chance to be near you folks—not that I'm not <u>very</u>, very happy here!" Only half-heartedly open to this solution, my father nevertheless did apply for jobs in Ohio, though nothing came of this.

One kind of job stress was resolved when, on September 7, my mother recorded that "Tony received his release from the Employment Service yesterday, effective the 15th, because they're having a wholesale layoff because of too many employees and slackened work." With the placement of most returning veterans in the two years following the war, the U. S. Employment Service was remanded to the states, offices were closed, and many employees were let go. My mother took her usual sanguine view of the matter: "He had too much worry and responsibility for what he made. I feel if this hadn't happened, he'd have beaten his brains out for the Service all his life and never would have broken away. We're both relieved, after a fashion, that he's out."

By September 9, however, my mother writes that "Tony is so anxious to get work, I'm afraid he'll take the first thing that comes along. Of course something like this upsets his stomach and he won't get right until he's back at the grind." In desperation, my father contemplates opening a "beer parlor" in a building owned by his father in White Castle, which, according to my ever-optimistic mother, should enable him "to retire after a few years." She concludes her naïve outline of this particularly inadvisable plan hatched by my near-teetotaler and introverted father with "Tony will go nuts without anything to do." She need not have worried: by the middle of November, my father became office manager of a lucrative local furniture and appliance concern in Donaldsonville, having fortunately given up on the "beer parlor" and the removal to Ohio plans.

The signal event of 1947, however, was my mother's pregnancy and the birth of my older brother, Andrew, in June. On January 5, then at the beginning of her second trimester, she wrote her sisters "that we're to be proud parents in June, and I <u>do</u> mean proud!" and throughout her term she apprised them of the easy pregnancy she was enjoying: no morning sickness, no back strain, no significant weight gain. In her announcement letter, she notes that "I've undergone a complete mental metamorphosis—I always thought I'd be scared if I were in such a position, and I used to pity pregnant women—felt real sorry for them—and now to think I'm neither scared nor the least bit sorry for myself!"

Her delivery on June 25 was, however, beset by some worrisome complications. On July 2, the day she was released from the hospital, she acknowledges that "I can tell you now we were really worried about Andy—at first because of his great difficulty in breathing, and then later

Tony noticed that he was twitching convulsively." "Tony must be psychic," she continues, "because he didn't bubble over with the joy that I thought most fathers should display." "I keep <u>worrying</u> about the little fella," he repeatedly noted to the doctor who explained that their baby had suffered a mild "cerebral edema" common in babies after delivery, but that it would soon correct itself, the baby being "perfectly normal in every respect," his only difficulty being his too-apprehensive parents.

During the baby's delivery, however, my mother noted on July 2 that she "thought he was dead because he didn't cry, and I could see he was blue. I could also see them working with him, and I was praying hard," reminding the Infant Jesus of Prague of her bargain with Him for "a <u>normal</u>, healthy baby." This bargain involved a donated statue of the Infant to a new parish church in Cincinnati after the successful delivery of a healthy baby: "The Infant has made good, hearing all our prayers." Their priest friend visited her in the hospital to bring her a book entitled *This Tremendous Lover* to help her wile away her hospital time. "Sounds torrid, doesn't it," my mother quips, noting with disappointment that it was instead "religious."

On June 27, my mother could write from her hospital bed, "I'm truly a favored one: Here I am with a wonderful husband and son, my two wonderful sisters, and most considerate relatives by marriage. I feel surrounded by love on every side, and I in turn wish I could make all my dear ones realize how much they mean to me." She expresses her love and gratitude from "a bower of flowers" sent to perfume her sterile hospital room.

The remainder of my mother's letters of 1947 are replete with news of her infant, fortunately a boy. A girl would have labored under the name "Antoinette." After her initial scare, her baby thrives, and she describes each advance he makes: "I just can't wait till you see this buster of ours," she writes to her sisters on July 30; "he's getting huge, loves to eat, and looks just <u>like</u> a little boy. It's almost like a show to watch his facial expressions. He looks angelic, stupid, coy, shy, eager, bored, comical, mean, and happy. You'll just have to see for yourselves!" "He's really got a beautiful face, full on," she writes on August 15: "I can't say much for his profile—it's sort of Andy Gump-ish. His expressions change so rapidly with every mood that one never tires of gazing at him." On December 8, she notes that "Andy is so bright and cute he notices everything now. When Tony left this noon, he said, 'You're lucky to get to stay with him this afternoon.'" "Andy is too active to sleep much," she continued; "Sunday morning from 1:30 to 3 he was wide awake. When he knew his crying had us both awake, he lay with his tongue between his lips, blowing and making noises" like raspberries. As a consequence, "Tony had a talk with Andy and pretended to warm his pants, and Andy laughed roguishly. Tony and Andy are such pals that Andy hasn't eyes for anyone when Tony's around."

The year 1947 was thus preserved in a sheaf of my mother's happy, engaged letters. These letters never reveal episodes of unhappiness or tension, for her at least: even my father's worries about his stomach and his job prospects seem to my mother only slight waverings of fortune, soon steadied. Her letter of November 9 says it all: "The time seems to slip by so fast. It's such a wonderful time, and I just want to hold onto it with both hands." Her enthusiasm for life is unbounded; her love for family and infant son is jubilant and entire, sweeping all around her into her exultant reality.

VIII
1948: The Domestic Circle

My aunts retained well over 100 letters written to them in 1948, the great majority from my mother's pen, though my father contributed more than his usual few, even as he repeated how little he relished letter-writing. On November 29, my mother assures her sisters that "any letters you get from Tony are entirely on his own hook and because he <u>wants</u> to write them."

My mother makes no apology for focusing her letters on a completely domestic sphere. On October 5, she notes that her letters "have so much to say about little things." On June 6, she says again that she writes to record "all the little homely things we do." These domestic communications are a winsome account of days treasured by an exuberant new wife and mother.

Occasionally and for variation, the letters leave the domestic circle to capture vignettes of local color, as in the letter of February 11 where my mother describes how on Mardi Gras, "only the colored people had a parade" in Donaldsonville, which she viewed with field glasses from her balcony, "rather a pathetic attempt of a down-trodden race to do a little something." She regrets having to miss the "King Zulu colored parade in White Castle," which she describes as "really something—noisy and boisterous with maskers dancing in the streets," it being sponsored by my father's aunt, who realizes a handsome profit from those who frequented the "Negro bar and dance hall" she operates with her husband. Stout as a fire plug, my father's aunt herself presided behind the bar, squatting on a stool, a derringer stuffed into her ample bosom.

For the most part, however, the letters resound with domestic contentment. On September 12, the day following the "wonderful anniversary" of their second year of married life, my mother writes that they amused themselves over a candlelit dinner recalling "what we were doing at that particular time on our wedding day." "I hope," she added, "we'll always be as happy as we are now. It seems we grow so much closer, and Tony said last week he loves me more and more as time goes by." The love of her husband is "my compensation for being separated from you, and I hope your compensation comes from knowing that I've made a good choice and am really happy in it." On November 29, she returns to this regret at her separation from her sisters: "The only fly in my ointment" is this inability to live closer to them. In a rare moment of uneasiness at the arbitrariness of fate, she notes that "maybe if I had that <u>too</u> something else would go wrong because everything can't be too perfect, and for my money everything else is!"

My mother continually attests to the closeness of the marriage she shares with my father, claims which seem genuine and not just assurances to her sisters that she made a good choice. The pleasure my parents took in each other's company is a repeated theme in the letters. For example, my mother writes on January 18 that my father so looks forward to "us being together whenever he has time off, and I consider myself very lucky that he does feel that way." On April 16, she notes that she has to discontinue writing her letter and go to bed when my father does "because neither of us has ever gone to bed before the other as long as we've been married." Their inseparability is taken up again on June 3, where she notes her lonely neighbor, "79 years old but loves young people and is most interesting, has begged me to go to the movies with her, but I don't like to go without Tony." And on August 11, she notes how much she looks forward to her evenings when "we can enjoy each other's company and share our recreation or just talk."

Two events of 1948 focus many of my mother's happy letters of that year: their January move after over a year in their cramped apartment into half of a remodeled duplex and the birth on July 10 of their second child.

The move did not go well, but their excitement about relocating into a roomier, cleaner, more private duplex carried them through the difficulties. Their landlady was ready for them to move on: my brother's crying at all times of the day and night, the landlady's disapproval of what she saw as my mother's unrefined practice of hanging her laundry out on the apartment's front balcony, the approaching birth of yet another baby all caused her to hint broadly that their tenancy needed to conclude. Before this move, their landlady decided to have natural gas piped into her house during the last days of their occupancy so as not to inconvenience her next tenants, resulting in dusty debris and noxious odors to pervade the apartment while my parents were packing. Then my parents could not secure a telephone line for their new dwelling. As of January 11, the electricity had not yet been connected, the new linoleum not yet laid, and the kitchen not yet painted. In addition, their new landlord had to take whatever laborers he could round up to work on the house at "double expense" and variable reliability, and he had to "beg, borrow, and hoard the materials," always in short supply and without much selection. So frequent were the resulting delays in finishing the house that my father had to step in and do some of the carpentry in the kitchen. On January 27, nearly a month after they were to vacate their first apartment, my mother laments: "We're so disgusted—it looks as if we'll never, never get into That House! First the carpenter, then the plumber, then the painter have held us back, then during the freeze a pipe in the kitchen burst, so we were finally to move this Sunday and lo' and behold the main pipe sprung about six cracks, preventing us."

Their difficulties mounted. They decided to move temporarily into the other half of the duplex, then still unoccupied, but on moving day, "it's raining pitchforks, and Tony came home sick." They had to ask their impatient landlady to let them stay on another week. "Did you ever see anything like it?" my mother asks on January 27, noting that everything they owned or wore was packed, so anything they needed required a frustrating search through their boxes.

My father's illness was a flu so incapacitating that he had to rely on his brother and a cousin to coordinate the move over the last day of January. The 1948 flu epidemic in Louisiana was so severe, as my mother noted on January 30, that "all schools are closed in Baton Rouge and 500 workers failed to report" at Esso (now Exxon-Mobile), the largest petro-chemical plant in the South. On February 5, my mother notes that my father "has been ill for an entire week," and as late as February 19, she notes that he "hasn't felt equal to doing much since the flu." Though delayed in settling in by my father's illness, they were happy with their move into what my mother, on February 13, describes as a "shot gun house" where "one can stand in the front or back and fire a shot clear through the house" because "all the doors to all the rooms open in a direct line" through the middle of the dwelling.

The second major event of 1948 for my parents was my birth on July 10. I am actually writing of this event on my 72nd birthday, July 10, 2020, poring over my mother's letters in their faded ink on sepia-toned paper. I am on this day almost twice as old as my mother was when she completed her labor. She has now been dead for over 20 years, but in these letters she is engaged with life and bringing new life forth, looking forward to her future. There is a trust in the letters that all will be well in spite of their knowing of the possibilities of a problematic delivery. Once again, my mother and her sisters make a compact with their beloved Infant Jesus of Prague: a healthy infant for a donated statue of the divine child, gilt-crowned and adorned with its full complement of bejeweled liturgical vestments.

My mother announced her pregnancy to her sisters on March 14, marked "private," explaining that she withheld this information so long to spare them the lengthy wait for the outcome. "Almost unbelievable, isn't it," my mother confides: "We could hardly believe it ourselves, that this could happen despite the living up to the very letter of the Rhythm Method." Now, she concludes, "I know why doctors have no faith" in the only birth control method "approved by the Catholic Church." She hastens to assure her sisters that they "must not get the impression that we are displeased because we planned for this not to happen so soon, but how can we deny this of God Who has been so good to us?" She assures her sisters that the pregnancy has been so smooth and easy that were it not for "progressing bulkiness" and "signs of life" she would "not know a thing was different—fact is, I really think I have more pep this way!" Financially, they would be stretched, she admits, but my father "feels God will always help him provide for those He sends." She concludes by assuring her sisters that "We have no consciences to ease and are really looking forward to this second child as eagerly as we did to our first." "Tony," she adds, "is such a wonderful father, it would be a shame not to have more children, and we want boys!"

My mother tries to amuse her sisters in her next letter, March 18, where she records that their parish priest called to retrieve his book on the Rhythm Method he had earlier lent them. When my mother told this priest that "it didn't work," he "said if we cooperate wholeheartedly with God even if He should choose to surround us with a dozen children, we'll be all the happier for it!" He assured my mother that "the Method really does work where God wants it to" and confided to her that his close friend, a physician, and his nurse wife "really believe in it" and that "they've attempted to practice it ever since their second child was born, and they now have nine but are very happy." My mother notes the irony that this priest could relate this to her with a straight face.

The Infant of Prague manifests Himself in many letters during my mother's pregnancy, but is especially prominent in her letter of July 12, penned two days after my birth: "The Infant went out of His way to hear our prayers this time!" Not only was I a healthy 7.5 pound boy, but my delivery was "practically painless": "I never dreamed delivery could progress so quickly and smoothly," my mother marveled, "probably our compensation for being satisfied about having them close together. There were so few pains, unbelievably mild and far apart, that I was convinced it was a false alarm" and almost did not alert Tony.

My aunts held the Infant of Prague to stern bargaining terms: they wrote in mid-September to my mother asking if, two months after my birth, they should "go ahead and order the statue, making sure Lucien was okay first." My mother responded on September 20 that "Lucien is perfect and there was no reason to delay." Part of their deal with the Infant had been their wish for "a little boy, as we were definitely praying for a vocation to the priesthood" for at least one son.

My donated statue of the Infant of Prague found its niche at the Church of the Ascension in Donaldsonville, as my mother notes on November 8: the Monsignor "has already designated Its place in the sanctuary very near the Communion rail" and believes "this statue may be exactly what's needed to change the luck of this parish, especially financially," his church being "so desperately poor." She adds, "Lucien will always be proud of that statue." On visiting this church as an adult, I noted that the statue had disappeared, apparently a casualty of Vatican II reforms. When I inquired about it at the parish office, the octogenarian secretary retained only the vaguest recollection of the statue's ever having been there.

In her letter of July 12, my mother contemplates her newborn with "a wee bit of disappointment at discovering on close scrutiny that he actually looks like me," but she expresses a degree of satisfaction in my uninterrupted sleeping, having "to be prodded to take any nourishment and then just swallows in self-defense when it rolls into his mouth. Perfectly lazy, even too much so to cry." On July 14, my mother notes her newborn "is pleased with his world and seemingly glad to be in it." He has "a fat, placid little old face—looks sort of like a little old woman." They named me "Lucien" after my grandmother Lucy, whose birthday was celebrated July 11, the day after I was born.

"Lucien is a very quiet baby. He does very little crying," my father notes on August 1, while my mother writes on August 10 that I do not "demand any attention," but am "the slowest eater I've ever seen, eating only about an ounce or two at a time" so that my feeding "may stretch over two or three hours." And, she continues, "after he's decided he's had enough to eat, he sleeps positively for hours."

My mother's most complete assessment of me as an infant was penned on October 5: "He's so friendly that it's almost pathetic. He'll probably be the type of person that either will be so irresistible that everyone will try to please him or he'll be taken advantage of because he's so doggone sweet. If you just say one word to him, he smiles and laughs and gurgles all over himself, and is so good that people forget he's even in the house." (Neither of these predictions of my future self proved accurate.)

In contrast to my Zen placidity, my older brother Andy had been a difficult baby. Plagued with severe colic, he took nourishment greedily but soon gave it all up again. His digestive discomfort caused him to cry long and frequently and to sleep little. My mother's letters of 1948 were mostly focused on him, his development and his quirks and antics. Fortunately, by January 27, my mother noted that Andy's colic was abating and that he was developing robustly into "the strapping kid he is now." Andy "makes noises like a complete zoo at one time, with gusto," she notes on April 10, though he has developed a new habit, "very provoking and hard to cope with": when out in his stroller, he insists on dragging at least one foot on the sidewalk or placing a foot on a wheel. "He's become very helpful," my mother notes wryly on July 28: "He now takes the rubber cap off his bottles and empties them in his crib and playpen. He also takes his soiled diapers off, standing stark naked in the front doorway."

After my appearance, Andy began to exhibit severe separation anxiety, which my beleaguered mother decried on September 7: he "wants to be able to either keep me in sight all the time or be in the same room with me. If I leave and shut the door on him, he sobs as though his heart would break. If I leave the door open, he comes after me as fast as he can perambulate." In the letters, Andy comes across as a mischievous, excitable, and demanding toddler, and my parents take enormous delight in him.

My parents simply could not have been more Catholic. On April 16, their parish priest paid them a visit to bless them for "the sacred work which you have nobly undertaken with, and for, Him" in having Catholic children. However, when this priest visited to bless their home on June 16, he commented on how attractive their bedroom was, "but there was one thing wrong with it—the twin beds. He didn't seem to think it very Catholic, and suggested we get rid of them and get a double bed." Reflecting ironically on her having two children born a year apart, my mother concluded: "I thought it was kind of nervy."

My so-Catholic parents were constantly providing this priest and his colleagues with infusions of cash to offer Masses for their dead and living relatives. On June 10, their parish priest informs them that he will be offering Masses on June 15, 23 and July 11, 16, and 17 for various deceased members of my mother's family. Their greatest desire was to have sons in hopes of providing priests for the Church: "I hope Tony and I will be able to produce at least one priest," my mother noted on March 18 and in subsequent letters as well.

My parents' marriage continued to be a happy one. Their individual characteristics were becoming well understood and accepted by each of them. For example, my mother's near-narcolepsy grew even more pronounced, while my father continued an incurable insomniac. On January 8, my father notes that my mother is "now reading a magazine and sleeping at the same time. How she does it is beyond me because I can't hardly sleep in bed let alone sleeping while sitting up." On June 3, my mother provides evidence of her uncontrolled sleepiness in a letter marred by a series of smudges and smears: "Here I am falling asleep again and making this looks herrible (sic)."

My father's shyness and introversion were becoming more and more apparent to my mother: On September 8, she notes that my father is quite voluble with his family, but if he had to address others, "he'd probably freeze," and when he receives a gift or compliment "face to face, he becomes inarticulate." She notes on September 12 that my father "shows his very best side to me and the children in the privacy of our own home and I love him for it."

Threading throughout my mother's letters of 1948 were continuing concerns about my father's income and job prospects. Though initially happy and well treated at the furniture store, my father dreamed of owning his own business. On March 18, my mother noted that "I do think the advent of another baby for us will be the primary deciding factor in Tony jumping off the deep end and going into business for himself." Both my father's maternal aunt and his paternal uncle were in the bar/tavern business in two different towns and had each "mopped up." This recurrent idea of opening a bar strikes me as naïve: my father drank one Scotch-and-soda each New Year's Eve, complained of how much time away from his family his current job required, and was notably shy and diffident around those he did not know well, all three guarantors of failure for him as a bar owner. My mother seems to acknowledge this bad fit when she notes that "although the work may prove distasteful to Tony, he'll like the idea of working for himself, and when he makes enough money he can get out." Fortunately, this scheme never came to fruition nor did any of the others, like opening a shoe store or a paint shop or going into the furniture line with an old Army pal.

My mother's last letter of 1948 ends with my mother happily tending to her husband and children, rounding the domestic circle: "Our little schmoo was wriggling around, so I bathed him and gave him a bottle. Andy's still asleep, but I hear rustlings every now and then. He's getting restless." The year 1948 was thus a happy one for my parents. Their letters are filled with gratitude for their fortunate present and with a presentiment that their future was bright.

IX
1949: Change and Nostalgia

Except for two letters written in January, the earliest letter of 1949 was dated August 4. No explanation is offered for the absence of letters during the nearly seven months intervening. On August 4, my mother tells her sisters "all about Tony's new status" at the furniture store: he was given enough stock in the company to guarantee him a commission of 8.5% of net sales annually, a significant increase in his income. The local Donaldsonville newspaper announced my father's good fortune, quaintly heralding him as "a capable young man with a pleasing personality" who "pledges to undertake his new duties in such a way as to render the general public the usual courtesy and satisfaction always offered by the firm."

This good fortune was soon eclipsed by news of the death in an automobile accident of Pat Miller, constant companion of my Aunt Helen, church organist and choir director, bon vivant, Master of Revels, incorrigible wag, close family friend, and godfather to me. My mother's letter of August 22 acknowledges her several attempts to frame a response expressive of her shock and grief. After tearing up several drafts, she eulogizes Pat as "the center of everything, in every crowd. No matter where he went, things more or less pivoted around him." Drawing upon her Catholic faith for a consolation she hoped to extend to her sisters, she noted that Pat, who loved everyone, "must certainly be loved by God" who granted him the last rites of the Church and the good death wished for by any Catholic. My mother records my father's usual response to such news: Tony "sobbed and sobbed" and was unable to talk with my aunts during a consolatory long distance call.

Sometime around the end of August, my mother bundled up my brother and me and headed on the train to Ohio to be with my aunts in their grief. My parents had never been separated before. They made a compact to write to each other every day while they were apart. In Springfield, my mother found my Aunt Helen "utterly crushed, though she tries to put a brave face on things when she's around people." My mother concludes that if the children were not there, "I think the empty house would drive Helen mad." Both of my parents worried about how my aunts "will feel when we have to leave," as my father put it in his letter of October 3. With a clearer understanding of the chaos and raw energy two toddlers introduced into my maiden aunts' quiet home, my mother noted on October 31 on her return to Louisiana that my aunts evinced a "wonderful patience with the children" but "I'll bet you breathed a long, blessed sigh of relief and went to bed to hibernate for a while." Unlike their behavior in Ohio, her sons, now in their own home, "have been good as gold so far, I guess because we can sort of put them in a cage."

The contents of my parents' letters to each other differed greatly. My mother's letters detailed her social engagements in her reunion with family and friends and described the behavior of her sons. My father's letters expressed his loneliness and longing for us so far away. On September 23, his 32nd birthday, he noted that "It's not so bad that you are away on my birthday, but it was hard to realize that you had to be away on our anniversary. It was tough for the remainder of that day and the few days after." His letters sound a continuous refrain: "Miss you terribly, darling, and also the kids" (September 25); "Really I do miss all of you a lot. My thoughts were of you and the kids yesterday, especially at the dinner table" (September 26); "Boy, I really do miss you, and (in tiny, barely decipherable print) I want to be with you <u>badly</u>!!!" (September 29). On October 3, he writes two wistful letters, in the first of which he notes "that I could almost write a whole letter saying, 'I miss you, need you, and love you so much, darling.' I know you wouldn't like that type of letter, so I will write about other things and mean in my heart the other." In this letter, he protests his love for us four times and concludes with his assurances that "all thinking, good judgment, and bad judgment, success or failure, all is for the benefit of my family, you and our wonderful sons." He worries that my mother, on reading this, will begin "to wonder what is wrong with me that I am writing such a letter." "Writing such," he continues, "I feel that you are close to me although you are away." So strong was his missing us that on October 4, he notes that he has placed our photographs on the mantle, "and I stop to look at them every time I pass. When I am in the room, I just stand there and look at them."

In several of my father's letters, he writes in tiny, almost unreadable script, of his physical yearning for my mother. On October 8, however, he suspects that my mother may be sharing his letters with her sisters. He asks that my mother keep his letters to herself, begging her indulgence for having written so intimately: "Perhaps there are some things I shouldn't write about. I write these things because I love you and miss you so much." My mother is quick to respond to this. On October 12, she sputters, "Some things you shouldn't write about? Between husband and wife? Nonsense! You can't know how thrilled I always am when you get sentimental and lovey-dovey with me!"

Occasionally my father's rigorous sense of fairness took over when he felt that my mother was not upholding her side of their everyday letter-writing agreement. My father kept to the bargain, though at times resorting to brief postcards, a technical dodge to daily letters. My mother, steering two active boys away from constant meddling and being in demand for social gatherings with a large circle of friends, found it difficult to maintain a daily writing schedule, especially because her letters, unlike my father's, were long, fully detailed anecdotal accounts of her busy days. Then too, if she put off writing until the end of the day, as she preferred, she often fell asleep at the task. And the postal service made for late delivery of some of her letters.

If my father did not receive my mother's letters in what he considered a timely way, he was quick to scold. On October 5, for example, he complains that he had not received a letter from my mother for the "second straight day": "You know that before you left you said you would see to it that you would write a little something each day. I didn't ask you to do this. But since you said such, I am holding you to your word. I don't think it's very fair when I manage to find a little time each day to write." The next day, October 6, he acknowledges receiving two letters from her in the same post: "I didn't mean to be too hard with my letter yesterday, but when I don't hear from you, I lose interest in everything; thus you see what it means to me to hear from you."

By October 8, my mother had received his reprimand: "It's very unfair of you to revile me for not writing. I have never gone more than one day without writing, and Helen can vouch for that!" The next day, October 9, she tries to make light of his pique: "Say, you haven't taken on the role of misunderstood husband and found a pair of pink, shell-like ears that are most sympathetic, have you?" In his response to this on October 12, my father admits to "being so dumb" that he does not understand my mother's attempt at levity: "I really don't know what you're trying to get across to me." My father may not have understood my mother's joking allusion to possible infidelity here, such allusions not being compatible with the more prosaic way his mind worked. Or he may have understood perfectly well and was annoyed: I do not think there could ever have been a man more faithful to his wedding vows than my father, and even a bantering quip associating him with infidelity he would have found repugnant.

My mother's letters to my father differed considerably in tone, mood, and content from his to her. My mother's mission in Ohio was to keep her grieving sisters occupied and distracted, employing the energy and antics of her two boys as her main strategy for accomplishing this. She also uses her letters as a means of including my father in these distractions, describing amusing incidents involving us, but not foregoing descriptions of our destructive or annoying pranks. In her letters to my father, she attempts to include him in the family life he is missing.

On September 18, for example, my mother records my encounter with the four-year-old daughter of a friend: "Lucien got so affectionate, put his arms around her, and then bit her sharply on the knee, the vampire!" And on September 21, she described how Andy threw a tantrum before visitors, whereupon my mother tried ignoring him before spanking him and putting him in another room, but then "he really put on a show, the first time in front of people."

"It's so hard to make them mind," my mother complained in her letter of October 6, "as they forget their spankings as soon as received and are right back into mischief again." She ends her letter of October 7 with a plaintive note: "Lucien's eating the buttons on my skirt and Andy's back of the bookcase fooling with the cords and plugs to the lamps." This letter degenerates into a series of ink squiggles: "Lucien is pulling at the desk blotter."

308

My father implies at times that my mother's letters do not fully acknowledge how much he misses his family and loves her, that her letters do not adequately reciprocate his affection. She addresses this on October 12: "The reason I haven't said too much about my feelings for you is, I've expatiated so much about what I thought you especially wanted to hear—about the kids, what we were doing, etc.— that I'd find I'd used up all my paper and hadn't much space to write about anything else." This separation, she continues, "is paying off big dividends. Never having been separated before, we both are realizing fully how very much we mean to each other." She concludes that as much as she has always loved her hometown of Springfield, "I now think Donaldsonville is the greatest place on earth, because my home is there—<u>our</u> home."

On October 13, close to my father's joining his family in Ohio for two weeks, my mother writes: "Darling, I can hardly believe you'll soon be with us, and I'm absolutely thrilled. It will be like another honeymoon, only better, if possible, because of the children." I suspect that my father, well aware, through direct experience and recent hearsay, of his sons' waywardness, demanding constant vigilance and attention, had other ideas of what another honeymoon might involve.

Though our behaviors were easier to manage at home in Louisiana, we could still be trying, especially to my mother home alone with us through most of the day. Near equal parts of exasperation and amusement characterize my parents' reactions to our behaviors and probably safeguarded their sanity at times. For example, my mother calls Andy a "ruffian" and a "wild Indian" when he throws a tantrum on November 14. She threatens that when he is naughty, "Santa Claus won't like it and won't bring him any toys." Not to be taken in by this, Andy whips his head back and forth to scan the room and then calls out "in a smart-alecky voice—'Santa Caws—Oh Santa Caws—where are you?'"

Andy was not the only one acting out. On November 30, my mother notes to my aunts that I am a "mess" and go "through all sorts of tantrums. He gets angry at the least thing and is getting wilder than a March hare. Then he looks out of the corners of his eyes at you in the most killing manner to see what effect it has." "Talk about a ruffian, he's it!" (So much for my placid babyhood, my infantile Zen tranquility….) This ruffian behavior persisted for a while. On December 11, my mother describes my angry outbursts, during which I change expressions "about 50 times a minute. I have an awful time to keep from laughing at him, he's so comical." Her letters are filled with other descriptions of exasperating moments of child-rearing that she responds to with amusement and forbearance.

A mutual dependence on daily communication, an affectionate sharing of domestic occurrences, and a constant assurance of love and attachment course through the 1949 letters of my parents while apart and when writing to my aunts. Their letters portray an intimate marriage, a delight in the dailyness of living. In them, one finds a voice, a tone, a mood, a presence outmoded in today's world but ever fresh despite the faded ink and brittle, sepia stationery on which the letters are written. They are relics of a time far different from our own.

In my mother's nostalgic letter of December 18, she remembers Pat Miller: "He loved Christmas so much, as all our family did." "I was just thinking," she continued, of the many who "formerly shared our Christmases—they were so jolly and full of people, and now so few of us are left. Sometimes memories seem so close that one could almost relive those times as one grows older. It was always such a joyous time for us!"

In her last letter of 1949 to her sisters, dated December 27, she notes that "We had such a wonderful Christmas, and it would have been so grand for me too had it not been that this year I was more homesick for you two than I've ever been, probably because I knew this Christmas would be such a different one for you." "I couldn't help but be blue," she continues, "thinking of all our dear ones who have gone." This last letter of 1949 draws into the circle of my mother's love all her family and friends, those living and those dead, those nearby and those far away.

X
1950-1952: The Last Letters

My mother's letters of 1950 focus primarily on the deeds of her two sons. The year starts with Andy's diphtheria diagnosis, "scarier than it sounds," my mother assured her sisters. On January 4, she notes "his running fire of conversation" as she tries to compose her letters: "Andy's sitting in the high chair and hasn't left off talking for a minute." The doctor had told her "to keep him in bed yet this week because if just around in a room, it might do damage to his heart."

Andy's recovery was rapid. The letters describe his tolerance and at times irritation with his little brother: On July 21, my mother notes that "sometimes Andy is very sweet toward Lucien, but sometimes he becomes irked (and I don't blame him!) when he is engrossed in 'building a house' with his blocks and Lucien gets the urge to wreck it." "Then," she adds, "I have to step in to avert bloodshed." She was proud of Andy's developing acuity: On May 31, she admires his ability to follow the dots in his coloring book to reveal a picture: "Not only did he grasp the idea at once, but his lines were quite straight and put in the right places."

At almost two, I had become a handful in comparison with Andy who, at almost three, had become more self-sufficient in behavior, in language, and in his ability to entertain himself. "Talk about a roughneck!" my mother complained on January 4: "Lucien's it! The original roughneck, and independent as they make them." By January 11, my mother refers to me as "the great climber (he climbs anything)." That day, for instance, she found me "hanging onto the curtains" from which I promptly fell and "battered the corner of his mouth quite a bit" but, fortunately, did not "knock out an eye." This climbing phase persisted: On May 13, my mother noted that I was "getting to be exactly like a monkey." After climbing high onto the back gate and falling on my head, I did the same thing that evening by falling again on my head from "the guard rail of his crib" where she saw me teetering but was unable to reach me in time. "He's really funny," she continued; "He juts his mouth out just like a monkey too, and when he gets angry jumps around like one."

My mother used frequent animal imagery to describe me. On January 26, she wrote that I sounded "like a cockatoo," ill-tempered and explosive: "He has the most raucous, shrill screams, and if he has something others want to play with, he just won't surrender it, just stands there shielding it and shrilling." Andy had begun to refer to me as "that child," clearly a sobriquet for me picked up from my mother's bouts of exasperation." "He's <u>bad</u>!" my mother laughs in describing me at this letter's conclusion.

I was "bad," maybe, but adults often are more amused by the romps of "bad" children than they are with the blander behaviors of "good" children. That seemed to be the case with my parents, who noted that I looked "like a goblin, just like a pixie or little sprite—and is as mischievous as one" (May 8). On May 31, my mother noted that I had the "laugh of a fat person, and it's contagious": "He's so cute that it's hard to look at him without laughing, I mean at all times." On July 12, my parents confess to liking the way I talk at two: "He's so serious and confidential when he tells you something." And they seem endlessly amused by what they call "Lucienisms": "He's so quaint and still twisting his speech. We don't correct him too often" because "his mistakes are so delightful." Examples of "Lucienisms": "draft" for "giraffe"; "losper" for "lobster"; "cup car" for "club car"; "black water what you could drink" for "coke." My mother recounts my crowing about how well I made my bed: "there are big hills and little hills all over it." "Ifashada," I would intone in my evening prayer "Now I Lay Me Down to Sleep"; my mother finally figured out that was my version of "If I should die." Finally, my mother laughed that I called the damson plum preserves at breakfast one morning "dancing damned plums preserved."

In reflecting on her children and determined to provide us with a pleasant and tolerant childhood, my mother noted to her sisters on April 3 that "nothing seems worse to me than not to have had a happy childhood, maybe because we can look back on ours as being beautiful." "No matter what happens after," she continued, "nothing can take it away, and somehow one can almost always continue to be happy after that, or at least have the right philosophy about life which enables us to more or less make our own happiness." I have come to recognize the rightness of these maternal ideas and to see in her parenting of us the greatest kindness she could offer her children. The cumulative outlay of her love for her children was far greater than any of us could ever reciprocate.

My mother was so convinced of the necessity to foster children well that when she received a plea from my father's cousin in Sicily for five vials of streptomycin to treat her son's serious illness, she insisted that they send, not five, but ten vials secured from her doctor. She notes in her letter of May 15 that "we both feel we should help as much as possible and decided that if anyone belonging to us were in such a fix we'd be frantic and think that someone just had to help." While the medicine was in transit, the boy's frantic mother wired again "and asked us to please help her secure it" with a desperation that would move any mother. The money for the drug was to have been used for her Mother's Day gift that year.

My mother was humble enough to acknowledge that her good fortune in her husband and her children was not due to her own merits. As has been noted, she and her sisters had great devotion to the Infant of Prague, a representation of the Child Jesus with a golden crown studded with gems and a "globus cruciger" (or an orb representing the earth topped with a cross) in his left hand, his right raised in benediction. He is routinely clothed in sumptuous bejeweled robes of colors coordinated with the liturgical season. My aunts promised to donate an image of the Infant for each of my mother's pregnancies resulting in a successful delivery.

The letters of 1950 offer information regarding the installation of my statue of the Infant in Ascension Church and the commission of appropriate liturgical robes for it. On January 11, my mother noted that the Infant, recently installed, had again "a fresh red rose. He's never without it. I reminded Him of the donors, as I always do, also the reasons for the donations—our two kids." On Ash Wednesday, my mother was irked that the Infant's robes had not yet been changed to Lenten purple, and when my father suggested that she take over from the nuns the task of dressing the Infant appropriately, she concluded that "it's not a bad idea at all."

Still peeved by the tardiness in keeping the Infant's robes liturgically current, my mother reported on February 26 that this sartorial negligence was due to the Monsignor's annoyance at parishioners who could not refrain from entering the sanctuary, "fingering the statue, putting rosaries about Its neck, turning It around to face wherever they sit in church, and all sorts of wild things like that, SO he is having a GLASS CASE made, if you please, where the outfits will be safe from dirty hands and superstitious practices." My parents decided, if "not too prohibitive," to donate the glass case as well as dry-cleaning costs incurred to maintain the Infant's elaborate robes. They worried, however, that this glass dome would prevent flower offerings from being placed on the Infant's pedestal, also donated by my parents.

They need not have worried: On April 3, my mother wrote that her sisters "could never visualize how beautiful the addition of the dome has made the statue. It glows like a jewel. I think your statue is the most popular object of worship, outside, of course, of the Blessed Sacrament, in the church. It seems to have captured the imagination of the people."

A reason for intensifying devotion to the Infant of Prague was announced to my aunts in February: "The Agostas are making the Third Important Announcement of their career as a team. We strongly suspect we will become Five along about October!" "This next bundle will have been ideally spaced," she continued, adding that "we feel just two children in the family is almost as bad as having just one, and that there is greater benefit to all concerned in greater numbers." Perhaps a bit defensively, she asserted that "there is no reason on earth why we should not continue to have a family" and concluded with "we hope you like the idea, as we do." She asked them to "pray that the coming heir will be another boy."

This news did meet with my aunts' approval: "Your pledge of an Infant for our new infant is again most wonderful," my mother noted on March 4. My mother may have suspected that her sisters might meet the news of this new pregnancy with less than enthusiasm because they were aware of the precarious state of my parents' finances and the dissatisfaction my father was evincing about his job. In her letter of February 13, my mother noted their need for a newer car, their current one having become so unreliable that they were afraid to drive it. Acknowledging that buying a new used car would involve "quite a bit of money to put out," they had to face the expenditure, ruinous or not. "Well," my mother buoyantly concluded in the same letter, "you gotta take a chance and trust in God that you'll always have enough to get along on. I don't think He ever lets you down."

My father became increasingly disaffected with his job during 1950. On January 4, my mother noted that "Tony has just about reached the end of his rope" with his employer. "He definitely has made up his mind to leave." Then my mother segued revealingly: "Don't get excited, but Tony said he wouldn't be averse to living in Springfield or its environs," so "if you hear of anything, let us know." Meanwhile, "we can make a Novena to the Infant." On January 16, my mother noted her sisters' immediate offer for them to move up to Ohio and live with them until they got settled. "Tony," she cautioned, "would be too proud to sponge." "Someday," she added, "we might have to do that," but Tony "believes we should postpone until he absolutely has to ask for help."

Then began an earnest search for a new job, calling on relatives, former business associates and employers, veterans from his old squadron, and friends for help, all of whom advised him "to hang on because there was nothing else worthwhile in sight, not near what he was getting." By May 31, my mother is making "a Novena for Tony so that he'll land a job he'll like, preferably in Ohio," though she concluded that wherever God "thinks it best for me to be is all right. Only you might do some tall praying too!"

My father continued to scheme about opening his own business: a shoe repair shop, a furniture store, a bar (again) specializing in the "Negro trade" like his aunt's lucrative Blue Heaven Bar and Dance Hall in White Castle. After putting in an application at surrounding school boards to teach social studies and physical education, he was offered—and declined—a job, with minimal pay, teaching on a "school boat" that plied bayou waters, offering instruction at several backwater communities several times a week.

By March 15, nothing had come of my father's job searches, as my mother noted: "Things are really getting his goat at the store, and whenever I can wedge it in I always say, 'Well, you have a way out—there's always one course open to you'—meaning, of course, Springfield." "Maybe we'll wind up there," he would always respond. My father's stomach doctor strongly advised him to find other employment as soon as possible. My mother concluded this letter with the encouraging news that my father "prays to the Infant all the time, so I know He won't let him down. By the way, the Infant had on His beautiful pink outfit yesterday and looked like a dream."

By May 22, their discouragement about job hunting was desperate: Tony is "literally at a standstill—jobs are hard to find." On May 31, the idea of a move to Ohio, even without a job prospect there, became more urgent. My father confessed that "if something didn't show up for him here, he didn't expect to stay in this part of the country." At every opportunity, my mother was encouraging him to the move, "following up the idea whenever I think it's feasible. I can't keep pounding at him, but am trying to be subtle when I think the occasion arises." "I have an answer for any question he brings up," my mother assured her sisters.

The birth of a daughter in October decided him against taking the risk of moving to Ohio that my mother and her sisters were encouraging. My mother was prepared for this disappointment: she ended her May 31 letter by assuring her sisters that "I've never been happier in spite of living down here, but I do think we should all be together, especially now when there are so few of us." There was little left for my aunts in Ohio. Their older brother Alphonse had died that April 1950 in Springfield.

Having given up on their relocating to Ohio, my mother conceived of the idea that her sisters should join her in Louisiana. As late as January 29, 1952, my mother asked them, "<u>Are</u> you giving any thought to coming here to live? I'm going to pester you till I get your answer." My Aunts Helen and Jo departed for Louisiana in 1953, leaving good friends behind in Springfield as well as a family cemetery section full of their dead loved ones. They left the ghosts behind for a new life in the South, after which there was, obviously, no need for my mother to continue a correspondence with them.

The letters of 1950 conclude with my father's letter of November 16 to my aunts. Apparently his move to Baton Rouge from Donaldsonville occurred sometime in 1950 or 1951 as did his simultaneous acquisition of a new job as office manager of a tractor dealership, a job he kept for the remainder of his working life. This last letter of 1950 details my parents' family life: "Our family has reached a stage where management, supervision, PATIENCE, and psychology must be practiced. It is really a <u>deal</u> to keep these little people happy. None of the three will be happy or peaceful at the same time. After a while all are happy and we start over again. This cycle goes on for each 24-hour day. It's tough but Louise and I enjoy it and we are very proud and thankful for the wonderful family we have." They would welcome two more children, a daughter in 1951 and another son in 1953.

For some reason, my mother—or perhaps her sisters—reduced her letters of late 1950, 1951, and 1952 to fragments, cut up into strips dealing largely with the antics and pranks of her children and marking through the back information on these fragments, indicating that they were not to be read. I can only speculate about the reasons for editing these letters so radically, the primary one being an attempt to safeguard private concerns. The years 1950-1952 saw the births of two daughters, my father's finding employment in Baton Rouge and their subsequent move into a rented house in that city, their buying the house they were to live in for the remainder of their lives, and the decision of my aunts to join them in Baton Rouge and the building of a house for them next door to our own. These letters must have involved extended discussions of finances, assets, obligations, architectural and contractor decisions, loan applications, and other private fiscal considerations that my mother and her sisters felt should not be shared. In addition, there were some difficulties with my mother's pregnancies, all successful, but involving intimate discussions with her sisters. Perhaps for these reasons, the letters from late 1950 through 1952 are disappointingly mutilated and rigorously edited.

These letters of my parents to each other and to my mother's sisters in Ohio from 1943 to 1952 are a record of a time long past. Nearly everyone who figures in these letters is now dead, though they still live in my parents' vital words. My mother emerges as the central figure in this collection of letters. During my childhood, my mother was often harried, keeping a house together, five children fed and oriented according to a strict schedule, a husband satisfied, a job outside of the house under control. In these earlier letters, her spirit shows—her hopes, her joys, her wit, her worries, her buoyancy, her essential goodness. These letters provide a privileged aperture into the heart and mind of a woman remarkable for her embrace of all of life and for her engagement with the lives of those surrounding her whom she loved and who loved her.

I am reading these letters late in my own life. They help me to configure my past more clearly, especially now that I have more of that past left to me than I have a future. Reading these letters allows me a final and augmented vision and understanding of my father and my aunts, but most especially of my mother. What I already knew of all of them was how noble and good they were. They gave me life. Now, in turn, I am giving them renewed life through this writing and in my own living. I hope they would be pleased with the life I am giving them now.

The following passages display my parents' spirits and provide their epitaphs:

> When I have you in mind, I can think of nothing but happiness even though I know this won't be true always—although it might be different with us. I hope so, darling!
>
> (My father to my mother, August 8, 1946, a month before their marriage)

> Sometimes I think I'm getting whatever reward is due me here on earth instead of the next world. Having

always believed in Providence, and everything happening for the best, I'm nevertheless always a bit taken aback with such definite proof in my own life of God's beneficence.

(My mother to her sisters, July 1, 1951)

We realize that we can't always have everything as wonderful as we have right now, and so are trying to savor every moment because it seems we're at the peak of happiness, with almost everything that's possible for happiness as complete as we can expect.

(My mother to her sisters, undated fragment)

XI
How It All Turned Out

My parents did not, in fact, always "have everything as wonderful as we have right now," nor did they remain throughout their lives "at the peak of happiness" that my mother claimed for them in the early 1950s. Like all human beings, they suffered over time the disappointments inevitable in the course of the long lives they enjoyed together during their 54-year marriage. No matter with what verve and buoyancy life is embraced, life is always alternately fulfilling and disappointing.

But overall, my parents did "live happily ever after," if this ending to fairytales is understood aright. The fairytales did not promise in their formulaic conclusions that their heroes and heroines go on to enjoy at the end of their stories a magical exemption from all that life brings them, both joy and sorrow. To live "happily ever after" means that one has succeeded at learning, through trials and difficulties, how to live well, how to negotiate the vagaries of life successfully in order to live happily even in the face of the downturns of fortune that sometimes come as long as life lasts.

My parents' occasional disappointments forced them at times to re-examine what they had construed as the essential rightness of life. In their early faith, everything had an explanation and worked to the good because ruled by the gentle God they personified as a bejeweled Infant clothed in dazzling fabrics. No doubt they would have preferred to remain in this first comfortable explanation of how life was supposed to be, but life would challenge their early innocent views. Faced at times with sadness and uncertainty, their early faith was confronted in ways that forced them to grow. Their life outlook was at times challenged by a sterner God as their lives progressed.

For them, life had purpose and order, until at times it no longer seemed to, forcing them to confront doubt and disappointment. They were called at times to move from bedrock assurances through a dark landscape where affirmations would be hard won. They always did find their way again to the end. The beacon that led them, glimmering over the dark terrain, was love.

My sister once told me that she was only as happy as the least happy of her children. Certainly the happiness or unhappiness of their children alternately buoyed or weighted my parents as well. They were proud of their children, all of whom graduated from college or earned professional degrees, one a university professor, another a middle-school teacher, a third a registered nurse, and their last a technician in a petrochemical laboratory. This is not to say that events or circumstances in their children's lives did not at times cause them distress and concern, whether it was my homosexuality or another sibling's divorce or the conversion from their staunch Catholicism to a fundamentalist evangelical faith by another or one of their children's occasional difficulties with severe anxiety. But my parents took great satisfaction that their children all pursued successful careers, remained financially secure, were responsible, happy for the most part, and law-abiding, and produced five grandchildren whom they doted on. My parents' love for their children flowed back to them abundantly and was added to by their five grandchildren, all of whom grew into responsible and socially contributing adults during my parents' lifetimes.

The great tragedy of my parents' lives, however, from which they never fully recovered, was the accidental drowning death at 20 of their eldest son, Andrew, while he was stationed at an Air Force base in Michigan.

Though over 50 years have elapsed since his death, I still find it difficult to write of it. I remember everything about that loss with a sharp immediacy. Late on the evening of Saturday, May 18, 1968, I was at home in my bedroom studying for a final exam I was to take the following Monday. I looked up from my textbook on hearing a loud rap on the knocker at the front door, followed by the slap of my mother's slippers across the wooden floor of the living room as she went to open it.

Then erupted my mother's crying out for my father, a strangle of his name that carried in its tone the most intense fear and grief I have ever heard, before or since. I emerged from my bedroom to see her fleeing across the living room to find my father, afraid to face alone what she intuited was coming. Entering quietly, almost furtively, through the open front doorway were two Air Force officers.

They told my parents that my brother was missing in a lake after a boating accident earlier in the day, that the boat he was riding in had overturned and he had not surfaced. They would drag the lake in the morning.

I know what keening sounds like because I fell into a continuous rocking and moaning, so deep in misery and shock that I cannot recall much more than my mother's face, dry-eyed, swollen and mottled in bruised plum and bone-white anguish, and my father's broken phone call to his sister and brother-in-law, who came over immediately. My keening disturbed them. My mother gave me a sleeping pill and urged me to go to bed.

I woke the next morning early to the sound of my father weeping at the dining room table, my mother soothing him in low words I could not make out. I was afraid to join them.

Soon the house crowded with relatives. They persuaded my mother to lie down. At about 3:00 that Sunday afternoon, the same Air Force officers arrived at the front door. I went into my parents' bedroom to awaken my mother. "They're here," I said. She scanned my face, desperate for any glimmer of hope reflected there, saw none, looked down in despair. Her black dress was rumpled and dusted with blanket lint.

The officers delivered their dreaded news in voices low but crisp as their starched uniforms, told my parents when Andy's body would arrive, indicated that there would be a full military funeral in addition to any religious rites my parents desired.

Later that evening after everyone had gone, I was talking quietly with my mother while she was ironing dress shirts for my father and me. "Do you think he was right with God at the end?" she asked in a strained voice.

We stared at each other, both of us numb and mute with a grief intensified by this consideration. I could only nod an affirmation to her question. I am relieved that I cannot relocate myself physically in this sad scene, made even sadder that then we could only imagine judgment, not be comforted by mercy instead, saw possible severity rather than the compassion my mother made herself feel when she considered her God. I would now have responded differently to her question: "Mother, he was a boy of 20! How could he ever have done anything so eternally wrong as to deserve the kind of punishment you fear? Measure your love for him, then treble it in the heart of God." There seemed to be no recollection for her at this time of the mild Infant of Prague whom they had venerated for so long and whose statue beckoned with blessings from their bedroom. Here she tasted the bitter gall of the dark side of a faith then more legalistic than loving, a faith that toted up "sin" on a black and white balance sheet.

My parents never got over this shock. They had a memorial bench erected in the cemetery near Andy's grave, which they visited most Sundays after Mass, bringing fresh flowers and a small whisk broom they used to clear his marker of leaves. They hung the crucifix from over his coffin by the front door to remind them of him daily. They rarely spoke of him, and then only in words tender and edged in grief.

One Sunday a few weeks after his burial and before the sod had greened over his grave, I sat on the memorial bench at the cemetery with my mother. "I'll never laugh again," I said. "You will," she assured me, "and if you don't, you will have failed to live well."

Etched in my memory is the last time I saw Andy alive on his final visit home, on leave from where he was stationed. He was in his uniform, which he was proud of, standing lean and tall, about to board his plane. My parents and I stood just inside the large airport windows in those days when one could see a person off before a flight. At the top of the stairs to the plane, just before boarding, Andy turned to us to wave once, glowing in a rich amber light from the sun setting over his shoulder.

Time passed, and the jagged edges of my grief rounded for me. I came to a time when I did not think of Andy very often. But in 1989, 21 years after his death, I was attending an orientation session in preparation for becoming a volunteer at the Sacramento AIDS Foundation. The moderator reminded us of the obvious: we were volunteering to work with people who were dying. He asked us to recall someone close to us who had died and how we had dealt with death and grief. I suspect my nerves were frayed because of the gravity of what we were learning; I know I had damned up my feelings for too long a time, but suddenly I began to sob. Convulsive heavings. I could only manage to get out embarrassed apologies and exclamations of mortified surprise at this paroxysm I could not contain for all my trying.

In their last years, my parents took to visiting me in California just after my spring teaching term ended in mid-May. I arranged excursions throughout the West for them and for my sister who accompanied them. On my mother's last visit, we toured the Grand Tetons and Yellowstone National Park. My mother had begun to wander in time occasionally. She had become a diminished variation of herself, had lost emphasis somehow. She suffered from severe osteoporosis. She was in pain much of the time, especially on arising in the mornings.

Over coffee one morning, it became clear to me that her pain had escalated and, though she was attempting to disguise it, she was suffering. "I'm so sorry to see you like this, Mother," I said, taking her hand.

"This is the price one pays for living a long life," she said. With a squeeze of my hand before releasing it, she added: "It's worth it."

Several nights later, my mother and I sat before a blaze in the lobby of the Old Faithful Lodge in Yellowstone, with its heavy tiers of timbered balconies towering above us. We were waiting for my father and sister who had not yet come down from our rooms. A late snow descended in an impenetrable white swirl outside a large window we sat next to. My mother looked at the falling snow, her face, white and delicate as porcelain, blanching silver in the snowlight.

"Do you ever think about Andy?" she asked.

"Oh yes," I answered. "I have never gotten over his death. All my youthful sense of secure rightness in the universe disappeared with him."

"It's time you made your peace with his death," she noted after a pause. "I think I have at last. I've never told anyone about this, but several months ago, I had a dream about him. Do you remember we had that side arbor of red climbing roses over the black wrought-iron gate to the backyard? In my dream, the gate was wide open, and Andy was standing on the other side of it from me, framed among the roses. He was smiling and happy....so young! 'Look, Mother!' he laughed: 'I made it through. You will too. There's nothing to fear.'"

"I know it was only a dream," she concluded, "but it brought me comfort." She turned then from the snow at the window to gaze at the fire, a warm rose-surge now suffusing her face, a quiet smile settling over her thin lips.

My mother died a little over two years after this conversation, just short of her 89th birthday. My father died eleven years later at almost 94. He did not often speak of my mother in his last years. His funeral Mass was sparsely attended: He had outlived everyone except one sister and four of his five children.

As I hope I have shown, my parents' early letters were charged with a pervading enthusiasm and optimism, such eager joie-de-vivre, with an openness to life and all its promises and possibilities. Were they happy? They had all the usual requirements for happiness—they prospered materially, had a comfortable home, a vacation beach house, successful children and healthy grandchildren who loved them, years of a secure retirement, and long lives. In spite of all these contributions to happiness, it is difficult to know for sure if someone else was happy. But yes, I think my parents were happy on the whole.

On one of my last Christmas visits from California to my family in Louisiana while my mother was yet alive, I came home late one evening from a holiday party thrown by an old high-school classmate. I saw my parents' bedroom light glowing through the chill, damp Louisiana night, and when I went toward their room, I saw my father lying down, my mother sitting on the edge of his bed beside him, holding his hand. They were conversing in the low, uninflected tone people use who share a long intimacy. They did not at first notice me standing in their doorway. Then they both looked up at me at once, their lined faces radiant in their delight in each other and with me home with them again.

Helen Landes 1901-1992
Josephine Landes 1908-1961
Louise Landes Agosta 1911-2000
Anthony Alexander Agosta 1917-2011
Andrew Anthony Agosta 1947-1968

CONCLUSION:
A Valediction Forbidding Mourning

Occasionally I flash into a penetrating awareness of my own interiority. In these epiphanic moments of clarity, I recognize myself as the conservator of a vast inner world of thoughts and experiences and sensations known to no one else, an immense repository of all my actions and insights, of all sense impressions since I first opened my eyes in amazement, bleared by the amniotic fluids through which I swam to the light. I am not unique in this: every human being who has lived long enough similarly harbors a colossal accretion of experiences often unique to them, accumulated day by day, year by year.

This immensity is encased within the mortal flesh of a body prone to perish. The life load my body bears and will in time relinquish has long remained unprobed and unsorted. That is the work of this book, a dredging and ordering exercise.

People who read passionately can usually point to a few books that have affected them profoundly. Thoreau's *Walden* is one of those books for me. The opening of *Walden* provides the inspiration for all the personal writing I have done recently: "I should not talk so much about myself if there were anybody else whom I knew as well." Thoreau required that a writer provide "a simple and sincere account of his own life, and not merely what he has heard of other men's lives."

Thoreau's direct literary descendant, the American essayist and children's writer, E. B. White, penned a letter at the end of 1951 wherein he described writing as "translation, and the opus to be translated is yourself." "If a writer succeeds in communicating with a reader," he added in 1956, "I think it is simply because he has been trying... to get in touch with himself—to clarify the reception." I cannot offer a better rationale for having written this book.

This book's account of what I can reconstruct of my progress from initial confusion about who and what I am to glimmerings of understanding to my final courage in accepting myself fully has been filled with dodges and windings and wrong turns, blunders and slipups that, on recalling them, make me wince at times. The gay life I attempt to reconstruct in this book is replete with false starts, lucky accidents, some wise deliberations, at last a dogged determination to follow my own interests, my own academic pursuits, my own bent—and I no longer give a damn about how wayward others may now judge that bent to be.

I have, during the course of my life, thrown up in the air a succession of trial floats. Too many of them plummeted quickly to earth, the gas I filled them with too giddy to bear them up for long. Others, leaden-weighted with consequences I had not anticipated, soon crashed down on top of me. Still others, fortunately, remained aloft and spun into orbit, beneficent stars that rained their radiance on me throughout my life.

Fortunately, there have been many of these charms, perhaps more than I have deserved: loving parents, many delicious lovers who delighted all my senses, a career I have loved, partners who have stayed with me to expand my heart and heighten my joy. In this empty, cold universe, its darkness flashing with violent collision and cosmic accident, I was born, a speck in all that vastness, on a planet suffused with light and softened by love, which has countenanced me with kindness. It is difficult to see how my eventual passing from my good fortunes could warrant any mourning!

II
Atropos Nearing

Much of my good fortune derives from my having always reveled in life's sensuous details. From my dawning consciousness onwards, I have celebrated color, sound, and form, roistered in the specific, been dazzled by the particular, the precisely delineated. I have eschewed, as far as possible, "big ideas." I have found God only in the details of creation, when I have been able to find Him at all.

It is a sacrilege to dwell in this opulent and sumptuous world and not note in every rift and ledge and sill its richness and plenitude and abundance. Deeply suspicious of ideas unattached to phenomena, I have attempted always to savor the definite and fixed and unique, the minute and determinate, all that is pertinent and particular, even if considered inconsequential by those attuned to "the grand scheme of things," a phrase that has always seemed meaningless to me.

I believe it is salvific to note the perfect gather of a stitch on the immaculate placket of a tailored silk shirt, the threshing of light through wheat undertones in a lover's tousled hair, the curve of a lampshade finial echoing the s-curve of a chair splat. I would have sinned in failing to note the fading from crimson to ashy mauve on the sepal petals of a rose I once cut from Dore's garden. The cobalt to kohl <u>sfumato</u> blur, perfect and poignant, in my favorite late Rothko painting still brings holy tears to my eyes. It is prayer to rise at dawn to regard the subtle gradations of cloud light tinctured with aqua, a creamy green, Tintoretto blue, and mauve deepening from horizon to zenith just before the sun first glances over the hills, its radiance obliterating all other hues in a dazzle of gold. Not to discern these fleeting pleasures as they pass is to fast-slip the fabric of life through one's fingers without feeling its texture. It is a transgressive fall from grace to ignore these consecrated sacraments offered by life in this world.

I have cultivated a mind ravenous for all of earth's images and sensory impressions, a mind aware that at some soon time it must relinquish this largesse, this benefaction, and dissolve in ether.

My mind has always floated on the eddies and ripples of a stream of digressions and driftings. For the life of me, I cannot think straight: My mind does not mesh congenially with abstract ideas or logical syllogisms. Instead, it walks deflections like fluffed amber Pomeranians loosed from their black patent-leather leashes. When I try to rein the little yappers in, they go all swollen-tongued and bug-eyed. They gargle and splutter and strangle. It seems too cruel. So I have given them their frisky ways. They pee on what posts they sniff out.

These thought-windings and sensuous images have served me well, providing for me life's plenitude and abundance, its extravagance, its consequent engagement. They are also providing me, now in my mid-70s, with yet another service. They distract me from a frowzy crone whom I sometimes glimpse approaching in my peripheral vision. She wavers there in the ruffles and brooches that I trick her out in to divert my gaze from her wrinkles and rheumy eyes and sour breath. My mind's savoring of digressions, its hunger for impressions is now its way of distancing my gaze from a reality it acknowledges but tries to turn aside.

I know that this crone can never be denied for long, no matter how my mind attempts to disguise her. She is Atropos, the final Fate, the last of the Moirai (Greek for "Apportioners"), the three somber daughters of Nyx, primeval night. Atropos succeeds her sisters Clotho, the spinner of the thread of life, and Lachesis, determiner of the life-thread's length. Atropos, the Inflexible, cuts the thread of life with her gleaming knife.

So Atropos now shambles beneath my mind's attempted distractions, mumbling with withered lips, her knife-blade poised over my fraying life-thread as she ravels it through gnarled fingers. Out of the corner of my eye, I see her as she regards me levelly, still staying her hand. But she must be met at last.

III

My mother maintained that we walk in mystery; we walk the earth among the angels who ushered us into the world and will accompany us out of it. I agree with her that we walk in the incomprehensible miracle of our lives, that we are enveloped in wonder. I hope the angel part is true as well: I would be elated to see those I have loved ever alive again in a luminous afterglow where all are forever blissful. I suspect, however, that Atropos does not hand us over to any recording Angel in an afterlife, hunched over a glowing parchment of documented human lives, his inscribing quill plucked from his own iridescent wing. I suspect that there is no chronicle-keeping in Heaven, no indelible accounts of individual lives. My own life, without some inconceivable intervention, will almost certainly be swallowed whole by hungry death. So my reason tells me—and I have no reason to believe it is mistaken. It is, though, almost inconceivable that a mind can evanesce, that capacious private universe forever dispelled, a scintillating consciousness gone dark for all time. But so it seems in time it must....

Some of us may live on a little while through our sown genes, shadow outlines suggested in the color of eye or cleft of chin in the children we leave behind. But even these strewn genes will eventually become so diluted in the tides of birth and death as to be dispersed for good. In the memories of others, the dead live only a little while. I do not even know the names of my great-grandparents.

This book, with its heft of details and its recollections of people and events, its weight of images, is my chronicle. I have striven to recall and examine my skewed memories, even those a reader may feel I should not have divulged, should certainly take no pride in. I wrote these remembered fictions so that I might tread water, waft on the wind, float over continents since it is so difficult to conceive of any other form of immortality. I, fleet and fragile, will be preserved in this book. Nothing will be lost. All will be conserved.

This is an ambition I know I have failed at. And my failure is appropriate. Few of the living left after we abandon them will remember us for very long. The disembodied voice heard in this book will soon be stilled, the name on the cover forgotten, the photograph at the book's end unattached to anything corporeal. That is the way it should be. My life here has been sufficient. I am reconciled to my fate.

This opulent earth is meant to renew itself perpetually, the old outlived and forgotten, the world made ever new again for all who enter it, the dead reduced to the sustenance that maintains new life. All that should be left of us are the nutrients leached from the bodies we no longer need and the shared knowledge and beauty born in our stilled hearts and minds. I hope that future readers of this book, should there be any, will find in it at least a fading glow from the experiences that have enriched my mind and the beauty that has so lifted my heart.

ABOUT THE AUTHOR

Lucien L. Agosta (left in photo), Emeritus Professor of English Literature at California State University, Sacramento, earned his Ph.D. at the University of Texas, Austin, in 1977. In addition to publishing numerous articles in his field, he is the author of three books: HOWARD PYLE (G. K. Hall, 1987); E. B. WHITE: THE CHILDREN'S BOOKS (Simon and Schuster Macmillan, 1995); and LOSING TIME: AIDS LESSONS IN LOVE AND LOSS (BookLocker Press, 2019). He appears on the DVD for the 2006 film version of CHARLOTTE'S WEB under the segment "What Makes a Classic." He received the outstanding teaching award at California State University, Sacramento, for the 1999-2000 academic year. He is married to Bud Sydenstricker (right in photo) and now resides in Palm Springs, CA.

9 798885 313025